P9-BBU-862

P9-BBU-862

THIS BOOK IS DEDICATED TO
the crew of the Space Shuttle Columbia, STS-107.

Their memory shall remain in the hearts of the NASA family.
Their bravery and courage shall forever bind them to this dynamic century of flight.

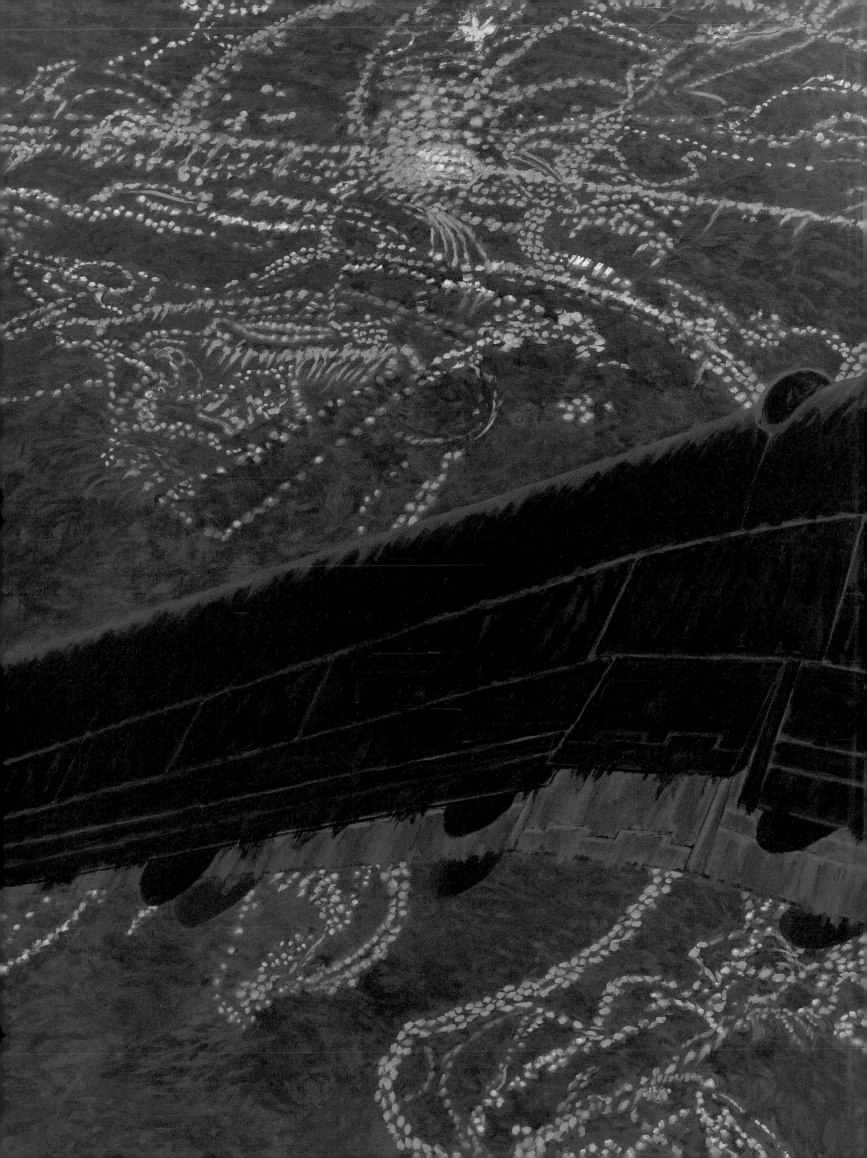

CENTENNIAL OF
FLIGHT

1903-2003

Flight

A Celebration of 100 Years in Art and Literature

Edited by

*Anne Collins Goodyear, Roger Launius,
Anthony Springer, and Bertram Ulrich*

Dear Jimmy and Pat,
  with very best wishes for
Christmas and the New Year.
       love, Anne
          December 2003

welcome
BOOKS

NEW YORK ✳ SAN FRANCISCO

Contents

Phantom Interceptors, Gerhard Richter, 1964

Introduction

"[W]hen one examines carefully into the possible utility of flying machines, he is forced to the conviction that no great benefits to mankind are reasonably to be expected from even the most triumphant success in this line of invention. It is really curious that so many people assume without reflection that a successful flying machine would mean either increased speed or increased carrying power over our present methods of transportation....This is sheer nonsense; and it is worthy of confutation only because it is a kind of nonsense to which people who talk on this subject seem to fall victims in a very unthinking way."

—ARTHUR MARK CUMMINGS, *The Uselessness of Flying Machines*

EVEN IN THE DECADE preceding the advent of the first "flying machine," proponents of the quest for such a vehicle faced widespread opposition and the dismissal of their aspirations as nonsense. As late as 1900, Wilbur Wright opened his letter to the French aeronautical expert Octave Chanute with the following qualification: "For some years I have been afflicted with the belief that flight is possible to man. My disease has increased in severity and I feel that it will soon cost me an increased amount of money if not my life."

The first powered, heavier-than-air flight lasted only twelve seconds. Yet Wilbur and Orville Wrights' success at Kitty Hawk on the morning of December 17, 1903 marked the beginning of a new era in human history. Before the day was out their inven-

tion had moved through the air for nearly a full minute. Together the two brothers from Dayton, Ohio, unlikely heroes, launched what may arguably be the defining technology of the twentieth century: the airplane. Their accomplishment represents the triumph of the human imagination, stimulated and disciplined by dedication and perseverance. "The average person," Anne Morrow Lindbergh reminds us in *North to the Orient*, "is apt to forget, or perhaps he never knew, the centuries of effort which have finally enabled man to be a bird, centuries of patient desiring, which reach back at least as far as the Greek world of Icarus."

Within a half century of its appearance, the airplane revolutionized transportation, warfare, and exploration. By 1953, two world wars had been fought with bombers and aerial reconnaissance, and thousands of passengers around the world had flown from one destination to another with revolutionary speed. New heroes had emerged, capable of pushing the airplane beyond its perceived limits: Louis Blériot, who first flew over the English Channel; Charles Lindbergh, who became the first man to cross the Atlantic alone, Amelia Earhart, who proved that women could do it too; Benjamin O. Davis, Jr., who demonstrated the mettle of African-American pilots in battle during World War II; and Chuck Yeager, who first dared to fly faster than sound.

Stimulated by such successes, the second fifty years of powered flight has witnessed the shattering of even more boundaries. "Why should we try for space travel?" asked Willy Ley in 1945. "It cannot be a substance of any kind that can be expected to pay. It can only be something intangible, not involving haulage, which is, at the same time, more valuable. There is something like that: Knowledge." As though answering Ley on cue, President John F. Kennedy would inspire a nation to put an astronaut on the moon for just such a reward. "We choose to go to the moon," Kennedy told an audience at Rice University in September, 1962: "We choose to go to the moon in this decade and do the other things, not only because they are easy, but because they are hard, because that goal will serve to organize and measure the best of our energies and skills, because that challenge is one that we are willing to accept, one we are unwilling to postpone, and one which we intend to win, and the others, too."

Prodded by Soviet accomplishments, such as putting the first man in space, and accomplishing the first space walk, American astronauts Buzz Aldrin and Neil Armstrong succeeded in reaching the lunar surface in July 1969. The moon landing of 1969 had the extraordinary distinction of closely paralleling a fictional account of the event published almost a century earlier. Just as Jules Verne had imagined in his *From Earth to the Moon* and *Round the Moon*, three adventurers participated in the mission, took off from Florida, reached the moon, and returned to splash down in the Pacific Ocean.

Norman Rockwell's painting *Suiting Up* suggests how such men were transformed into revered star-walkers, donning the suits to travel beyond earth's atmosphere, and Mitchell Jamieson's portrayal of astronaut Gordon Cooper in *First Steps* suggests the larger-than-life persona these individuals enjoyed back on earth. In recent years, yet another long-standing vision of space travel, one suggested by Chesley Bonestell's painting Space Station over Yucatan and Robert McCall's depiction of Space Station no. 1, created to publicize Stanley Kubrick and Arthur Clarke's film 2001: A Space Odyssey, has been achieved, with the inauguration of construction on the International Space Station.

The history of flight and of space flight is one which has benefited repeatedly from the imagination of writers and artists, who have presaged events to come. We conclude by considering what new visions may be realized in the next century of flight. Will we witness the success of four-dimensionally powered flying saucers, such as that imagined by the artist Panamarenko? Will tourists colonize the moon, as suggested by the digital photography of Yoshio Itagaki?

This anthology pays tribute to a century of flight, exploring a multitude of responses to the airplane and its descendants in times of peace and war, triumph and despair. An instrument that has both literally and metaphorically expanded our horizons and shaped our view of the world, the flying machine has not lost its capacity to inspire. Collected here are accounts, literary and pictorial, by those who have made history as pilots, those who have experienced the thrill of flight as passengers, those who have witnessed the destructive potential of aircraft, and those who have imagined what the future might hold. A century after he addressed his high school class in 1904, the wisdom of Robert Goddard, who pioneered the development of rockets, still applies: "The dream of yesterday is the hope of today and the reality of tomorrow."

Anne Collins Goodyear
Assistant Curator of Prints and Drawings
National Portrait Gallery, Smithsonian Institution

Part 1

The Invention of the Airplane

Anthony Springer

A CENTURY AGO, on the barren, windswept dunes of North Carolina's outer banks, two Ohio brothers were to make history. On December 17, 1903, Orville and Wilbur Wright, bicycle mechanics by profession and aeronautical pioneers by avocation, prepared their frail wood and fabric machine for flight. The brothers, dressed in coats and ties—the fashion of the day—even as they were working in the blowing sand, prepared their hand-made craft, with its wings of fabric-covered wood and a unique gasoline-powered engine and hand carved propellers, to set off on a test of their flying machine. The craft had just been repaired from the last series of tests, which ended with broken parts and no true flight of the vehicle. Today would be different. The craft was prepared and launched, rolling along the launch rail and in no uncertain terms gracefully lifting into the air with Wilbur at the controls. The airplane would fly for 12 seconds and travel 120 feet. By the fourth flight that day, the brothers had flown for 59 seconds and 852 feet before the wind blew over the fragile craft, leaving it unflyable. The brothers had succeeded where others had previously failed, technical midwives presiding at the birth of modern aviation.

At the turn of the century many thought those interested in flight eccentric; at best crazy, and insane at the worst. "If we were meant to fly we would have been born with wings" was a common thought at the time. The thought that man could take flight was pursued by both trained scientists and engineers and interested novices. The people involved in the study would communicate with each other to share ideas and progress.

One of the cornerstones of the dissemination of knowledge amongst the reactionary was Chicago civil engineer-turned-aeronautical engineer Octave Chanute, who kept in touch with those of like mind interested in the conquest of flight throughout the world. In 1894, Chanute published *Progress in Flying Machines*, a compilation of the latest research on flight from around the world. The Wrights wrote to him to ask for advice on flight, since they were interested in the subject and preparing to look into the possibility of trying what no one previously had succeeded in doing—building a powered flying machine capable of carrying a man.

The Wrights began their study with research on how objects fly and what had been accomplished up to this point. They realized that much could be learned from the people who had gone before them, and it was a waste to relearn what had already been learned. Once they had contacted others involved in the study, such as Chanute and the Smithsonian they began to test their theories of why objects fly. The Wrights built kites, and as others did, tested gliders to gain experience in both the design of an aircraft and the process of controlling these craft during flight. After many failures and more research into the process of flight undertaken using a small wind tunnel they constructed, and other apparatus—such as mounting a small-scale proposed wing section on a bicycle, their design evolved. Each year they would return to Kitty Hawk to flight test their new designs.

At this time, the turn of the twentieth century, the nation's top scientist, Samuel P. Langley, head of the nation's premier research institution, the Smithsonian, had been studying flight for the last decade, at first quietly and then in the open. He began with studying the aerodynamics of flight, or how objects move through the air, and over the year advanced to models—from steam powered later versions to his final, full-scale man carrying aerodromes. Langley's later work on flight was funded by the United States government, and ended in December 1903 in failure when his aerodrome, piloted by Charles Manly, crashed upon takeoff from his houseboat into the Potomac River. This public failure in part led to the initial lack of recognition of the Wright's accomplishment. If the nation's greatest scientist with the funding of the United States government could not build a man carrying flying machine, how could two novice bicycle mechanics from Dayton have succeeded?

On that blustery December day, the Wrights accomplished their goal. With Wilbur at the controls the brothers would fly the first piloted, powered, controlled, heavier-than-air flying machine. The only witnesses to this feat were the men of the nearby lifesaving station—who had helped the Wrights over the years as they sent their strange contraptions into the air in short hops, and a few local residents.

The barren, inaccessible sand dunes of Kill Devil Hills are now gone, replaced with pine trees and grass to prevent the ever-shifting dunes from erosion. The place where this first flight occurred, preserved as a national park, is now engulfed by one of the top summer tourist destinations, the outer banks, with multitudes of tourists, hotels, and mini-malls. It is difficult to imagine this place as it was in 1903. For these Ohio boys it was the ends of the earth, accessible only by boat with a few locals and a life saving station as your neighbors. The words, pictures and artists' renderings of the place are all that ties us with a moment in time that forever changed the world. Today it is hard to imagine a world without flight; a concept we take for granted as just another mode of transportation. The items which follow discuss the first steps in flight through poetry, literature, and art.

Progress in Flying Machines

1894

Octave Chanute

To the possible inquiry as to the probable character of a successful flying machine, the writer would answer that in his judgment two types of such machines may eventually be evolved: one, which may be termed the soaring type, and which will carry but a single operator, and another, likely to be developed somewhat later, which may be termed the journeying type, to carry several passengers, and to be provided with a motor.

The soaring type may or may not be provided with a motor of its own. If it has one this must be a very simple machine, probably capable of exerting power for a short time only, in order to meet emergencies, particularly in starting up and in alighting. For most of the time this type will have to rely upon the power of the wind, just as the soaring birds do, and whoever has observed such birds will appreciate how continuously they can remain in the air with no visible exertion. The utility of artificial machines availing of the same mechanical principles as the soaring birds will principally be confined to those regions in which the wind blows with such regularity, such force, and such frequency as to allow of almost daily use. These are the sub-tropical and the trade-wind regions, and the best conditions are generally found in the vicinity of mountains or of the sea.

This is the type of machine which experimenters with soaring devices heretofore mentioned have been endeavoring to work out. If unprovided with a motor, an apparatus for one man need not weigh more than 40 or 50 lbs., nor cost more than twice as much as a first-class bicycle. Such machines therefore are likely

Nature Morte: "Notre Avenir est dans l'Air," Pablo Picasso, 1912

to serve for sport and for reaching otherwise inaccessible places, rather than as a means of regular travel, although it is not impossible that in trade-wind latitudes extended journeys and explorations may be accomplished with them; but if we are to judge by the performance of the soaring birds, the average speeds are not likely to be more than 20 to 30 miles per hour.

The other, or journeying type of flying machines, must invariably be provided with a powerful and light motor, but they will also utilize the wind at times. They will probably be as small as the character of the intended journey will admit of, for inasmuch as the weights will increase as the cube of the dimensions, while the sustaining power only grows as the square of those dimensions, the larger the machine the greater the difficulties of light construction and of safe operation. It seems probable, therefore, that such machines will seldom be built to carry more than from three to 10 passengers, and will never compete for heavy freights, for the useful weights, those carried in addition to the weight of the machine itself, will be very small in proportion to the power required. Thus M. [Hiram] Maxim provides his colossal aeroplane (5,500 sq. ft. of surface) with 300 horse power, and he hopes that it will sustain an aggregate of 7 tons, about one-half of which consists in its own dead weight, while the same horse power, applied to existing modes of transportation, would easily impel—at lesser speed, it is true—from 350 to 700 tons of weight either by rail or by water.

Although it by no means follows that the aggregate cost of transportation through the air will be in proportion to the power required, the latter being but a portion of the expense, it does not now seem probable that flying machines will ever compete economically with existing modes of transportation. It is premature, in advance of any positive success, to speculate upon the possible commercial uses and value of such a novel mode of transit, but we can already discern that its utility will spring from its possible high speeds, and from its giving access to otherwise unreachable points.

It seems to the writer quite certain that flying machines can never carry even light and valuable freights at anything like the present rates of water or land transportation, so that those who may apprehend that such machines will, when successful, abolish frontiers and tariffs are probably mistaken. Neither are passengers likely to be carried with the cheapness and regularity of railways, for although the wind may be utilized at times and thus reduce the cost, it will introduce uncertainty in the time required for a journey. If the wind be favorable, a trip may be made very quickly; but if it be adverse, the journey may be slow or even impracticable.

The actual speeds through the air will probably be great. It seems not unreasonable to expect that they will be 40 to 60 miles per hour soon after success is accomplished with machines provided with motors, and eventually perhaps from 100 to 150 miles per hour. Almost every element of the problem seems to favor high speeds, and, as repeatedly pointed out, high speeds will be (within certain limits) more economical than moderate speeds. This will eventually afford an extended range of journey—not at first probably, because of the limited amount of specially prepared fuel which can be carried, but later on if the weight of motors is still further reduced. Of course in civilized regions the supply of fuel can easily be replenished, but in crossing seas or in explorations there will be no such resource.

It seems difficult, therefore, to forecast in advance the commercial results of a successful evolution of a flying machine. Nor is this necessary; for we may be sure that such an untrammeled mode of transit will develop a usefulness of its own, differing from and supplementing the existing modes of transportation. It certainly must advance civilization in many ways, through the resulting access to all portions of the earth, and through the rapid communications which it will afford.

It has been suggested that the first practical application of a successful flying machine would be to the art of war, and this is possibly true; but the results may be far different from those which are generally conjectured. In the opinion of the writer such machines are not likely to prove efficient in attacks upon hostile ships and fortifications. They

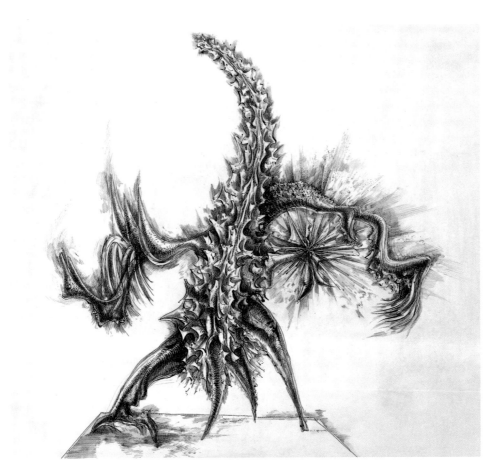

Spectre of Kitty Hawk, Theodore Roszak, 1946

cannot be relied upon to drop explosives with any accuracy, because the speed will be too great for effective aim when the exact distance and height from the object to be hit cannot be accurately known. Any one who may have attempted to shoot at a mark from a rapidly moving railway train will probably appreciate how uncertain the shot must be.

For reconnoitering the enemy's positions and for quickly conveying information such machines will undoubtedly be of great use, but they will be very vulnerable when attacked with similar machines, and when injured they may quickly crash down to disaster. There is little question, however, that they may add greatly to the horrors of battle by the promiscuous dropping of explosives from overhead, although their limited capacity to carry weight will not enable them to take up a large quantity, nor to employ any heavy guns with which to secure better aim.

Upon the whole, the writer is glad to believe that when man succeeds in flying through the air the ultimate effect will be to diminish greatly the frequency of wars and to substitute some more rational methods of settling international misunderstandings. This may come to pass not only because

of the additional horrors which will result in battle, but because no part of the field will be safe, no matter how distant from the actual scene of conflict. The effect must be to produce great uncertainty as to the results of maneuvers or of superior forces, by the removal of that comparative immunity from danger which is necessary to enable the commanding officers to carry out their plans, for a chance explosive dropped from a flying machine may destroy the chiefs, disorganize the plans, and bring confusion to the stronger or more skillfully led side. This uncertainty as to results must render nations and authorities still more unwilling to enter into contests than they are now, and perhaps in time make wars of extremely rare occurrence.

So may it be; let us hope that the advent of a successful flying machine, now only dimly foreseen and nevertheless thought to be possible, will bring nothing but good into the world; that it shall abridge distance, make all parts of the globe accessible, bring men into closer relation with each other, advance civilization, and hasten the promised era in which there shall be nothing but peace and goodwill among all men. ✳

"I have been afflicted with the belief that flight is possible to man."

1900

Wilbur Wright

Dayton, May 13, 1900

FOR SOME YEARS I HAVE BEEN AFFLICTED with the belief that flight is possible to man. My disease has increased in severity and I feel that it will soon cost me an increased amount of money if not my life. I have been trying to arrange my affairs in such a way that I can devote my entire time for a few months to experiment in this field.

My general ideas of the subject are similar to those held by most practical experimenters, to wit: that what is chiefly needed is skill rather than machinery. The flight of the buzzard and similar sailers is a convincing demonstration of the value of skill, and the partial needlessness of motors. It is possible to fly without motors, but not without knowledge & skill. This I conceive to be fortunate, for man, by reason of his greater intellect, can more reasonably hope to equal birds in knowledge, than to equal nature in the perfection of her machinery.

Assuming then that [Otto] Lilienthal was correct in his ideas of the principles on which man should proceed, I conceive that his failure was due chiefly to the inadequacy of his method, and of his apparatus. As to his method the fact that in five years' time he spent only about five hours, altogether, in actual flight is sufficient to show that his method was inadequate. Even the simplest intellectual or acrobatic feats could never be learned with so short practice, and even Methuselah could never have become an expert stenographer with one hour per year for practice. I also conceive Lilienthal's apparatus to be inadequate not only from the fact that he failed, but my observations of the flight of birds convince me that birds use more positive and energetic methods of regaining equilibrium than that of shifting the center of gravity.

With this general statement of my principles and belief I will proceed to describe the plan and apparatus it is my intention to test. In explaining these, my object is to learn to what extent similar plans have been tested and found to be failures, and also to obtain such suggestions as

Kitty Hawk, Richard Serra, 1983

your great knowledge and experience might enable you to give me. I make no secret of my plans for the reason that I believe no financial profit will accrue to the inventor of the first flying machine, and that only those who are willing to give as well as to receive suggestions can hope to link their names with the honor of its discovery. The problem is too great for one man alone and unaided to solve in secret.

My plan then is this. I shall in a suitable locality erect a light tower about one hundred and fifty feet high. A rope passing over a pulley at the top will serve as a sort of kite string. It will be so counterbalanced that when the rope is drawn out one hundred & fifty feet it will sustain a pull equal to the weight of the operator and apparatus or nearly so. The wind will blow the machine out from the base of the tower and the weight will be sustained partly by the upward pull of the rope and partly by the lift of the wind. The counterbalance will be so arranged that the pull decreases as the line becomes shorter and ceases entirely when its length has been decreased to one hundred feet. The aim will be to eventually practice in a

Poster for the *Stoned Moon* Series, Robert Rauschenberg, 1969

wind capable of sustaining the operator at a height equal to the top of the tower. The pull of the rope will take the place of a motor in counteracting drift. I see, of course, that the pull of the rope will introduce complications which are not met in free flight, but if the plan will only enable me to remain in the air for practice by the hour instead of by the second, I hope to acquire skill sufficient to overcome both these difficulties and those inherent to flight. Knowledge and skill in handling the machine are absolute essentials to flight and it is impossible to obtain them without extensive practice. The method employed by Mr. Pilcher of towing with horses in many respects is better than that I propose to employ, but offers no guarantee that the experimenter will escape accident long enough to acquire skill sufficient to prevent accident. In my plan I rely on the rope and counterbalance to at least break the force of a fall. My observation of the flight of buzzards leads me to believe that they regain their lateral balance, when partly overturned by a gust of wind, by a torsion of the tips of the wings. If the rear edge of the right wing tip is twisted upward and the left downward the bird becomes an animated windmill and instantly begins to turn, a line from its head to its tail being the axis. It thus regains its level even if thrown on its beam ends, so to speak, as I have frequently seen them. I think the bird also in general retains its lateral equilibrium, partly by presenting its two wings at different angles to the wind, and partly by drawing in one wing, thus reducing its area. I incline to the belief that the first is the more important and usual method. In the apparatus I intend to employ I make use of the torsion principle. In appearance it is very similar to the "double-check" machine with which the experiments of yourself and Mr. Herring were conducted in 1896–97. The point on which it differs in principle is that the cross-stays which prevent the upper plane from moving forward and backward are removed, and each end of the upper plane is independently moved forward or backward with respect to the lower plane by a suitable lever or other arrangement. By this plan the whole upper plane may be moved forward or backward, to attain longitudinal equilibrium, by moving both hands forward or backward together. Lateral equilibrium is gained by moving one end more than the other or my moving them in opposite directions. If you will make a square cardboard tube two inches in diameter and eight or ten long and choose two sides for your planes you will at once see the torsional effect of moving one end of the upper plane forward and the other backward, and how this effect is attained without sacrificing lateral stiffness. My plan is to attach the tail rigidly to the rear upright stays which connect the planes, the effect of which will be that when the upper plane is thrown forward the end of the tail is elevated, so that the tail assists gravity in restoring longitudinal balance. My experiments hitherto with this apparatus have been confined to machines spreading about fifteen square feet of surface, and have been sufficiently encouraging to induce me to lay plans for a trial with [a] full-sized machine.

My business requires that my experimental work be confined to the months between September and January and I would be particularly thankful for advice as to a suitable locality where I could depend on winds of about fifteen miles per hour without rain or too inclement weather. I am certain that such localities are rare.

I have your *Progress in Flying Machines* and your articles in the *Annuals* of '95, '96, & '97, as also your recent articles in the *Independent*. If you can give me information as to where an account of Pilcher's experiments can be obtained I would greatly appreciate your kindness.

—Wilbur Wright

Picasso and Braque, Mark Tansey, 1992

A Fractious Horse

SEPTEMBER 18, 1901

Wilbur Wright

NOW, THERE ARE TWO WAYS of learning to ride a fractious horse: one is to get on him and learn by actual practice how each motion and trick may be best met; the other is to sit on a fence and watch the beast awhile and then retire to the house and at leisure figure out the best way of overcoming his jumps and kicks. The latter system is the safer, but the former, on the whole, turns out the larger proportion of good riders. It is very much the same in learning to ride a flying machine, if you are looking for perfect safety, you will do well to sit on a fence and watch the birds, but if you really wish to learn, you must mount a machine and become acquainted with its tricks by actual trial.

Mr. Chanute in Paris

APRIL 11, 1903

Ernest Archdeacon

Figurine Honoring Gordon-Bennett

A GREAT FLURRY IN THE "AERIAL" WORLD was provoked in recent days, by the arrival in Paris, and reception at the Aéro-Club, of Mr. Chanute, the American inventor who, if not extremely well-known among ordinary mortals, is a veritable celebrity among "aviators."

For several years, Mr. Chanute has been working with indefatigable earnestness on the difficult problem of aerial navigation by heavier-than-air means.

A great German scientist, Lilienthal, was the first in this field to make lastingly memorable experiments. He built machines with stationary wings which were attached to the body and permitted him, by launching himself from the top of a small hill, to glide for a certain time in space, exactly like soaring birds. Lilienthal had dedicated several years of his life to this study and had attained very remarkable results. He had made over two thousand gliding experiments, succeeding at times in rising higher than the starting point, and covering by this means distances up to 300 meters.

Success seemed more and more to encourage his efforts; so that he constructed another machine, much more important than his preceding ones, which, it was his hope, would produce excellent results. Unfortunately at the first trials of his new apparatus, having risen to a good height, he, for some unexplained reason, crashed in full flight. The inventor, hurled violently to earth, died a few hours later.

Immediately after the death of Lilienthal, which occurred in 1896, Mr. Chanute resumed his own experiments with tireless patience and precision of method, never allowing himself to swerve from the unalterable path he had laid out.

I shall not speak here of the innumerable apparatus built successively by Mr. Chanute, each new one marking a slight improvement over the former.

Admitting that he was no longer very young, he took pains to train young, intelligent, and daring pupils, capable of carrying on his researches by multiplying his gliding experiment to infinity.

Principal among them, certainly, is Mr. Wilbur Wright, of Dayton (Ohio), who for his part has made some extremely remarkable experiments, and whose most recently built machine now seems to be the model for its type. I shall therefore only describe this last one, lest my article become excessively long.

In Lilienthal's machines, the man was upright and obtained equilibrium by shifting the lower part of his body in the appropriate direction; in those of Mr. Wright, on the other hand, the man is placed in horizontal position on the machine.

In order to regulate the equilibrium in the transverse direction, he operates two cords which act, by means of warping, upon the right and left sides of the wing and, simultaneously, by the movement of the vertical rear rudder.

In order to steer the machine in the longitudinal direction, he can, in the same manner, using the cords, operate the horizontal forward rudder, which must be vigorously pointed vertically downward when the speed is to be killed for landing.

We know that, in order to benefit from the full supporting action of the wind, the "glide" is always made against the wind; it will be understood, then, that in pointing the horizontal rudder vertically downward, the machine turns up suddenly, presents an enormous surface to the opposing wind and finds itself stopped dead.

Mr. Wright's present machine weighs about 53 kilos.

The total supporting surface is about 28 square meters, divided into two surfaces, each about 10 by 1.40 m. each.

The distance between the two surfaces is 1.50 m.

The curvature of the wing is about 1/20 of its chord, the point of deepest curvature being 1/3 of the chord back from the front.

Here, in summary, are the results obtained at the present time:

The experimenters are launched from the top of a hill of about 30 meters, the slope of which is very gentle, not exceeding 10°.

Their longest "glides," to use Mr. Chanute's picturesque expression, have reached 200 meters, and they have several times risen higher than their starting point. Much longer flights could be made *with equal ease* by starting from a higher point.

In order to launch the machine, which the experimenter cannot himself do by running, as Lilienthal did, two assistants are sufficient: carrying the machine together, they take several steps against the wind and then let go when they feel the lifting action of the wind take effect.

With good conditions, a mean angle of descent of about 6° can be achieved, and this, according to Mr. Chanute, will diminish considerably with the incessant progress of the machines.

What is especially remarkable in these experiments is that they have been conducted with such

prudence and so methodically that, from the beginning, Mr. Chanute has not had to report a single accident—except a pair of torn trousers! And this although a very large number of people, even but slightly initiated, have already attempted and accomplished "glides."

It is also true that the experimenters, with their extraordinary care, have marvelously chosen their ground, which is all of soft sand and like that of our dunes. A terribly violent shock would be necessary on such-soil to lead to serious bruises.

Mr. Chanute is justly proud of this absence of accidents in his trials. Moreover, it is the only proud thing I know about him, for he is the most modest man in the world, always willing to attribute his own merits to others.

Finally, here is what Mr. Chanute said in closing:

"Our experiments, methodically conducted, will permit us, little by little, to learn completely 'the art of the bird'—an art which, without seeming so, is extremely difficult.

"In a year, then, or perhaps not for two, we will know it thoroughly.

"Until then, it is useless, and even dangerous, to burden oneself with a motor, and I much prefer to use such an untroublesome and simple motor as gravity.

"Besides," added Mr. Chanute, "these glides provide the most original and most enticing of sports; as proof of which, several of my friends, great sportsmen and hunters, have put aside their favorite sports to devote themselves with enthusiasm to aerial glides!"

Mr. Chanute, on his return to America, is to send us complete plans of his latest machines, so as to allow us to execute similar ones in France.

Moreover, I do not doubt that, before long, some of our dauntless automobile sportsmen will happen to make themselves some similar machines and seek out somewhere a favorable spot for competing in these exciting glides.

The machine fully equipped comes to about 350 francs. A little cheaper than an automobile!

If there are any orders, I will undertake to handle them. Let's go, gentlemen, take out your subscriptions. Just write me at La Locomotion. ✳

Experiments with the Langley Aerodrome

1904

Samuel Pierpont Langley

THE EXPERIMENTS UNDERTAKEN BY the Smithsonian Institution upon an aerodrome, or flying machine, capable of carrying a man have been suspended from lack of funds to repair defects in the launching apparatus without the machine ever having been in the air at all. As these experiments have been popularly, and of late repeatedly, represented as having

failed on the contrary, because the aerodrome could not sustain itself in the air I have decided to give this brief though late account, which may be accepted as the first authoritative statement of them.

It will be remembered that in 1896 wholly successful flights of between one-half and one mile by large steam-driven models, unsupported except by

Lieutenant Frank Lahm—1st Serviceman to Fly, Richard M. Green

the mechanical effects of steam engines, had been made by me. In all these the machine was first launched into the air from "ways," somewhat as a ship is launched into the water, the machine resting on a car that ran forward on these ways, which fell down at the extremity of the car's motion, releasing the aerodrome for its free flight. I mention these details because they are essential to an understanding of what follows, and partly because their success led me to undertake the experiments on a much larger scale I now describe.

In the early part of 1898 a board, composed of officers of the Army and navy, was appointed to investigate these past experiments with a view to determining just what had been accomplished and what the possibilities were of developing a large-size man-carrying machine for war purposes.

The report of this board being favorable, the Board of Ordnance and Fortification of the War Department decided to take up the matter, and I having agreed to give without compensation what time I could spare from official duties, the Board allotted $50,000 for the development, construction, and test of a large aerodrome, half of which sum was to be available immediately and the remainder when required. The whole matter had previously been laid before the Board of Regents of the Smithsonian Institution, who had authorized me to take up the work and to use in connection with it such facilities of the Institution as were available.

Before consenting to undertake the construction of this large machine, I had fully appreciated that owing to theoretical considerations, into which I do not enter, it would need to be relatively lighter than the smaller one; and later it was so constructed, each foot of sustaining surface in the large machine carrying nearly the same weight as each foot in the model. The difficulties subsequently experienced with the larger machine were, then, due not to this cause, but to practical obstacles connected with the launching, and the like.

The flying weight of the machine complete, with that of the aeronaut, was 830 pounds; its sustaining surface, 1,040 square feet. It therefore was provided with slightly greater sustaining surface and materially greater relative horsepower than the model subsequently described which flew successfully. The brake horsepower of the engine was 52°, the engine itself, without cooling water, or fuel, weighed approximately 1 kilogram to the horsepower. The entire power plant, including cooling water, carburetor, battery, etc, weighed materially less than 5 pounds to the horsepower. Engines for both the large machine and the quarter-size model were completed before the close of 1901, and they were immediately put in their respective frames and tests of them and their power-transmission appliances were begun.

It is well here to call attention to the fact that although an engine may develop sufficient power for the allotted weight, yet it is not at all certain that it will be suitable for use on a machine which is necessarily as light as one for traversing the air, for it would be impossible to use, for instance, a single cylinder gasoline engine in a flying machine unless it had connected to it prohibitively heavy flywheels. These facts being recognized, the engines built in the Smithsonian shops were provided with five cylinders, and it was found upon test that the turning effect received from them was most uniform, and that, by suitable balancing of rotating and reciprocating parts, they could be made to work so that there was practically no vibration, even when used in the very light frames of the aerodromes.

There are innumerable other details, for the whole question is one of details. I may, however, particularly mention the carburetors, which form an essential part of every gas engine, and such giving fair satisfaction for use in automobiles were on the market at the time, yet all of them failed to properly generate gas when used in the tests of the engine working in the aerodrome frame, chiefly because of the fact that the movement of the engine in this light frame must be constant and regular or the transmission appliances are certain of distortion. It was, therefore, necessary to devise carburetors for the aerodrome engines which would meet the required conditions, and more than half a dozen were constructed which were in advance of anything then on the market, and yet were not good enough to use in the aerodrome, before a satisfactory one was made. These experiments were made in the shop, but with an imitation of all the disturbing influences which would be met with in the actual use of the machine in the air, so as to make certain, as far as possible, that the first test of the machine in free flight would not be marred by mishaps or unseen contingencies in connection with the generation and use of power.

It is impossible for anyone who has not had experience with such matters to appreciate the great amount of delay which experience has shown is to be expected in such experiments. Only in the spring of 1903, and after two unforeseen years of assiduous labor, were these new engines and their appurtenances, weighing altogether less than 5 pounds to the horsepower and far lighter than any known to be then existing, so coordinated and adjusted that successive shop tests could be made without causing injury to the frame, its bearings, shafts, or propellers.

And now everything seemed to be as nearly ready for an experiment as could be, until the aerodrome was at the location at which the experiments were to take place. The large machine and its quarter-size counterpart were accordingly placed on board the large houseboat, which had been completed some time before and had been kept in Washington as an auxiliary shop for use in the construction work, and the whole outfit was towed to a point in the Potomac River; here 3 miles wide, directly opposite Widewater, Va., and about 4 miles below Washington and midway between the Maryland and Virginia shores, where the boat was made fast to moorings which had previously been placed in readiness for it.

Although extreme delays had already occurred, yet they were not so trying as the ones which began immediately after the work was thus transferred to the lower Potomac....

Finally, however, on the 3d of September [1903], everything seemed to be in readiness for the experiments, and the large aerodrome was accordingly placed in position and all orders given and arrangements made for a test that day. After stationing the various tugs, launches, etc., at their predetermined positions so that they might render any assistance necessary to the engineer or the aerodrome, in case it came down in the water at a point distant from the houseboat, and after the photographers, with special telephoto cameras, had been stationed on the shore in order that photographs with their trigonometrical data might be obtained, from which speed, distance, etc., might be later determined, and when everyone was anxiously expecting the experiment, a delay occurred from one of the hardly predictable causes just mentioned in connection with the weather. An attempt was made to start the engine so that it might be running at its proper rate when the aerodrome was launched into free air after leaving the track, but the dry batteries used for sparking the engine, together with the entire lot of several dozen which were on hand as a reserve, had become useless from the dampness....

Following the 3d of September, and after procuring new batteries, short preliminary tests inside the boat were made in order to make sure that there would be no difficulty in the running of the engine the next time a fair opportunity arrived for making a test of the machine in free flight.... [On] the 7th of October (1903) when it became sufficiently quiet for a test, which I was now beginning to fear could not be made before the following season. In this, the first test, the engineer took his seat. The engine started with ease and was working without vibration at its full power... and the word being given to launch the machine, the car was released and the aerodrome sped along the track. Just as the machine left the track, those who were watching it, among whom were two representatives of the Board of Ordnance, noticed that the machine was jerked violently down at the front (being caught, as it subsequently appeared, by the falling ways), and under the full power of its engine was pulled into the water, carrying with it its engineer. When the aerodrome rose to the surface it was found, that while the front sustaining surfaces had been broken by their impact with the water, yet the rear ones were comparatively uninjured. As soon as a full examination of the launching mechanism had been made, it was found that the front portion of the machine had caught on the launching car, and that the guy post, to which were fastened the guy wires which are the main strength of the front surfaces, had been bent to a fatal extent....

Entirely erroneous impressions have been given by the account of these experiments in the public press, from which they have been judged, even by experts; the impression being that the machine could not sustain itself in flight. It seems proper, then, to emphasize and to reiterate, with a view to what has just been said, that the machine has never had a chance to fly at all, but that the failure occurred on its launching ways; and the question of its ability to fly is consequently, as yet, an untried one.

There have, then, been no failures as far as the actual test of the flying capacity of the machine is concerned, for it has never been free in the air at all. The failure of the financial means for continuing these expensive experiments has left the question of their result where it stood before they were undertaken, except that it has been demonstrated that engines can be built, as they have been, of little over one-half the weight that was assigned as the possible minimum by the best builders of France and Germany; that the frame can be made strong enough to carry these engines, and that, so far as any possible prevision can extend, another flight would be successful if the launching were successful; for in this, and in this alone, as far as is known, all the trouble has come....

Failure in the aerodrome itself or its engines there has been none; and it is believed that it is at the moment of success, and when the engineering problems have been solved, that a lack of means has prevented a continuance of the work. ✳

Diary of First Flight

1903

Orville Wright

Thursday, Dec. 17th

WHEN WE GOT UP A WIND of between 20 and 25 miles was blowing from the north. We got the machine out early and put out the signal for the men at the station. Before we were quite ready, John T. Daniels, W. S. Dough, A. D. Etheridge, W. C. Brinkley of Manteo, and Johnny Moore of Nags Head arrived. After running the engine and propellers a few minutes to get them in working order, I got on the machine at 10:35 for the first trial. The wind according to our annemometers at this time was blowing a little over 20 miles (corrected) 27 miles according to the Government annernometer at Kitty Hawk. On slipping the rope the machine started off increasing in speed to probably 7 or 8 miles. The machine lifted from the track just as it was entering on the fourth rail. Mr. Daniels took a picture just as it left the trucks. I found the control of the front rudder quite difficult on account of its being balanced too near the center and thus had a tendency to turn itself when started so that the rudder was turned too far on one side and then too far on the other. As a result the machine would rise suddenly to about 10 ft. and then as suddenly, on turning the rudder, dart for the ground. A sudden dart when out about 100 feet from the end of the tracks ended the flight. Time about 12 seconds (not known exactly as watch was not promptly stopped). The flight lever for throwing off the engine was broken, and the skid under the rudder cracked. After repairs, at 20 min. after 11 o'clock Will made the second trial. The course was about like mine, up and down but a little longer over the ground though about the same in time. Dist not measured but about 175 ft. Wind speed not quite so strong. With the aid of the station men present, we picked the machine up and carried it back to the starting ways. At about 20 min. till 12 o'clock I made the third trial. When out about the same distance as Will's, I met with a strong gust from the left which raised the left wing and sidled the machine off to the right in a lively manner. I immediately turned the rudder to bring the machine down and then worked the end control. Much to our surprise, on reaching the ground the left wing struck first showing the lateral control of this machine much more effective than on any of our former ones. At the time of its sidling it had raised to a height of probably 12 to 14 feet. At just 12 o'clock Will started on the fourth and last trip. The machine started off with its ups and downs as it had before, but by the time he had gone three or four hundred feet he had it under much better control, and was traveling on a fairly even course. It proceeded in this manner till it reached a small hummock out about 800 feet from the starting ways, when it began its pitching again and suddenly darted into the ground. The front rudder frame was badly broken up, but the main frame suffered none at all. The distance over the ground was 852 feet in 59 seconds. The engine turns was 1071, but this included several seconds while on the starting ways and probably about a half second after landing.

Photo of the first Wright brothers' flight, December 17, 1903

The jar of landing had set the watch on machine back so that we have no exact record for the 1071 turns. Will took a picture of my third flight just before the gust struck the machine.

The machine left the ways successfully at every trial, and the truck was never caught by the track as we had feared.

After removing the front rudder, we carried the machine back to camp. We set the machine down a few feet west of the building, and while standing about discussing the last flight, a sudden gust of wind struck the machine and started to turn it over. All rushed to stop it. Will who was near the end ran to the front, but too late to do any good. Mr. Daniels and myself seized spars at the rear, but to no purpose. The machine gradually turned over on us. Mr. Daniels, having had no experience in handling a machine of this kind, hung on to it from the inside, and as a result was knocked down and turned over and over with it as it went. His escape was miraculous, as he was in with the engine and chains. The engine legs were all broken off, the chain guides badly bent, a number of uprights, and nearly all the rear ends of the ribs were broken. One spar only was broken.

After dinner we went to Kitty Hawk to send off telegram to M. W. While there we called on Capt. and Mrs. Hobbs, Dr. Cogswell and the station men. ✳

Airport Structure, Theodore Roszak, 1932

Kitty Hawk

1957

Robert Frost

PART ONE

Kitty Hawk, O Kitty,
There was once a song,
Even a rather great
Emblematic ditty,
I might well have sung
When I came here young
Out and down along
Past Elizabeth City
Sixty years ago.
I was to be sure
Out of sorts with Fate,
Wandering to and fro
In the earth alone,
You might think too poor-
Spirited to care
Who I was or where

I was being blown
Down along the coast
Like a crumpled better-
Left-unwritten letter
I to waste had thrown—
Given up for dead.
Oh, but not to boast
Ever since Nag's Head
Had my heart been great,
Not to say elate,
With a need the gale
Filled me with to shout
Summary riposte
To its dreary wail
There's no knowing what
Love is all about.
Poets know a lot.
Never did I fail

Of an answer back
To the zodiac
When in heartless chorus
Aries and Taurus
Gemini and Cancer
Mocked me for an answer.
I felt in me wing
To have up and flung
A heroic fling;
And might well have sung
The initial flight
That was to be flown
Into the sublime
Off these sands of Time
Time had seen amass
From his hourglass.
That initial flight
I can see now might

Well have been my own.
Once I told the master
Later when we met
I had been here too
As a young Alastor
When the scene was set
For the flight he flew
Long before he flew it.
Would he mind had I
Had him beaten to it?
Could he tell me why
Be original?
Why was it so very,
Very necessary
To be first of all?
How about the lie
Someone else was first?
He saw I was daffing.
He took this from me.
Still it was not laughing
Matter I could see.
He made no reply.
There *was* such a lie
Money and maneuver
Foster overlong
Until Herbert Hoover
Raised this tower shaft
To undo the wrong.
That was why this craft
Man was first to waft
Like a kiss to God
Stayed so long abroad
In repository

And appreciation
With a foreign nation
Of all crime the worst
Is the theft of glory,
Even more accursed
Than to rob the grave.
'Twas a sorry story.
But we needn't rave:
All has been redressed
And as for my jest
I might have one claim

To the Runway's fame
Had I only sung,
That was all my tongue.
I can't make it seem
More than that my theme
Might have been a dream
Of Cape Hattaras,
Or else Roanoke,
One more fond alas
For the seed of folk
Sowed in vain by Raleigh,
Raleigh of the cloak,
And some other folly.
Getting too befriended,
As so often, ended
Any melancholy
I was to have sung
For I fell among
Some kind of committee
From Elizabeth City,
Each and every one
Loaded with a gun
And a demijohn
(Need a body ask
If it was a flask?)
Out to kill a duck
Or perhaps a swan
Over Currituck.
This was not their day
Anything to slay
Unless one another.
Being out of luck
Made them no less gay,
No, nor less polite.
They included me
Like a little brother
In their revelry
Even to the height—
All concern to take
Care my innocence
Should at all events
Tenderly be kept
For good gracious' sake.
And if they were gentle
They were sentimental.

One drank to his mother
While another wept.
Something made it sad
For me to break loose
From the need they had
To make themselves glad
They were of no use.
Something made it sad;
Manners made it hard,
But that night I stole
Off on the unbounded
Beaches where the whole
Of the Atlantic pounded.
There I next fell in
With a lone coast guard
On midnight patrol,
Who as of a sect
Asked about my soul
And whereall I'd been.
Apropos of sin,
Did I recollect
How the wreckers wrecked
Theodosia Burr
Off this very shore?
'Twas to punish her
But her father more —
We don't know what for:
There was no confession.
Things they think she wore
Still sometimes occur
In someone's possession
Here at Kitty Hawk.
We can have no notion
Of the strange devotion
Burr had for his daughter:
He was too devoted.
So it was in talk
We prolonged the walk,
On one side the ocean
And on one a water
Of the inner sound;
And the moon was full,
As the poet said
And I aptly quoted,
That old laurel-crowned

Lord of a John Bull.
The moon's being full
And right overhead,
Small but strong and round,
By its tidal pull
Made all being full.
Here it was again
In the self-same day,
I at odds with men
Came twice on their pity,
Equally profound
For a son astray
And a daughter drowned.

Kitty Hawk, O Kitty,
Know you no dismay.
Men will get away.
And some time in some
Mood akin to pity
You would weep no less
For man's small success
Than his unsuccess.
You'd be overcome
In the deathless scene
When that common scoff,
Poor Darius Green,
And his fool machine
Finally took off.

PART TWO

When the chance went by
For my Muse to fly
From this Runway beach
As a figure of speech
In a flight of words,
Little I imagined
Men would treat the sky
To a flying pageant
Like a thousand birds.
Neither you nor I
Ever thought to fly,
Oh, but fly we did,
Literally fly.

That's because though mere
Lilliputians we're
What Catullus called
Somewhat (*aliquid*).
Mind you we are mind.
We are not the kind
To stay too confined.
After having crawled
Round the place on foot
And done yeoman's share
Of just staying put,
We arose from there,
And we scaled a plane
So the stilly air
Almost pulled our hair
Like a hurricane.

This we're certain of,
All we do and try
All we really love
Is to signify.
Pulpiteers will censure
Our godless adventure
Since we took that fall
From the apple tree
Into what they call
The Material.
But God's own crescent
Into flesh was meant
As a demonstration
That the supreme merit
Lay in risking spirit
In substantiation.
Westerners inherit
A design of living
Deeper into matter
(Not without some patter
Of the soul's misgiving).
All the science zest
To materialize
By on-penetration
Into earth and skies
(Don't forget the latter
Is but further matter),
Has been West-Northwest.

If it was not wise
Tell me why the East
Seemingly has ceased
From its long stagnation
In mere meditation
And made such a fuss
To catch up with us.
Can it be to flatter
Us with emulation?

The uplifted sight
We enjoyed at night
When instead of sheep
We were counting stars,
Not to go to sleep,
But to stay awake
For good gracious' sake,
Naming stars to boot
To avoid mistake,
Jupiter and Mars,
Just like Pullman cars,
Was no vain pursuit.
Some have preached and taught
All there was to thought
Was to master Nature
By some nomenclature.
But if not a law
'Twas an end foregone
Anything we saw
And thus fastened on
With an epithet
We would see to yet —
We would want to touch
Not to mention clutch.

Someone says the Lord
Says our reaching toward
Is its own reward.
One would like to know
Where he says it though.

I don't like that much.

Let's see where we are.
What's that sulphur blur

Off there in the fog?
Go consult the log.
It's some kind of town,
But it's not New York.
We're not very far
Out from where we were.
It's still Kitty Hawk.

We'd have got as far
Even at a walk.

Don't you crash me down.
Though our kiting ships
Prove but flying chips
From the science shop
And when motors stop
They may have to drop
Short of anywhere,
Though our leap in air
Prove as vain a hop
As the hop from grass
Of a grasshopper,
Don't discount our powers;
We have made a pass
At the infinite,
Made it as it were
Rationally ours,
To the most remote
Swirl of neon-lit
Particle afloat.
Ours was to reclaim
What had long been faced
As a fact of waste
And was waste in name.

That's how we became
Though an earth so small,
Easy to asperse
For its size and worse,
Justly known to fame
As the Capital
Of the universe?

We make no pretension
Of projecting ray

We can call our own
From this ball of stone,
None I don't reject
As too new to mention.
All we do's reflect
From our rocks, and yes,
From our brains no less.
And the better part
Is the ray we dart
From the head and heart,
The mens animi.

Till we came to be
There was not a trace
Of a thinking race
Anywhere in space.

We know of no world
Being whirled and whirled
Round and round the rink
Of a single sun
(So as not to sink),
Not a single one
That has thought to think.

Pilot, though at best your
Flight is but a gesture,
And your rise and swoop
But a loop the loop
Lands on someone hard
In his own back yard
From no higher heaven
Than a bolt of levin,
I don't say retard.
Keep on elevating.
But while meditating
What we can't or can,
Let's keep starring man
In the royal role.
It will not be his
Ever to create
One least germ or coal.
But let's get this straight
There creation is.
More or less control

Of it is the whole
Business of the soul.

And this flight we wave
At the stars and moon
Means that we approve
Of things on the move,
Be they stars or moon.
Ours is to behave
Like a kitchen spoon
Of a size Titanic
To keep all things stirred
In a blend mechanic,
Saying that's the tune
That's the pretty kettle!
Matter mustn't curd
Separate and settle.
Motion is the word.

Nature's never quite
Sure she hasn't erred
In her vague design
Till on some fine night
We two come in flight
Like a king and queen
And by right divine
Waving scepter-baton
Undertake to tell her
What in being stellar
We're supposed to mean.

God of the machine,
Peregrine machine,
Some consider Satan,
Unto you the thanks
For this token flight,
Thanks to you and thanks
To the brothers Wright
Once considered cranks
Like Darius Green
In their home town, Dayton.

Statement to the Associated Press

JANUARY 5, 1904

Orville and Wilbur Wright

I⸤T⸥ HAD NOT BEEN OUR INTENTION to make any detailed public statement concerning the private trials of our power "Flyer" on the 17th of December last; but since the contents of a private telegram, announcing to our folks at home the success of our trials, was dishonestly communicated to the newspapermen at the Norfolk office, and led to the imposition upon the public, by persons who never saw the "Flyer" or its flights, of a fictitious story incorrect in almost every detail; and since this story together with several pretended interviews or statements, which were fakes pure and simple, have been very widely disseminated, we feel impelled to make some correction. The real facts were as follows:

On the morning of December 17th, between the hours of 10:30 o'clock and noon, four flights were made, two by Orville Wright and two by Wilbur Wright. The starts were all made from a point on the level sand about two hundred feet west of our camp, which is located a quarter of a mile north of the Kill Devil sand hill, in Dare County, North Carolina. The wind at the time of the flights had a velocity of 27 miles an hour at ten o'clock, and 24 miles an hour at noon, as recorded by the anemometer at the Kitty Hawk Weather Bureau Station. This anemometer is thirty feet from the ground. Our own measurements,

made with a hand anemometer at a height of four feet from the ground showed a velocity of about 22 miles when the first flight was made, and 20 ½ miles at the time of the last one. The flights were directly against the wind. Each time the machine started from the level ground by its own power alone with no assistance from gravity, or any other source whatever. After a run of about 40 feet along a monorail track, which held the machine eight inches from the ground, it rose from the track and under the direction of the operator climbed upward on an inclined course till a height of eight or ten feet from the ground was reached, after which the course was kept as near horizontal as the wind gusts and the limited skill of the operator would permit. Into the teeth of a December gale the "Flyer" made its way forward with a speed of ten miles an hour over the ground and thirty to thirty-five miles an hour through the air. It had previously been decided that for reasons of personal safety these first trials should be made as close to the ground as possible. The height chosen was scarcely sufficient for maneuvering in so gusty a wind and with no previous acquaintance with the conduct of the machine and its controlling mechanisms. Consequently the first flight was short. The succeeding flights rapidly increased in length

Form No. 168.

THE WESTERN UNION TELEGRAPH COMPANY.
—————— INCORPORATED ——————
23,000 OFFICES IN AMERICA.   CABLE SERVICE TO ALL THE WORLD.

This Company **TRANSMITS** and **DELIVERS** messages only on conditions limiting its liability, which have been assented to by the sender of the following message. Errors can be guarded against only by repeating a message back to the sending station for comparison, and the Company will not hold itself liable for errors or delays in transmission or delivery of **Unrepeated Messages**, beyond the amount of tolls paid thereon, nor in any case where the claim is not presented in writing within sixty days after the message is filed with the Company for transmission.
This is an **UNREPEATED MESSAGE**, and is delivered by request of the sender, under the conditions named above.
ROBERT C. CLOWRY, President and General Manager.

RECEIVED at Dayton, Ohio   170

176 C KA CS 33 Paid.   Via Norfolk Va

Kitty Hawk N C Dec 17

Bishop M Wright

        7 Hawthorne St

Success four flights thursday morning all against twenty one mile

wind started from Level with engine power alone average speed

through air thirty one miles longest 57 seconds inform Press

home ##### Christmas .   Orevelle Wright   525P

Wright brothers' telegram to their father, December 17, 1903
OVERLEAF: *Orville Wrights First Powered Flight-Kitty Hawk, North*, Harvey K. Kidder

and at the fourth trial a flight of fifty-nine seconds was made, in which time the machine flew a little more than half mile through the air, and a distance of 852 feet over the ground. The landing was due to a slight error of judgment on the part of the aviator. After passing over a little hummock of sand, in attempting to bring the machine down to the desired height, the operator turned the rudder too far; and the machine turned downward more quickly than had been expected. The reverse movement of the rudder was a fraction of a second too late to prevent the machine from touching the ground and thus ending the flight. The whole occurrence occupied little, if any, more than one second of time.

Only those who are acquainted with practical aeronautics can appreciate the difficulties of attempting the first trials of a flying machine in a twenty-five mile gale. As winter was already well set in, we should have postponed our trials to a more favorable season, but for the fact that we were determined, before returning home, to know whether the machine possessed sufficient power to fly, sufficient strength to withstand the shocks of landings, and sufficient capacity of control to make flight safe in boisterous winds, as well as in calm air. When these points had been definitely established, we at once packed our goods and returned home, knowing that the age of the flying machine had come at last.

From the beginning we have employed entirely new principles of control; and as all the experiments have been conducted at our own expense without assistance from any individual or institution, we do not feel ready at present to give out any pictures or detailed description of the machine. ✳

My Story of the Wright Brothers

1948

Charles E. Taylor

IT WAS A HOT JUNE NIGHT IN DAYTON. It must have been a Saturday because I was at the Wright Cycle Company gassing with Wilbur and Orville. They used to stay open Saturday nights to take care of the folks who worked all week and couldn't get around any other time.

One of the brothers, I forget which, asked me how would I like to go to work for them, There were just the two of them in the shop and they said they needed another hand. They offered me $18 a week. That was pretty good money; it figured to 30 cents an hour. I was making 25 cents at the Dayton Electric Company, which was about the same as all skilled machinists were getting.

The Wright shop was only six blocks from where I lived—at Calm and Gale streets—and I could bicycle to lunch. Besides, I liked the Wrights. So I said all right and I reported in on June 15th. That was in 1901.

I was a machinist and had done job work for the boys in my own shop. Once I made up a coaster brake they had invented but they dropped it later. I knew they were interested in box kites and gliders, and that they had gone South to Kitty Hawk, North Carolina, in 1900 with a glider. I didn't know any-thing about that stuff but I did know something about the bicycle business.

Three weeks after I went to work for the Wrights they took off for the South with another glider and I was alone in charge of their bicycle company. They trusted me to handle not only their customers but their money.

When they returned that year they decided to build a small wind tunnel to test out some of their theories on wings and control surfaces. We made a rectangular-shaped box with a fan at one end powered by the stationary gas engine they had built to drive the lathe, drill press and band saw. I ground down some old hack-saw blades for them to use in making balances for the tunnel. Nowadays, wind tunnels run into the millions of dollars and some are big enough to hold full-scale airplanes.

That was the first work they asked me to do in connection with their flying experiments. For a long while, though, I was kept busy enough repairing bicycles and waiting on customers. The Wrights did most of their experimenting upstairs where they had a small office and workroom. I worked in the shop in the back room on the first floor.

It was part of my job to open up at 7:00 A.M. They would get in it little later, between eight and nine o'clock. We all stayed until closing time at six. We went home for lunch, but at different times so we didn't have to close the shop. Their father, Milton Wright, was a bishop, in the United Brethren Church and the boys never worked on Sunday....

So far as I can figure out, Will and Orv hired me to worry about their bicycle business so they could concentrate on their flying studies and experiments. I suppose the more of the routine work I shouldered, the faster they were able to get on with their pet project—and I must have satisfied them for they didn't hire anyone else for eight years. If they had any idea in June of 1901 that someday they'd be making a gasoline internal-combustion engine for an airplane and would need some first-rate machinework for it, they sure didn't say anything about it to me.

Photo of Wilbur Wright at Le Mans, Leon Bolle, 1908

But when they returned from the South in 1902, they said they were through with gliders and were going to try a powered machine. They figured they'd need a larger machine to carry the motor and they started work on the new biplane right away. At the same time they tried to locate a motor. They wrote to a dozen companies, some of them in the automobile business, requesting one that would produce 12 horsepower but wouldn't weigh too much. Nothing turned up.

So they decided to build one of their own. They figured on four cylinders and estimated the bore and stroke at four inches. While the boys were handy with tools, they had never done much machinework and anyway they were busy on the air frame. It was up to me. My only experience with a gasoline engine was an attempt to repair one in an automobile in 1901.

We didn't make any drawings. One of us would sketch out the part we were talking about on a piece of scratch paper and I'd spike the sketch over my bench.

It took me six weeks to make that engine. The only metal-working machines we had were a lathe and a drill press, run by belts from the stationary gas engine.

The crankshaft was made out of a block of machine steel 6 by 31 inches and one and five-

eighths inches thick. I traced the outline on the slab, then drilled through with the drill press until I could knock out the surplus pieces with a hammer and chisel. Then I put it in the lathe and turned it down to size and smoothness. It weighed 19 pounds finished and she balanced up perfectly, too.

The completed engine weighed 180 pounds and developed 12 horsepower at 1,025 revolutions per minute....

While I was doing all this work on the engine, Will and Orv were busy upstairs working on the air frame. They asked me to make the metal parts, such as the small fittings where the wooden struts joined the spars and the truss wires were attached. There weren't any turnbuckles in the truss wires, so the fit had to be just so. It was so tight we had to force the struts into position....

We never did assemble the whole machine at Dayton. There wasn't room enough in the shop. When the center section was assembled, it blocked the passage between the front and back rooms, and the boys had to go out the side door and around to the front to wait on the customers.

We still had bicycle customers. The Wright Brothers had to keep that business going to pay for the flying experiments. There wasn't any other money.

While the boys always worked hard, and there never was any horseplay around the shop, they always seemed to find time to stop and talk with a customer or humor the neighborhood children who wandered in. Sometimes I think the kids were the only ones who really believed that Will and Orv would fly. They hadn't learned enough to say it couldn't be done....

We finally got everything crated and on the train. There was no ceremony about it, even among ourselves. The boys had been making these trips for four years, and this was the third time I had been left to run the shop. If there was any worry about the flying machine not working, they never showed it and I never felt it.

You know, it's a funny thing, but I'm not sure just how or when I learned that Will and Orv had actually flown the machine. They sent a telegram to the bishop saying they had made four successful powered flights that day—December 17, 1903—and would be home for Christmas.

I suppose their sister Katharine or maybe the bishop came over and told me about it. I know I thought it was pretty nice that they had done what they set out to do; and I was glad to hear that the motor ran all right. But I don't remember doing any jig steps. The boys were always so matter-of-fact about things; and they never made any effort to get me excited.

Even when they got home there was no special celebration in the shop. Of course they were pleased with the flight. But their first word with me, as I remember, was about the motor being damaged when the wind picked up the machine and turned it topsy-turvy after Wilbur had completed the fourth flight. They wanted a new one built right away. And they were concerned with making improvements in the controls. They were always thinking of the next thing to do; they didn't waste much time worrying about the past.

The Wrights didn't go into the airplane experiment with the idea of making a lot of money. They just seemed to be curious about the problems involved—I suppose you would call it a challenge—

and they determined to find out why they couldn't make it work. It was not a game with them or a sport. It may have been a hobby at the start, but now it was a serious business.

I was happy, working for Will and Orv, and I know they were pleased with my work. They showed it in many ways. Orville even left me an $800 annuity in his will. When I finally left his employ in 1919 he could have forgotten about me then and there. But the fact he did not helps me believe he appreciated that I had a part in giving the airplane to the world, though nobody made any fuss about it and I didn't either....

It was Orville who gave me my first flight....

In May, 1910, Orv finally took me up. It was at Simms Station, and he did what a lot of pilots have done in later years with their first-flight passengers. He tried to give me a scare. We were flying around over the field when suddenly the plane began to pitch violently. I grabbed hold of a strut and looked over at Orv. He didn't seem upset, although he appeared to be having a hard time controlling the machine. Pretty soon the pitching stopped and we landed. Orv asked me if I were scared. I said, "No, if you weren't, why should I be?" He thought it was very funny.

I always wanted to learn to fly, but I never did. The Wrights refused to teach me and tried to discourage the idea. They said they needed me in the shop and to service their machines, and if I learned to fly I'd be gadding about the country and maybe become an exhibition pilot, and then they'd never see me again.

One of my jobs that Summer of 1904 was as sort of airport manager at Simms Station. I suppose it was the first airport in the country, with all due respect to the sands of Kitty Hawk. It was a small pasture the boys had arranged to use. We built a shed for the machine and a catapult to assist in the take-offs, because the field was small and rough.

It was made up of a wooden track and a tower at the starting end. We drew heavy weights to the top of the tower on ropes which were rigged through pulleys to the bottom of the tower, out to the take-off end of the track, and back to the airplane. When the weights were released, the machine would dart forward. Now people are fooling around with assisted take-offs again for big planes.

We were all very busy out at Simms Station that summer testing out the new airplane we built to replace the Kitty Hawk machine. We scarcely had time to keep the bicycle business going, and by the following summer the boys gave it up entirely.

I must have built half-a-dozen engines for the boys before the airplane company was formed in 1909 and they took on additional help....

[After nearly five years on the West Coast] in the fall of 1912 I took my family back to Dayton, but left the baby in Los Angeles in the care of Mrs. I. C. Shafer. We had known her family for many years back in Ohio. Mrs. Taylor was again hospitalized and she remained so until her death in 1930.

Back East, it wasn't like old times. Wilbur had died on May 30th, from typhoid fever and there were a lot of new faces around the Wright plant. The pioneering days seemed about over for me.

Maybe that's why that Christmas of 1912 stands out in my memory. It wasn't

going to be a very happy one, for either the Wrights or the Taylors. Christmas Eve there came a knock at the door, and there was Orville with a big basket filled with everything for a big Christmas dinner. He just handed me the basket, wished us a "Merry Christmas," and went away. It was the first time he had ever come to our house.

I stayed on with Orville, after he sold the company in 1915 and retired to his laboratory. I helped out with some of his inventions and experiments, and kept his car in good running order. But there was less and less work to do, and finally I got restless and took a job downtown with the Dayton-Wright Company in 1919.

In 1916 we took the Kitty Hawk plane out of storage and fixed it up for it first exhibition, at the Massachusetts Institute of Technology in Cambridge, Massachusetts. If it hadn't been for [Roy] Knabenshue, there might not have been the historic relic to exhibit there or in Washington, now. Roy tells how he approached Wilbur early in 1912 and asked him

what he was going to do with the Kitty Hawk and Wilbur told him, "Oh, I guess we'll burn it; it's worthless." Roy argued it was historic and finally talked him out of destroying the plane.

It was then forgotten until Orville got this request to show it in Massachusetts. It came from Lester D. Gardner (then publisher of Aviation magazine, later an officer in the Army Air Service in the first World War and founder of the Institute of the Aeronautical Sciences) who was in charge of the aeronautical part of the dedication program of the new buildings of MIT at Cambridge. Orville was reluctant at first, but consented when Gardner and Roy convinced him how interesting it would be to the public.

Orville and I continued to see each other frequently after 1919. He used to bring odd jobs to me at the plant where I was working, and I would visit him at his laboratory. Then in 1928 I moved to California, and I didn't see him again until 1937. That was when Henry Ford hired me to help restore the original Wright home and shop when he moved them to his Greenfield Village museum at Dearborn, Michigan. They were installed on the grounds near the first Ford workshop and Thomas Edison's original laboratory.

I helped Fred Black, the director of the project, track down the original machinery and furniture, and then I built a replica of the first Wright engine. The home and shop were dedicated in April, 1938, with all the big names in aviation on hand.

I met Orville often during this period, both in Dayton and in Dearborn. When I left the Village to return to California in 1941, I called on him in Dayton. That was the last time I saw him, but he wrote to me regularly about his work and I kept him posted on what I did. He wrote every December 17th. It was sort of a personal anniversary with us and it was also a Christmas message....

In the last note I got from him, shortly before he died; he wrote:

"I hope you are well and enjoying life; but that's hard to imagine when you haven't much work to do." It was signed. "Orv."

He knew me pretty well. ✳

Ode for
Orville and Wilbur Wright

2000

David Moolten

Robert Rauschenberg in his <u>Pelican</u> (Dedicated to the Wright Brothers), photo by Peter Moore, 1963

I DON'T YEARN FOR THEIR STEEP EXCURSION
Into fame and fortune, for it had
The usual price, and Orville died bitter
And Wilbur died young. I envy them
Only the slender and empty distance they left
Between them and a seaside's grassy bluffs
In mild December, the frail ingenuity
Of dreams, a lifetime's hopes made of string and cloth
And a little puttering motor that might have run
A lawnmower if the brothers had put their minds
To one first. For dumb exhilaration, nothing
Not an F-16 thundering from its base
In Turkey, nor my red-eye circling O'Hare—
Comes close to what they must have felt
For less than a shaking, clattering minute,
Clearing all attachment to the world
Of dickering and petty concerns: for some,
No other heaven. So I take note of them
As they took notes from the lonely buzzard, obsessed
To the point of love with the ghostly air
And the small fluttering things that wandered
Through it. Eccentric but never flighty,
Bookish but not above nicking their hands
In bicycle shops and basements, they lived
With their sister and tinkered with the future.
Propelled by ambition, the mandate
It invents, they still heeded the laws
Of nature, trimmed needless weight, saw everything,
Even themselves, as burden, determined
Not to crash and burn. Sheer will launched them,
Good will, because those first forty yards
Skimming shale and reeds were for everyone.
Facedown between the struts, staring at the ground
As it blurred past, they failed like anyone
To grasp the implications. But legs flailing,
They hung on, buoyed by never and almost
And then just barely. I could do worse
Than their brief rapture, their common sense
Of purpose. Or I could, if only
For a moment, exalt them, go along
With the jury-rigged myth, the quaint
Contrivance that lets them rise above it all.

The Heroic Age of Aeronautics

Part 2

Dominick Pisano

IN HIS BOOK *CELEBRITY*, Chris Rojek explains that "to the anthropologist Mircea Eliade, nearly all religions posit the existence of sky gods or celestial beings. Human experience is typically divided into three realms: sky, earth and underworld. Men and women are of the earth, but their lives are invested with heightened meaning by the journeys—offered through religious rites and ceremonies—to the sky or the underworld." Pilots' passages into the air and back to earth in an attempt to conquer time and space reflect the arduousness of human existence; simultaneously, their journeys give them a heroic and even godlike aspect. Given this archetypal significance, it is not surprising that government, industry and the media, using the techniques of mass communication, have fashioned celebrity personas for pilots, attributing glamorous status to them and making them into public figures, often for nationalistic and propagandistic purposes.

One could argue that the Wright brothers were the first aviation celebrities because they were the first to achieve piloted controlled, sustained flight in December 1903, but more importantly because the press took note of what they had done. Notwithstanding the claims of others to this distinction, celebrity status was thrust on the naïve Wrights.

World War I brought about interest in a new form of aviation celebrity—the ace, a fighter pilot who gained prominence by the number of victories (aircraft shot down) scored against the enemy. Businessmen like André Michelin, the French tire mogul, established a million-franc fund for aviators who had distinguished themselves in battle. By 1916, governments began to recognize aviators and exploit their nationalistic and propagandistic value. German ace Manfred von Richthofen was the most prominent member of the new fraternity, with 80 victories, but the French had Réné Fonck (75 victories), the British had E.C. "Mick" Mannock (73 victories), and the Americans had Edward V. "Eddie" Rickenbacker (26 victories). Although the ace's public image reflected actual courage and daring, that image was often distorted by wartime propaganda and the postwar memoirs written by the pilots themselves.

It was in the 1920s, however, when all of the conditions for modern-day celebrity— radio, motion pictures, magazines, press photography—were in place, that there was a veritable sea change in the way celebrities were perceived by the public. Columnists like Walter Winchell created an obsession with celebrity, and the public hungered for information about them as never before. Earlier in the century, newspaper magnates like Alfred Harmsworth (later known as Lord Northcliffe), owner of the *London Daily Mail* and *London Times/Daily Mirror*, and Ralph Pulitzer and his two brothers, Joseph Jr., and Herbert, owners of the *New York World* and the *St. Louis Post Dispatch*, offered aviation prizes and trophies in an attempt to boost circulation. But the ability to transmit information to masses of people paved the way for Charles Lindbergh, the most renowned aviation celebrity of the twentieth century.

Lindbergh's celebrity grows out of what historian Warren Susman defined as a cultural shift in emphasis from "a Calvinist producer ethic with its emphasis on hard work, self-denial, savings and the new, increasing demands of a hedonistic consumer ethic: spend, enjoy, use up." The problem is that Lindbergh refused to be shaped by the forces of consumerism; he chose rather to insist that he represented the old Calvinist values, and the press never forgave him for his refusal to go along in their attempts to make him a celebrity. Hollywood bolstered the Lindbergh persona as pilot-hero, and aviation as a significant activity, in its representation of flying during the late 1920s and throughout the 1930s.

If Lindbergh fought against celebrity, Amelia Earhart, Lindbergh's counterpart in public recognition as a pilot, actively sought it out. Some have argued that it was Earhart's persistent pursuit of celebrity—and the physical and psychological toll it took on her—that eventually led to her disappearance and apotheosis as the dead pilot heroine, struck down by fortune in mid-career. Ironically, the celebrity she achieved after death has become more important than what she accomplished during her lifetime.

World War II in the air created its own type of celebrity. Jimmy Doolittle, once famous for being an exciting air race pilot, became equally famous for his military leadership, especially for planning and executing the raid on Tokyo in April 1942. But as in World War I, the ace dominated the news. Nevertheless, by the time of World War II, the ace had become largely superfluous, combat flying had become a corporate activity, and opportunities for the "lone wolf," who was entirely free to seek out his prey without regard to the dictates of the mission, had diminished.

The terrible destruction wrought by air power in World War II, especially the atomic bombing of Japan in 1945, made aviation celebrity on a wide scale a thing of the past in the postwar period. Aviation had lost a good deal of its glamorous innocence as a result of the war, and pilot celebrities began to recede from the forefront of public consciousness. While the early Cold War kept aviation in the news, the enterprise had

44

HOME JOURNAL NEW YORK *EVENING* JOURNAL PRICE 5 CENTS
June 11, 1927
Copyright, 1927, New York Evening Journal, Inc.

"LINDY"

WE Captain Charles A. Lindbergh, Who Conquered the Atlantic in the New York to Paris Flight in 33 Hours and 30 Minutes, and His Plane, "Spirit of Saint Louis." *Charles A. Lindbergh* become more and more corporate, and less and less individualistic. All of the technological breakthroughs had taken place, and with fewer opportunities for celebrity-making than before, the press and public lost interest. Before long, pilotless guided missiles began to replace aircraft and pilots as attention getters; the era of space travel had begun with the Mercury, Gemini and Apollo programs designed to place American astronauts on the moon in an attempt to show the United States' technological superiority over the Soviet Union.

While the Mercury astronauts achieved considerable fame for their bravery, Life magazine and the National Aeronautics and Space Administration helped to construct their celebrity. Howard McCurdy points out that the company of test pilots, from which the astronauts were drawn, "were thought to be a hard-living, hard-drinking lot." But "to a public clamoring for personal details, the Mercury Seven were presented by the press as the personification of the clean-cut, all-American boys whose mythical lives popularized family-oriented television programs of the 1950s and 1960s." Interestingly, Tom Wolfe, in The Right Stuff, pits the Mercury astronauts against Charles E. "Chuck" Yeager, a late-blooming aviation hero whose unlikely celebrity as a test pilot came years after he was the first man to fly faster than the speed of sound, in 1947. In Wolfe's view the astronauts, despite their former careers as test pilots, come out second-best when compared to Yeager, who exemplifies the "Right Stuff," the ineffable quality that distinguishes the elite fighter pilot from the ordinary one.

In these post-heroic contemporary times, large numbers of people perceive that piloting an airplane may be a potentially dangerous, but not particularly heroic activity. Aircraft are used routinely in war; air routes crisscross the globe; aviation has become so familiar that no one thinks much about it. If the idea of a pilot-hero-celebrity exists at all, it may only be in terms of nostalgia for a bygone era.

Advertising poster for the New York Evening Journal, June 11, 1927

Blériot Tells of His Flight Across the English Channel

1909

Louis Blériot

Special Cable to The New York Times
Dispatch to the London Daily Mail
Dover, England, July 25 [1909]

I ROSE AT 2:30 THIS (SUNDAY) MORNING, and finding that the conditions were favorable, ordered the torpedo boat destroyer, *Escopette*, which had been placed at my disposal by the French Government, to start. Then I went to the garage at Sangatte and found that the motor worked well. At 4 A.M. I took my seat in the aeroplane and made a trial flight around Calais of some fifteen kilometers (over nine miles), descending at the spot chosen for the start across the Channel.

Here I waited for the sun to come out, the conditions of *The Daily Mail* prize requiring that I fly between sunrise and sunset. At 4:30 daylight has come, but it was impossible to see the coast. A light breeze from the southwest was blowing the air clear, however, and everything was prepared.

I was dressed in a khaki jacket lined with wool for warmth over my tweed clothes and beneath my engineer's suit of blue cotton overalls. A close-fitting cap was fastened over my head and ears. I had neither eaten nor drunk anything since I rose. My thoughts were only upon the flight and my determination to accomplish it this morning.

Hommage à Blériot, Robert Delaunay, ca. 1913–14

"All Ready" at 4:35

At 4:35 "All's ready." My friend Leblanc gives the signal, and in an instant I am in the air, my engine making 1,200 revolutions, almost its highest speed, in order that I may get quickly over the telegraph wires along the edge of the cliff.

As soon as I am over the cliff I reduce speed. There is now no need to force the engine. I begin my flight, steady and sure, toward the coast of England. I have no apprehensions, no sensation—pas du tout—none at all.

"The Escopette" Follows

The Escopette has seen me. She is driving ahead at full speed. She makes perhaps 42 kilometers (26 miles) an hour. What matters it? I am making at least 68 kilometers (over 42 miles). Rapidly I overtake her traveling at a height of 80 meters (260 feet). Below me is the surface of the sea, disturbed by the wind, which is now freshening. The motion of the waves beneath me is not pleasant. I drive on.

Ten minutes are gone. I have passed the destroyer, and I turn my head to see whether I am proceeding in the right direction. I am amazed. There is nothing to be seen—neither the torpedo boat destroyer nor France nor England. I am alone, I can see nothing at all.

For ten minutes I am lost; it is a strange position to be in—alone, guided without a compass in the air over the middle of the Channel.

I touch nothing; my hands and feet rest lightly on the levers. I let the aeroplane take its own course. I care not wither it goes.

Sees England's Cliffs

For ten minutes I continue, neither rising nor falling nor turning, and then twenty minutes after I have left the French coast, I see green cliffs and Dover Castle, and away to the west the spot where I had intended to land.

What can I do? It is evident the wind has taken me out of my course. I am almost at St. Margaret's Bay, going in the direction of Goodwin Sands.

Now it is time to attend to the steering. I press a lever with my foot and turn easily toward the west, reversing the direction in which I am traveling. Now I am in difficulties, for the wind here by the cliffs is much stronger and my speed is reduced as I fight against it, yet my beautiful aeroplane responds still steadily.

Flies Over Dover Harbor

I fly westward, chopping across the harbor, and reach Shakespeare Cliff. I see an opening in the cliff. Although I am confident I can continue for an hour and a half, that I might, indeed, return to Calais, I cannot resist the opportunity to make a landing upon this green spot.

Once more I turn my aeroplane, and describing a half circle, I enter the opening and find myself again over dry land. Avoiding the red buildings on my right, I attempt a landing, but the wind catches me and whirls me around two or three times. At once I stop my motor, and instantly my machine falls straight upon the ground from a height of twenty meters (seventy-five feet). In two or three seconds I am safe upon your shore.

Soldiers in khaki run up, and policemen. Two of my compatriots are on the spot. They kiss my cheeks. The conclusion of my flight overwhelms me.

Thus ended my flight across the Channel—a flight which could easily be done again. Shall I do it? I think not. I have promised my wife that after a race for which I have already entered I will fly no more. ✳

Propellers, Fernand Leger, 1918

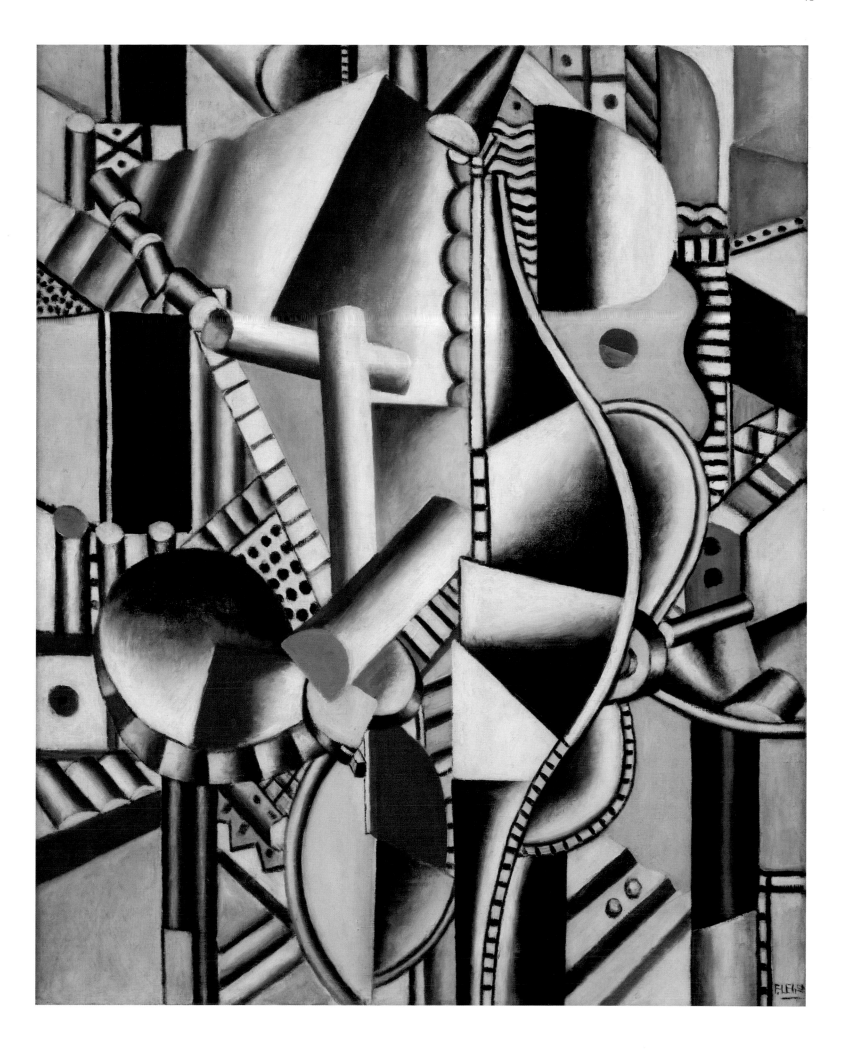

How a Woman Learns to Fly

1911

Harriet Quimby

IF A WOMAN WANTS TO FLY, first of all she must, of course, abandon skirts and don a knickerbocker uniform. I speak of this particularly, because so many have asked me about my flying costume. It may seem strange, but I could not find an aviation suit of any description in the great city of New York—and I tried hard. In my perplexity it occurred to me that the president of the American Tailors' Association, Alexander M Grean, might be a good advisor; and he was, for it did not take him long to design a suit which has no doubt established the aviation costume for women in this country, if not for all the world, since French women still continue to wear the clumsy and uncomfortable harem skirt as a flying costume. My suit is made of thick wool-back satin, without lining. It is all in one piece, including the hood. By an ingenious combination it can be converted instantly into a conventional appearing walking skirt when not in use in knickerbocker form.

The speed with which the aviator flies and the strong currents created by the rapidly revolving propeller directly in front of the driver compel the latter to be warmly clad. There must be no flapping ends to catch in the multitudinous wires surrounding the driver's seat. The feet and legs must be free, so that one can readily manipulate the steering apparatus; for the steering on a monoplane is not done by a wheel guided by the hand as in an automobile. One who has to run a motorcycle or an automobile successfully is all the better qualified to begin his lessons as an aviator. Without experience of this kind, the noise of an unmuffled motor in an airplane will be nerve-racking.

The first lesson of the beginner in an airplane is intended to accustom her to the noisy jarring vibration of the engine. Before the student climbs into her seat, she will discover why it is well to cover her natty costume with washable jumpers or coveralls. Not only the chassis of the machine, but all the fixtures are slippery with lubricating oil, aid when the engine is speeded a shower of this oil is also thrown back directly into the driver's face. It is interesting to know that castor oil is used as lubricant for high-tensioned engines, like the Gnome.

The first instruction that my preceptor, Andre Houpert, gave me after taking my seat in the monoplane was regarding the manipulation of the switch, so that no injury would result to the mechanic, who was cranking the engine directly in front of me. The school machine I use is a Moisant monoplane, fitted with a Gnome engine of thirty horse-power. Four sturdy mechanics held on to the rudder until I had speeded the engine to the necessary velocity to start the aeroplane across the field. Under the impetus of a rapidly revolving propeller, the machine swept ahead, sometimes on the ground and, as the engine gained speed, sometimes a little above it. The aviator's first lesson is to learn to steer his airship in a perfectly straight line for a distance of a mile or over. This looks very easy, until you discover that an aeroplane possesses the perversity common to all inanimate objects. It always wants to go the other way, instead of the straight way that you seek to direct. Your first dash across the field and back takes two minutes, if no mishap occurs. After two dashes of this description, a discreet teacher will dismiss you for the day. You have had all that your nerves ought to be asked to stand. In the best schools of France—a land famous for its aviators—no pupil, however apt, is permitted to have a longer daily lesson than five minutes at the onset of his course; and Monsieur Houpert, who is a graduate of a leading French school of aviation, follows this plan. When we read about Grahame-White or some other noted aviator learning to fly to altitudinous heights after only three days' lessons, we must bear in mind that these three days do not represent all the time required in training, but simply the aggregate of hours devoted on many consecutive days to short lessons. Though I have been a student at the Moisant school for almost two weeks, my actual time in the monoplane would not exceed half an hour—yet I am already called a flyer!

After learning how to make a straight line on and off the ground, you are next taught how to manipulate the wings, so that when you leap off the ground you may preserve your balance in the air. Having accomplished so much, you are prepared for further instruction given in a course of lectures in connection with field practice, regarding emergencies requiring special knowledge. You are not yet prepared to make an application for a pilot's license, but are well on the way to reach your goal. Like learning to swim, the first requisite of one who would learn to fly is confidence and the knowledge that you can do it. The future mastery of the swimmer's art depends upon himself and how much time he can give to the recreation. The same may be said of the would be flyer.

Everyone asks me "how it feels to fly." It feels like riding in a high powered automobile, minus bumping over the rough roads, continually signaling to clear the way and keeping a watchful eye on the speedometer to see that you do not exceed the limit and provoke the wrath of the bicycle policeman or the covetous constable....

Part Two
August 17, 1911

Four o'clock in the morning! The light is just dawning as the telephone at the Garden City Hotel summons me to rise. The birds are chirping. The air is heavy with the odor of the fields, the trees and the flowers. It is the time when nature seems to be at rest and is, therefore, especially adapted for a lesson in flying. This is the reason why the students at the Moisant Aviation School must submit to the penalty of an early contemplation of nature, whether they appreciate it or not.

The student of aviation must be the earliest riser of all students in search of knowledge, for all the lessons can be given only while the air is still and while the little signal flag on the field clings close to its mast. Dressing in a hurry and waiting for a moment to enjoy the healthful precaution of a cup of hot coffee poured from a faithful vacuum bottle, the student is soon on the way across the field to the hangers, where the aeroplanes, with expanding white wings, are silently awaiting their flights. The activity of instructors and students here is in striking contrast with the quiet of the sleepy hotel just left. Even the little white dog with a black spot on his forehead, the much petted mascot of the school, is alert and seems thoroughly interested in the goings on. An anxious look is directed from time to time to a little red flag on the end of a tall bamboo pole, placed in the middle of the aviation field, and there is considerable misgiving as the light piece of bunting flutters from its mast. Each one hazards a guess as to the possibility of a flying lesson. All hope that the wind is not too strong or too puffy, but all fear that it may be, for this is not an unusual experience. Professor Houpert, the instructor, settles that matter by walking out into the open with an anemometer and measuring the velocity of the breeze, which he may report as blowing four or five miles an hour. If it is over this, the school is called off for the day, for a student of aviation who ventures into anything more than a six-mile wind, especially with a low-powered school machine, is almost certain to come to grief. This little measuring instrument resembles a small windmill, with cups instead of blades, and the strength of the breeze is measured by the rapidity with which cups revolve.

If Professor Houpert's verdict is favorable, there is a general scurrying toward the dressing rooms, where the students cover their natty aviation costumes with homely, one-piece mechanic suits, calculated to withstand any kind of wear and tear as well as oil. Each student picks up a chair and drags it from the hanger to the field, so as to rest comfortably until his or her turn comes to take a lesson. The beginner takes his first lesson in grass cutting. This means that he mounts the machine, the motor is started and he attempts to guide it as it moves swiftly on its wheels over the long stretch of grass to the far end of the aerodrome. Here a mechanic is posted to await the student's arrival, turn his machine around and start him back again over the course. He is, indeed, a promising student if he has made anything like a straight line in his grass cutting. If he succeeds in doing this five or six times without mishap, he is permitted to take short jumps of two or three feet in height in the air as he rushes across the field. An irreverent newspaperman termed this feat kangarooing, which name seems to fit the performance pretty well. It is at the kangarooing stage that the fascination of flying begins.

There is no exaggeration regarding the much reported sense of fascination which accompanies a flight, however low, through the air. The feel of the first freedom experienced as the wheels leave the ground makes the student eager for a longer flight. It is not surprising that sometimes a fledgling will forget what the instructor says and elevate his planes, which, of course, like a flash shoots the machine higher into the air. Finding himself much higher than he expected to go, he is more apt to seek a sudden descent, involving both a breakage and humiliation.

As the seniors enjoy the discomfitures of a freshman at college, so do the senior students of aviation enjoy the antics of the grass cutter. The length of time that the would-be aviator remains in the kindergarten class depends largely upon himself. It is no disgrace to spend weeks at the early stage of instruction, for some of the world's best flyers have been the slowest to learn. Nor should it be forgotten that the

lessons, depending on weather conditions, must necessarily be irregular. Learning to fly is like learning anything else. It requires patience and stick-to-itiveness to master the art. It requires these qualities, also, to learn to drive an automobile, but it does not follow that one who can run an automobile can drive a flying machine, for there is no similarity in the control of the two. But one who has easily learned how to drive an automobile and to pilot it with a clear head through congested traffic will undoubtedly find his experience an aid in learning to fly. I state this as the result of my own experience.

It is, indeed, a time for rejoicing in the school when Professor Houpert informs the student that he has graduated from the rather clumsy kindergarten machine and is to take his first flight in a lighter and more powerful machine fitted with a sensitive control. This means that he is really going to fly. The humor of the aviation school differs from any other. The students are invariably a light-hearted and a jolly crowd, seeing and enjoying the funny sides of things. A great deal of good natured banter is exchanged between those who return from a flight and the students who have watched them. Although one fledgling reached a height of only ten feet or so and that only one fraction of a minute, he returned with an exciting tale of having fallen into an air hole and a laughable explanation of how he dexterously straightened his machine and returned to earth with safety. Another created a roar of laughter, when he returned from a kangerooing trip, by his account of being attacked by a vicious sparrow on the way. M. Vedrine, who crossed the Alps and startled the world by reporting that in transit he had been attacked by an enormous eagle, has nothing on the students of the Moisant school.

It was a happy day for me when Professor Houpert told me that my grasscutting days were over and that I was ready for a flight in the air. It was the day I had longed for with an expectancy that I cannot describe, the fascination of flying had such a hold upon me. Every student tells me that he has the same feeling, except those who have had a mishap which has tested their nerve too much. A flying

Trainer Biplane in Flight with Pilot and Passenger

student cannot expect to go through the course of instruction without some breakage, for the most skillful of flyers have their bad moments. It must be remembered that the flying machine must be in perfect working order and that one false move of the student invites disaster. It may be only a broken fork or wheel or perhaps a chip off the propeller, but it is enough to disable the machine and put it out of commission until repairs have been thoroughly made. It is a remarkable fact that thus far the records show that only one beginner has had a fatal casualty. I refer to the case of Mlle. Moore, a student of a biplane school in France, a few weeks ago.

The second machine in which I was to take my first flight in the air differed in essentials from the first one, known as the grass cutter. The latter is equipped with three wheels, so that it can roll over the ground smoothly, while the former has two wheels in front and a skid instead of a wheel behind. The student must, therefore, rise above the ground promptly or run the risk of injuring the dragging skid. The chassis of the flyer is lighter than that of the grass cutter and the power of the former is considerably increased. The student who takes his first real flight is instructed to fly straight across the field and to alight near where a mechanic stands waiting to turn him around for his return trip. His first lesson as a

freshman is intended to teach him to manage his machine while running cover the ground. His first lesson as a graduate is to learn how to cut his pathway through the air. While grass cutting, the freshman learns how to steer. While air cutting, the graduate must not only steer, but he must learn the more difficult task of warping his wings and of manipulating his elevating and lowering planes. The warping is done by a wheel resembling the steering wheel of an automobile and which rests directly in front of the pilot. This wheel, by a movement back and forth, elevates or lowers the plane. After one successful straight-away flight, I was instructed by my pleased instructor to fly across the field and to turn around and come back without alighting at the other end. The fundamental requirements of a good student are that he shall be able to make a good ascent and a safe landing. These are the most difficult accomplishments of a flyer. When he has mastered them he has learned his lesson pretty well. After learning to make a circuit of the aerodrome, the student is asked to do what is considered difficult—a right-hand turn. After having done this without mishap, he is then capable of attempting to make a flight in the form of a figure eight, which the essential requirement before he can secure the much coveted pilot's license from the Aero Club of America.... ✳

Portrait of Amelia Earhart, Hugo Gellert, c.1932

A Pilot Grows Up

1937

Amelia Earhart

PILOTS ARE ALWAYS DREAMING DREAMS…

I think my mother realized before I did how much airplanes were beginning to mean to me, for she helped me buy the first one. It was second-hand, painted bright yellow, and one of the first light airplanes developed in this country. The motor was so rough that my feet went to sleep after more than a few minutes on the rudder bar. I had a system of lending the plane for demonstration so as not to be charged storage. Hangar rental would have annihilated my salary.

After a year my longest hop was from Long Beach to Pasadena, about 40 miles. Still I all but set off to cross the continent by air. The fact that I couldn't buy gasoline myself forced me to compromise and drive a car with Mother along. I am sure I wouldn't be here to tell the tale if I had carried out the original plan.

I did what flying I could afford in the next few years and then the "Friendship" came along. I was working in Denison House in Boston, one of America's oldest social settlements.

"Phone for you, Miss Earhart."

"Tell 'em I'm busy." At the moment I was the center of an eager swarm of Chinese and Syrian neighborhood children, piling in for games and classes.

"Says it's important."

So I excused myself and went to listen to a man's voice asking me whether I was interested in doing something dangerous in the air. At first I thought the conversation was a joke and said so. Several times before I had been approached by bootleggers who promised rich reward and no danger— "Absolutely no danger to you, Leddy."

The frank admission of risk stirred my curiosity. References were demanded and supplied. Good references. An appointment was arranged for that evening.

"Would you like to fly the Atlantic?"

My reply was a prompt "Yes"—provided the equipment was all right and the crew capable. Nine years ago flying oceans was less commonplace than today, and my own experience as a pilot was limited to a few hundred hours in small planes which work and finances permitted.

So I went to New York and met the man entrusted with the quaint commission of finding a woman willing to fly the Atlantic. The candidate, I gathered, should be a flyer herself, with social graces, education, charm and, perchance, pulchritude.

His appraisal left me discomforted. Somehow this seeker for feminine perfection seemed unimpressed. Anyway, I showed my pilot's license (it happened to be the first granted an American woman by the F.A.I.) and inwardly prepared to start back for Boston.

But he felt that, having come so far, I might as well meet the representatives of Mrs. Frederick Guest, whose generosity was making the flight possible, and at whose insistence a woman was to be taken along. Those representatives were David T. Layman, Jr., and John S. Phipps, before which masculine jury I made my next appearance. It should have been slightly embarrassing, for if I were found wanting in too many ways I would be counted out. On the other hand, if I were just too fascinating, the gallant gentlemen might be loath to risk drowning me. Anyone could see the meeting was a crisis.

A few days later the verdict came. The flight actually would be made and I could go if I wished. Naturally I couldn't say "No." Who would refuse an invitation to such a shining adventure?

Followed, in due course, after weeks of mechanical preparation, efforts to get the monoplane "Friendship" off from the gray waters of Boston Harbor. There were chill before-dawn gettings-up, with breakfasts snatched and thermos bottles filled at an all-night lunch counter. Brief voyages on the tugboat Sadie Ross to the anchored plane, followed by the sputter of the motors awakening to Mechanic Lou Gordon's coaxing and their later full-throated roar when Pilot "Bill" Stultz gave them the gun—and I crouched on the fuselage floor hoping we were really off.

Thrice we failed, dragging back to Boston for more long days of waiting. Waiting is apt to be so much harder than going, with the excitement of movement, of getting off, of adventure-around-the-corner.

Finally one morning the "Friendship" took off successfully, and Stultz, Gordon, and I transferred ourselves to Newfoundland. After thirteen days of weary waiting at Trepassey (how well I remember the alternating diet of mutton and rabbits!) the Atlantic flight started. Twenty hours and forty minutes later we tied up to a buoy off Burryport, Wales. I recall desperately waving a towel; one friendly soul ashore pulled off his coat and waved back. But beyond that for an hour nothing happened. It took persistence to arouse interest in an itinerant trans-Atlantic plane.

I myself did no piloting on that trip. But I gained experience. In London I was introduced to Lady Mary Heath, the then very active Irish woman flyer. She had just made a record flight from London to Cape Town and I purchased the small plane she had used. It wore on its chest a number of medals given her at various stops she made on the long route.

After the pleasant accident of being the first woman to cross the Atlantic by air, I was launched into a life full of interest. Aviation offered such fun as crossing the continent in planes large and small, trying the whirling rotors of an autogiro, making record flights. With these activities came opportunity to know women everywhere who shared my conviction that there is so much women can do in the modern world and should be permitted to do irrespective of their sex. Probably my greatest satisfaction was to indicate by example now and then, that women can sometimes do things themselves if given the chance.

Here I should add that the "Friendship" flight brought me something even dearer than such opportunities. That Man-who-was-to-find-a-girl-to-fly-the-Atlantic, who found me and then managed the flight, was George Palmer Putnam. In 1931 we married. Mostly, my flying has been solo, but the preparation for it wasn't. Without my husband's help and encouragement I could not have attempted what I have. Ours has been a contented and reasonable partnership, he with his solo jobs and I with mine. But always with work and play together, conducted under a satisfactory system of dual control.

I was hardly home when I started off to fly the continent—my 1924 ambition four years late. Lady Heath's plane was very small. It had folding wings so that it actually could fit in a garage. I cranked the motor by standing behind the propeller and pulling it down with one hand. The plane was so light I could pick it up by the tail and drag it easily around the field.

At that time I was full of missionary zeal for the cause of aviation. I refused to wear the high-bred aviation togs of the moment. Instead I simply wore a dress or suit. I carried no chute and instead of a helmet used a close-fitting hat. I stepped into the airplane with as much nonchalance as I could muster, hoping that onlookers would be persuaded that flying was nothing more than an everyday occurrence. I refused even to wear goggles, obviously. However, I put them on as I taxied to the end of the field and wore them while flying, being sure to take them off shortly after I landed.

That was thoroughly informal flying. Pilots landed in pastures, race courses, even golf links where they were still enough of a novelty to be welcome.

In those days domestic animals scurried to the fancied protection of trees and barns when the flying monsters roared above them. Now along the airways there's not enough curiosity left for a self-respecting cow even to lift her head to see what goes on in the sky. She's just bored. Stories of that happy-go-lucky period should be put together in a saga to regale the scientific, precision flyers of tomorrow.

Nineteen-twenty-nine was the year of the women's derby from California to Cleveland, the first time a cross-country race had ever been sponsored for women alone. I felt I needed a new plane for this extraordinary sporting event. So I traded in the faithful little Avion for my first Lockheed Vega. It was a third-hand clunk but to me a heavenly chariot.

I crossed the continent again from New York to California to stop at the Lockheed factory. I thought possibly there might be a few adjustments necessary before I entered the race. There I met the great Wiley Post for the first time. Wiley Post had not then had his vision of stratosphere flying, and was simply a routine check pilot in the employ of the Lockheed company.

It fell to him to take my airplane up for test. Having circled the field once, he came down and proceeded to tell everyone within earshot that my lovely airplane was the foulest he had ever flown. Of course the worse he made the plane, the better pilot I became. The fact that I should have been able to herd such a hopeless piece of mechanism across the continent successfully was the one bright spot in the ensuing half hour.

Finally Lockheed officials were so impressed by my prowess (or so sorry for me) that they traded me a brand new plane. The clunk was never flown again.

The Derby produced one of the gems which belong in the folklore of aviation. Something went wrong with her motor and Ruth Elder made a forced landing in a field thickly inhabited by cattle. The bovine population crowded around her plane and proceeded to lick the paint off the wings—there seemed to be something in the "doped" finish that appealed to them. Meanwhile, Ruth snuggled down in the safety of the cockpit. "You see," she explained, "I didn't know much about such things and was uncertain as to the sex of the visitors. My plane was red—very red. And I'd always heard what bulls did to *that*."…Apparently the cows were cows.

After the "Friendship" flight I did not immediately plan to fly the Atlantic alone. But later as I gained in experience and looked back over the years I decided that I had had enough to try to make it solo. Lockheed #2 was then about three years old. It had been completely reconditioned and a new and larger engine put in. By the spring of 1932 plane and pilot were ready.

Oddly, one of my clearest memories of the Atlantic solo concerns not the flight itself but my departure from home. On May 19th the weather outlook was so unpromising we had abandoned hope of getting off that day. So I had driven in to New York from our home in Westchester. Just before noon an urgent message caught up with me immediately to get in touch with Mr. Putnam at the Weather Bureau.

Our phone conversation was brief.

"It looks like the break we've waited for," he said. "Doc Kimball says this afternoon is fine to get to Newfoundland—St. John's anyway. And by tomorrow the Atlantic looks as good as you're likely to get it for some time."

I asked a few questions. A threatening "low" on the first leg of the route had dissipated to the southeast; a "high" seemed to be moving in promisingly beyond Newfoundland.

"Okeh! We'll start," I said. Mr. Putnam agreed he would corral Bernt Balchen, my technical adviser who was to go with me to Newfoundland to be sure that everything was as right as could be before I hopped off. I explained I would have to rush back to Rye to get my flying clothes and maps. We arranged to meet at two o'clock at the city end of the George Washington Bridge, which leads across the Hudson toward Teterboro Airport in New Jersey, where my plane waited.

As fast as I dared—traffic cops being what they are—I drove the twenty-five miles to Rye. Five minutes was enough to pick up my things. Plus a lingering few more to drink in the beauty of a lovely treasured sight. Beside and below our bedroom windows were dogwood trees, their blossoms in luxuriant full flower, unbelievable bouquets of white and pink flecked with the sunshine of spring. Those sweet blooms smiled at me a radiant farewell….That is a memory I have never forgotten.

Looking back, there are less cheering recollections of that night over the Atlantic. Of seeing, for instance, the flames lick through the exhaust collector ring and wondering, in a detached way, whether one would prefer drowning to incineration. Of the five hours of storm, during black midnight, when I kept right side up by instruments alone, buffeted about as I never was before. Of much beside, not the least the feeling of fine loneliness and of realization that the machine I rode was doing its best and required from me the best I had.

And one further fact of the flight, which I've not set down in words before. I carried a barograph, an instrument which records on a disc the course of the plane, its rate of ascent and descent, its levels of flight all co-ordinated with clocked time. My tell-tale disc could tell a tale. At one point it recorded an almost vertical drop of three thousand feet. It started at an altitude of something over 3,000 feet, and ended—well, something above the water. That happened when the plane suddenly "iced up" and went into a spin. How long we spun I do not know. I do know that I tried my best to do exactly what one should do with a spinning plane, and regained flying control as the warmth of the lower altitude melted the ice. As we righted and held level again, through the blackness below I could see the white-caps too close for comfort.

All that was five full years ago, a long time to recall little things. So I wonder if Bernt Balchen remembers as I do the three words he said to me as I left Harbor Grace. They were: "Okeh. So-long. Good luck." ✳

Amelia

1977

Joni Mitchell

Photo of Amelia Earhart

I WAS DRIVING ACROSS THE BURNING DESERT
When I spotted six jet planes
Leaving six white vapor trails across the bleak terrain
It was the hexagram of the heavens
It was the strings of my guitar
Amelia, it was just a false alarm

The drone of flying engines
Is a song so wild and blue
It scrambles time and seasons if it gets through to
you
Then your life becomes a travelogue
Of picture-postcard-charms
Amelia, it was just a false alarm

People will tell you where they've gone
They'll tell you where to go
But till you get there yourself you never really know
Where some have found their paradise
Others just come to harm
Amelia, it was just a false alarm

A ghost of aviation
She was swallowed by the sky
Or by the sea, like me she had a dream to fly
Like Icarus ascending
On beautiful foolish arms
Amelia, it was just a false alarm

Maybe I've never really loved
I guess that is the truth
I've spent my whole life in clouds at icy altitudes
And looking down at everything
I crashed into his arms
Amelia, it was just a false alarm

I pulled into the Cactus Tree Motel
To shower off the dust
And I slept on the strange pillows of my wanderlust
I dreamed of 747's
Over geometric farms
Dreams, Amelia, dreams and false alarms

Smash All Records Flying for Shell, Buehler, c. 1932

I Could Never Be
So Lucky Again

1991

General James H. "Jimmy" Doolittle

BY 1925, AVIATION IN AMERICA WAS very much on the public mind. The number of air races held in the good flying months proliferated; racing pilots became role models for the kids of America. For a pilot, there was a strong desire to participate, to compete, to set any kind of record or establish an aviation "first."…

The Pulitzer [race of 1925] was held in conjunction with the New York Air Races organization, and we Army pilots were encouraged to make the public aware that the races were scheduled. We did our best. We performed aerobatics all over downtown New York City. It was a rare thrill to fly down the city streets and look up at the tall buildings. It was also interesting to do it inverted. We also "fought" balloons and did low aerobatics wherever there was enough of a crowd to be impressed….

All of this, of course, was to keep public attention focused on aviation and what the airplane could do in time of war, which, as Billy Mitchell was preaching so vociferously, was bound to come.

I was designated to be the Army's alternate pilot for the 1925 Pulitzer Race; Lieutenant Cyrus Bettis was the principal pilot for the Army's lone R3C, fitted with wheels and powered by the 600-horsepower Curtiss V-1400 engine. In accordance with our orders we traveled from McCook to Mitchel Field "to witness certain phases of the construction work [on these airplanes] and for necessary training and test flights."

The race was held on October 12, 1925. Cy won it easily. His speed was officially set at 248.975 miles per hour. Al Williams placed second in his R3C with a speed of 241.695 miles per hour; and Army lieutenant Leo H. Dawson, flying a Curtiss P-1 Hawk, was third at 169.9 miles per hour.…

The Schneider Cup race, to be held at Baltimore two weeks after the Pulitzer, was reserved for seaplanes only. The race had been first run in 1913 and was sponsored by Jacques P. Schneider, pilot son of a wealthy French industrialist. It was considered the most important international air race at the time and received much press coverage in the flying nations of the world.

Since I had been the alternate pilot for the Pulitzer, I was to be the principal pilot for the Schneider competition. Cy was then the substitute for me if I couldn't fly for any reason. I had never flown a seaplane before; it behooved me to learn how....

There were two Italian and three British entries in the Schneider, plus the two Navy and one Army R3Cs. The British brought two impressive-looking Gloster-Napier III biplane racers and a Supermarine S.4 midwing monoplane. The Italians had two heavy Macchi M.33 flying boats, which were powered by Curtiss D-12 engines.

During the qualification tests before the speed runs, British pilot Henry C. Biard, flying the Supermarine S.4, had wing flutter problems and crashed into Chesapeake Bay. Biard suffered a broken wrist and was rescued from the icy water by speedboats. The S.4, was a washout.

The British lost one of the Gloster-Napiers when one of the struts bent and the pontoon structure collapsed so that it couldn't pass the navigability and watertightness tests. This left the second Gloster-Napier as the lone British entry.

The first of the two Macchis had engine trouble and was eliminated because the rules stated that all engines had to be sealed at the time of the navigability trials and no repairs or adjustments could be made. This left Giovanni de Briganti, one of the Italians; two U.S. Navy pilots—Lieutenants Cuddihy and Ofstie; and me.

The race committee had laid out a triangular course that was 31.07 miles in length, with pylons at three positions in Chesapeake Bay off Bay Shore Park, Maryland. Each plane had to fly around the course seven times for a total of about 217.5 miles,

or 350 kilometers, to satisfy the race rules....

There were many VIPs in the audience at Bay Shore Park. Generals, admirals, and army and navy attachés from all over the world were there; aircraft and engine manufacturers attended to see what information and tips they could pick up that would help improve their products. Orville Wright was also in the audience, and, much to my liking, Joe had been able to have the boys taken care of at McCook and had arrived by train.

I was first in line for takeoff over the speed course. The wind came from the right direction and I was airborne. My technique was simple. Climb slowly under full power before approaching the pylon, make a tight diving turn, and then level out until approaching the next pylon. It was in the steeply banked diving turns where I thought I could gain a critical speed advantage. Other pilots hadn't done this at the Pulitzer and, as far as I know, didn't do it during this race.

British captain Hubert Broad was next off, followed by Lieutenants Cuddihy and Ofstie. De Briganti trailed in the Macchi. I had no trouble staying in the lead, and it quickly became a U.S. Navy versus U.S. Army contest. Cuddihy crept up on me briefly, but Ofstie and the other two were never a threat.

Ofstie developed engine trouble during the sixth lap and dropped out; then Cuddihy's engine ran out of oil and burst into flames on the final lap. He managed to land not far from Ofstie and put the fire out with a hand extinguisher. My time over the course was fastest and set a new record for seaplanes of 232.573 miles per hour. Captain Broad was second at 199.169 miles per hour; and de Briganti came in third at 168.444 miles per hour. De Briganti, however, was not through flying. After he crossed the finish line, he continued out into the bay to look for Ofstie and Cuddihy, whom, he had seen down in the water. However, both pilots had already been taken in tow; de Briganti then ran out of gas and had to be towed himself. His act of courtesy and concern for his brother pilots earned him an ovation when he returned to shore. ✳

High Flight

1941

John Gillespie Magee, Jr.

OH, I HAVE SLIPPED THE SURLY BONDS OF EARTH
And danced the skies on laughter-silvered wings;
Sunward I've climbed, and joined the tumbling mirth
Of sun-split clouds—and done a hundred things
You have not dreamed of—wheeled and soared and swung
High in the sunlit silence. Hov'ring there,
I've chased the shouting wind along, and flung
My eager craft through footless halls of air.
Up, up the long delirious burning blue.
I've topped the windswept heights and easy grace
Where never lark, or even eagle flew.
And, while with silent, lifting mind I've trod
The high untrespassed sanctity of space.
Put out my hand, and touched the face of God.

Suprematist Composition: Airplane Flying, Kazimir Malevich, 1915

The Seaplane

Louise Stewart

EACH NIGHT ACROSS THE SUNSET SKIES
I watch a sailorman who flies.
Swifter than swallows are his wings
Mounting to where the pale moon swings
Above the solan's forkèd flight.
Far, far above the mad waves' spite
I catch his throbbing, laughing song,
Exultant 'neath the stars' bright throng,
While chasing cloud flotillas he
Conquers the air as well as sea.

Seaplane, Charles Bell, 1973

Spirit of St. Louis, Alexander Calder, 1929

The Thirty-Third Hour

1953

Charles A. Lindbergh

Almost thirty-five hundred miles from New York. I've broken the world's distance record for a nonstop airplane flight. The fuselage tank must be almost empty; and now there's no need to run it dry. I turn on the right wing-tank. In one hour more I should see the lights of Paris.

The sea is calm. Southward, just out of gliding range, lies the dusk-touched coast of Normandy. Little boats sail in toward shore, apparently motionless on the surface, leaving only their wakes as signs of movement to an airman's eye. A faint point of land, far ahead on my left, marks the location of Le Havre. The expanse of water, extending on eastward below it, is the estuary of the Seine.

I cross the coast again exactly on course, over Deauville. All the east foreshadows night. Day now belongs only to the western sky, still red with sunset. What more I see of France, before I land, will be in this long twilight of late spring. I nose the *Spirit of St. Louis* lower, while I study the farms and villages — the signs I can't read, the narrow, shop-lined streets, the walled-in barnyards. Fields are well groomed, fertile, and peaceful—larger than those of England. It's not hard to see how French farmers make a living; and there are plenty of places where I could land in emergency without cracking up.

People come running out as I skim low over their houses—blue-jeaned peasants, white-aproned wives, children scrambling between them, all bare-headed and looking as though they'd jumped up from the supper table to search for the noise above their roofs. Four-twenty on the clock. That's nine-twenty here. Why, it's past suppertime! I hold the stick with my knees, untwist the neck of the paper bag, and pull out a sandwich—my first food since take-off. *The Spirit of St. Louis* noses up. I push the stick forward, clamp it between my knees again, and uncork the canteen. I can drink all the water I want, now — plenty more below if I should be forced down between here and Paris. But how flat the sandwich tastes! Bread and meat never touched my tongue like this before. It's an effort even to swallow. I'm hungry, because I go on eating, but I have to wash each mouthful down with water.

One sandwich is enough. I brush the crumbs off my lap. I start to throw the wrapping through the window — no, these fields are so clean and fresh it's a shame to scatter them with paper. I crunch it up and stuff it back in the brown bag. I don't want the litter from a sandwich to symbolize my first contact with France.

All details on the ground are masking out in night. Color is gone. Only shades remain—woods darker than fields; hedgerows, lines of black. Lights twinkle in villages and blink in farmhouse windows. My instruments are luminous again. The rest of the flight will be in darkness. But I can't miss Paris, even if I find no other check point on my route. I'm too close. The sky's too clear. The city's too large.

I ease back on the stick and climb—to five hundred—to a thousand—to two thousand feet. A light flashes from the darkness, miles ahead. Could it be —I stare at the area from which it came, and wait. On our mail route at home, you count eleven between flashes—Another flash. Yes, it's an air beacon! And there are two more, blinking dimly in the distance, to the left. It must be the airway between London and Paris! Nobody told me it had flights.

From now on everything will be as simple as flying in to Chicago on a clear night. That line of beacons is converging with my course. Where the two lines meet—the beacons and my course—less than a hundred miles ahead—lies Paris. I can project them over the horizon, into the night, and already see the city in my mind's eye. Within half an hour, its glow will lighten the southeastern sky.

Down under my left wing, angling in from the north, winding through fields submerged in night, comes the Seine, shimmering back to the sky the faint remaining light of evening.

With my position known and my compass set, with the air clear and a river and an airway to lead me in, nothing but engine failure can keep me now from reaching Paris. The engine is running perfectly—I check the switches again.

The Spirit of St. Louis is a wonderful plane. It's like a living creature, gliding along smoothly, happily, as though a successful flight means as much to it as to me, as though we shared our experiences together, each feeling beauty, life, and death as keenly, each dependent on the other's loyalty. *We* have made this flight across the ocean, not *I* or *it*.

I throw my flashlight on the engine instruments. Every needle is in place. For almost thirty-three hours, not one of them has varied from its normal reading—except when the nose tank ran dry. For every minute I've flown there have been more than seven thousand explosions in the cylinders, yet not a single one has missed.

I'm leveled off at four thousand feet, watching for the luminosity in the sky ahead that will mark the city of Paris. Within the hour, I'll land. The dot on my map will become Paris itself, with its airport, hangars, and floodlights, and mechanics running out to guide me in. All over the ground below there are clusters of lights. Large clusters are cities; small ones, towns and villages; pin points are buildings on a farm. I can image that I'm looking through the earth to the heavens on the other side. Paris will be a great galaxy lighting up the night.

Within the hour I'll land, and strangely enough I'm in no hurry to have it pass. I haven't the slightest desire to sleep. My eyes are no longer salted stones. There's not an ache in my body. The night is cool and safe. I want to sit quietly in this cockpit and let the realization of my completed flight sink in.

Europe is below; Paris, just over the earth's curve in the night ahead—a few minutes more of flight. It's like struggling up a mountain after a rare flower, and then, when you have it within arm's reach, realizing that satisfaction and happiness lie more in the finding than the plucking. Plucking and withering are inseparable. I want to prolong this culminating experience of my flight. I almost wish Paris were a few more hours away. It's a shame to land with the night so clear and so much fuel in my tanks.

I'm still flying at four thousand feet when I see it, that scarcely perceptible glow, as though the moon had rushed ahead of schedule. Paris is rising over the edge of the earth. It's almost thirty-three hours from my take-off on Long Island. As minutes pass, myriad pin points of light emerge, a patch of starlit earth under a starlit sky—the lamps of Paris—straight lines of lights, curving lines of lights, squares of lights, black spaces in between. Gradually avenues, parks, and buildings take outline form; and there, far below, a little offset from the center, is a column of lights pointing upward, changing angles as I fly— the Eiffel Tower. I circle once above it, and turn northeastward toward Le Bourget.

The Thirty-fourth Hour

[Over France]

...Four fifty-two on the clock. That's 9:52, Paris time. Le Bourget isn't shown on my map. No one I talked to back home had more than a general idea of its location. "It's a big airport," I was told. "You can't miss it. Just fly northeast from the city." So I penciled a circle on my map, about where Le Bourget ought to be; and now the *Spirit of St. Louis* is over the out-skirts of Paris, pointed toward the center of that circle.

I look ahead. A beacon should be flashing on such a large and important airport. But the nearest beacon I see is fully twenty miles away, and west instead of east of Paris. I bank slightly, so I can search the earth directly ahead. There's no flash. But I'm flying at four thousand feet. The beacon may be sweeping the horizon. I'm probably far above its beam. It's probably like the beacons on our mail route, set low to guide pilots wedging underneath

clouds and storm, not for those who fly high through starlit nights. From my altitude, I shouldn't be hunting for a beacon, but for a darkened patch of ground, bordered by straight-lined, regularly spaced points of light, with a few green and red points among the yellow; that's how a landing field should look from four thousand feet.

Yes, there's a black patch to my left, large enough to be an airport. And there are lights all around it. But they're neither straight nor regularly spaced, and some are strangely crowded together. But if that's not Le Bourget, where else can it be? There's no other suitable grouping of lights—unless the location I've marked on my map is entirely wrong. I bank left to pass overhead. Are those flood-lights, in one corner of the dark area? If they are, they're awfully weak. They're hardly bright enough to be for landing aircraft. But don't I see the ends of hangars over at one side? Or are they just the build-ings of some factory?

It looks like an airport. But why would an airport be placed in such a congested section? There are thousands of lights along one side. They probably come from a large factory. Surely Le Bourget wouldn't have a factory that size right next to it. I'm almost overhead now. I can see no warning lights, no approach lights, and no revolving beacon. Looking straight down on a beacon, one can see the diffused light from its beam sweeping the ground under the tower. But those *are* floodlights, and they show the edge of a field. Maybe the French turn out their beacons when no planes are due, like that air-mail field at Cleveland. And even the people who think I have a chance of reaching Paris won't expect me here so soon. But why leave floodlights burning, and not the boundary lights and beacon? Of course I must remember I'm over Europe, where customs are strange....

I circle several times while I lose altitude, trying to penetrate the shadows from different vantage points, getting the lay of the land as well as I can in darkness. At one thousand feet I discover the wind sock, dimly lighted, on top of some building. It's bulged, but far from stiff. That means a gentle, constant wind, not over ten or fifteen miles an hour. My landing direction will be over the floodlights, angling away from the hangar line. Why circle any longer? That's all the information I need. No matter how hard I try, my eyes can't penetrate the blanket of night over the central portion of the field.

I straighten out my wings and let the throttled engine drag me on beyond the leeward border. Now the steep bank into wind, and the dive toward ground. But how strange it is, this descent. I'm wide awake, but the feel of my plane has not returned. Then I must hold excess speed—take no chance of stalling or of the engine loading up. My movements are mechanical, uncoordinated, as though I were coming down at the end of my first solo.

I point the nose just short of the floodlights, throttle half open, flattening out slightly as I approach. I see the whole outline of the hangars, now. Two or three planes are resting in the shadows. There's no time to look for more details. The lighted area is just ahead. It's barely large enough to land on. I nose down below the hangar roofs, so low that I can see the texture of the sod, and blades of grass on high spots. The ground is smooth and solid as far as the floodlights show its surface. I can tell nothing about the black mass beyond. But those several pin points in the distance look as though they mark the far border. Since Le Bourget is a major airport, the area between is probably also clear—I'll have to take a chance on that; if I land short, I may stop rolling before I reach it. . . .

In spite of my speed, the Spirit of St. Louis seems about to stall. My lack of feel alarms me. I've never tried to land a plane without feel before. I want to open the throttle wider, to glide faster, to tauten the controls still more. But—I glance at the dial—the needle points to eighty miles an hour. *The Spirit of St. Louis* is lightly loaded, with most of its fuel gone. Even at this speed I'll overshoot the lighted area before my tail skid strikes the ground. No, I'll have to pull the nose higher instead of pushing it down. I'll have to depend on the needle, on judgment more than instinct. I kick rudder and push the stick to one side, just to be sure—yes, controls are taut, there's plenty of speed. And feeling is not completely gone.

I still have a little left. I can feel the skid and slip. But the edge of perception is dull, very dull. It's better to come in fast, even if I roll into that black area after I land. And it's better to come in high—there may be poles or chimneys at the field's edge—Never depend on obstruction lights —especially when you don't see any.

It's only a hundred yards to the hangars now — solid forms emerging from the night. I'm too high— too fast. Drop wing—left rudder — sideslip — — Careful—mustn't get anywhere near the stall. I've never landed the *Spirit of St. Louis* at night before. It would be better to come in straight. But if I don't sideslip, I'll be too high over the boundary to touch my wheels in the area of light. That would mean circling again — — Still too high. I push the stick over to a steeper slip, leaving the nose well down — — Below the hangar roofs now — — straighten out — — A short burst of the engine — — Over the lighted area — — Sod coming up to meet me — — Deceptive high lights and shadows — Careful—easy to bounce when you're tired — — Still too fast — — Tail too high — — Hold off — — Hold off — — But the lights are far behind — — The surface dims — — Texture of sod is gone— —Ahead, there's nothing but night — — Give her the gun and climb for another try? — — The wheels touch gently—off again—No, I'll keep contact—Ease the stick forward — — Back on the ground — Off — Back — the tail skid too — — Not a bad landing, but I'm beyond the light—can't see anything ahead—Like flying in fog —Ground loop? — No, still rolling too fast — might blow a tire — The field must be clear — Uncomfortable though, jolting into blackness — Wish I had a wing light—but too heavy on the take-off — — Slower, now — — slow enough to ground loop safely —left rudder — reverse it —stick over the other way — — *The Spirit of St. Louis* swings around and stops rolling, resting on the solidness of earth, in the center of Le Bourget. ✳

The Airman

F. Vine Hall

WHAT THOUGHTS ARE HIS IN THE HIGH AIR,
What hazard does his spirit dare,
Or rapture, by what mystic rite
Does he approach the heaven's height.
By what mazes of what solemn dance
Does he to the still stars advance?
Exalted above earth he flies,
In the strange silence of the skies
Exultant: by steep steps he soars,
To gaze upon the golden doors
Of sunrise, if so he may trace
The springs of light, and the pure place
Of spirits. Nor the noon-tide sun,
Nor moon at midnight doth he shun;
He holds strange speech with storm and cloud,
He hears wild winds shout with the loud
Blast of a trumpet, as it were
A host of buglers in the air,
Or angel armies. In sheer height
He shelters, of the shining light
He builds a house, he is at home
Hung in the midst of heaven's dome.

Pêcheurs à la ligne avec aeroplane,
Henri Rousseau, 1907–1908

The Airplane at War

Part 3

Charles Gross

A PRODUCT OF THE TWENTIETH CENTURY, the achievement of sustained controlled powered flight in the first successful aircraft by the Wright brothers at Kitty Hawk, North Carolina, in December 1903 was the culmination of over a century of research and experimentation by various individuals in Europe, Great Britain, and the United States. The Wrights believed that their revolutionary invention would promote international peace and prosperity through commercial and private sales. When it became apparent that there was no significant civilian interest in their airplane, they turned to the armed forces.

Initially, the military was slow to recognize the potential of the Wrights' invention. Early aircraft were frail and unreliable contraptions with limited speed, distance, altitude, and load carrying capabilities. Instead, balloons and dirigibles were favored for reconnaissance and artillery spotting missions. However, increasing international tensions and the threat of war encouraged European powers to pour significant resources into aviation, including the establishment of several national laboratories for aeronautical research and development. Secure behind its ocean barriers, protected by a strong navy, and determined to remain aloof from Europe's quarrels, the United States allowed military aviation to languish.

During World War I, military aviators developed through a trial and error process most of the basic missions of air power that exist to the present day. At first they concentrated on the reconnaissance role of aircraft. Gradually, they explored the artillery spotting, air superiority, close air support, interdiction, strategic bombing, anti submarine warfare, air defense and airlift capabilities of aircraft. At sea, float planes and seaplanes were employed by several nations to support their surface fleets and hunt for submarines.

The Royal Navy introduced the aircraft carrier to the world's inventory of modern weapons during the conflict. Under the pressures of combat, the technology of flight made enormous progress. Contrary to the claims of some pioneer flyers, there was significant senior-level civilian and military support for aviation in some of the European powers both before and during the war. Propelled by mass circulation newspapers and magazines, as well as by the hunger for individual heroes amid the anonymous slaughter of trench warfare, pilots like Eddie Rickenbacker and Hermann Goering became national idols.

Massive military aircraft and engine production programs during World War I established the aviation industry as an economically significant enterprise grounded in modern science and engineering. There was an enormous increase in the performance characteristics of aircraft during the interwar period, driven by significant improvements in engine power and reliability. Equally significant, the "airframe revolution" of that era replaced box-like, open cockpit aircraft—made of wood and fabric and equipped with fixed landing gear, with streamlined all-metal planes that featured enclosed cockpits and retractable landing gear. The development of reliable lightweight airborne radios and the emergence of radar greatly increased the military potential of aircraft during the interwar period. Although commercial aviation emerged as a significant market for the industry in the 1930s, military aviation remained its most important customer and the primary stimulant of technological progress. Commercial aviation relied heavily on government regulation and subsidies as well as official research and development programs.

In America, aviation was portrayed as a benign and technologically progressive force during the interwar period by an informal coalition of businessmen, engineers and government officials as well as military and civilian pilots. According to Joseph Corn, this "air mindedness" was promoted as a way to improve human life, while encouraging the general development of aviation in the United States. Films, books, articles and radio broadcasts celebrated the exploits of pilots as reformers and individual heroes, aligned against bureaucracy, militarism, and private greed.

Aviation played key roles for both the Axis and Allied powers during World War II. While the United States and Great Britain followed what Richard Overy termed a "general air strategy" due to their strategic situations plus their vast industrial, scientific and technological resources, other nations adopted more limited approaches to the application of air power. The ability of the United States and Great Britain to successfully implement general air strategies gave those nations enormous flexibility in their global military operations. While providing critical support to ground and naval forces, aircraft also produced unprecedented death and destruction, especially among civilians, primarily through strategic bombing campaigns. Prewar forecasts that air power would produce quick, decisive and relatively bloodless victories proved to be erroneous. However, by the war's end, it was clear that air power had played at least an equal role with land and sea power in securing the Allies' global victory of the Axis.

Wartime books, magazines, newspapers and movies celebrated the exploits of individual pilots and exaggerated the contributions of aviation to Allied victory. But, as Joseph Corn observed, the wartime aerial Armageddon destroyed earlier millennial hopes that aviation would ensure international peace and prosperity. Ambiguity and skepticism replaced naïve optimism in the popular culture's post-war view of the airplane. It was seen as an extremely powerful weapon and an instrument of mass destruction that could eliminate civilization, as well as a means of promoting transportation and advanced technology. For the remainder of the twentieth century, ambivalence and uneasiness about aviation's impact on modern life continued to permeate American culture.

Despite the aerial Armageddon unleashed during World War II, military aviation and atomic weapons neither rendered war obsolete nor eliminated the need for armies and navies. Rather, it transformed modern warfare. While not changing the fundamental nature of armed conflict between states, it increased the speed, flexibility, scope and destructiveness of modern warfare. Military aviation made it possible to launch direct attacks on enemy cities, economies and civilian populations without the necessity of first defeating their armies and navies. That development contributed significantly to the fact that the twentieth century has been the bloodiest one in human history. At the operational level, aviation extended the zone of conflict from the immediate battle zone to the distant rear areas of armies and navies.

Jet aircraft, atomic weapons, radar, advanced electronics and missiles promised to revolutionize armed conflict between nations after World War II. Air refueling, which had been pioneered by the Americans and British during the interwar period, was perfected by the U.S. Air Force after World War II initially as a means to assure that its long range bombers could deliver atomic weapons to targets deep in the Soviet Union, and return safely to their bases. The airlift, which had played an important role in delivering troops and critical supplies during

World War II, emerged as a major element of American military power and diplomatic influence during the Cold War.

During the Cold War, the United States relied heavily on its land and sea-based aviation. Only the Soviet Union could begin to rival the strengths of American air power. Because of the political restraints placed upon its employment and its technological limitations, American military aviation could not secure victory over North Korean and Chinese forces during the Korean War. However, it did play a critical role in preventing the communists from winning that war.

During the 1950s, nuclear-armed American air power, especially the Strategic Air Command's bombers, gained an un-paralleled position in national strategy and probably prevented a global nuclear war with the Soviet Union. However, they were unable to either deter or win a number of lesser conflicts and international crises. The heavy reliance on nuclear weapons produced a dangerous and expensive arms race. Helicopters, which had played limited roles in World War II and the Korean War, were widely used by American forces in the Vietnam conflict for reconnaissance, search and rescue, transport and direct fire support missions. Although American air power achieved notable successes in Southeast Asia, its own technical and operational limitations, plus crippling political restrictions, placed upon its employment against North Vietnam, contributed to the defeat of the United States and its allies in that conflict.

The Vietnam War stimulated a post war military renaissance by the American armed forces, including their aviation arms. In order to fight and win against the numerically superior Soviet forces, the Americans modernized their aircraft, aircraft, missiles, and electronic

Whaam!, Roy Lichtenstein, 1963

systems, instituted far more rigorous combat training programs, and revamped their doctrines. Air-refueled fighter-bombers—equipped with precision guided munitions and sophisticated electronics gear, emerged from that period as the nation's aerial weapons of choice. Research and development programs were initiated to produce low observable or so-called "stealth" aircraft that could largely negate enemy radar coverage. Advanced sensors and high speed computers mated with missiles and bombs exponentially increased the destructiveness of American air power, while limiting collateral damage to civilian populations and structures. However, it still remained difficult for such "precision engagement" weapons to destroy small, mobile targets in mountains, forests, jungles and urban areas unless they were linked closely to friendly ground forces who could locate and identify them. Heavily armed helicopter gunships dedicated to the destruction of enemy armor and other close support missions for friendly ground forces were also deployed widely after the Vietnam War.

Since the Cold War's end, air power has once again emerged as the military instrument of choice among American civilian policymakers. Its leading role in the Persian Gulf, Kosovo and Afghanistan conflicts made it an attractive option for senior civilian and military officials who wanted a quick, decisive and relatively inexpensive means to achieve national policy objectives, with a minimum risk to American lives. The results of those post Cold War interventions abroad have been mixed at best. Moreover, they involved weak and isolated nations who could not begin to challenge the power of the United States and its allies.

By the twentieth century's final decade, the costs of the advanced technologies, as well as the vast training and logistics infrastructure needed to sustain a full spectrum of global air power, had become so huge that only the United States could afford them. In some specialized areas like stealth and advanced electronic warfare, only the world's one remaining superpower could pay the cost of full admission to the modern air power club. But, it was unclear what roles that air power could play in dealing with emerging asymmetrical threats like terrorism to national security.

An Eventful "D" Day

1919

Captain Edward V. "Eddie" Rickenbacker

Aeroplane Fight over the Verdun Front, Henri Farré

25 SEPTEMBER 1918 was my first day as captain of Squadron 94. Early that forenoon I started for the lines alone, flew over Verdun and Fort Douaumont, then turned east toward Etain. Almost immediately I picked up a pair of L.V.G. two-seater machines below me. They were coming out of Germany and were certainly bent on an expedition over our lines. Five Fokker machines were above them and somewhat behind, acting as protection for the photographers until the lines were reached.

Climbing toward the sun for all I was worth, I soon had the satisfaction of realizing that I had escaped their notice and was now well in the rear. I shut down my motor, put down my head, and made a beeline for the nearest Fokker.

I was not observed by the enemy until it was too late for him to escape. I had him exactly in my sights when I pulled both triggers for a long burst. He made a sudden attempt to pull away, but my bullets were already ripping through his fuselage, and he must have been killed instantly. His machine fell wildly away and crashed just south of Etain.

It had been my intention to zoom violently upward and protect myself against the expected attack from the four remaining Fokkers as soon as I had finished the first man. But when I saw the effect of my attack on the four dumbfounded pilots, I instantly changed my tactics and plunged straight on through their formation to attack the photographing L.V.G.s ahead. For the Fokkers were so surprised to find a Spad in their midst and to see one of their number suddenly drop that the remaining three *viraged* to right and left. Their one idea was to escape and save their own skins. Though they did not actually *piqué* for home, they cleared a space large enough for me to slip through and continue my dive on the two-seaters before they could recover their formation.

The two-seaters had seen my attack and had already put down their heads to escape. I plunged along after them, getting the rear machine in my sights as I drew nearer to him. A glance back over my shoulder showed me that the four Fokkers had not yet reformed their line and were even now circling about with the purpose of again solidifying their formation. I had a few seconds yet before they could begin their attack.

The two L.V.G. machines began to draw apart. Both observers in the rear seats began firing at me, although the range was too long for accurate shooting. I dove more steeply, passed out of the gunner's view under the nearest machine and zoomed quickly up at him from below. But the victory was not to be easy. The pilot suddenly kicked his tail around, giving the gunner another good aim at me. I had to postpone shooting until I had more time for my own aiming.

And in the meantime, the second photographing machine had stolen up behind me and I saw tracer bullets go whizzing and streaking past my face. I zoomed up diagonally out of range, made a *renversement* and came directly back at my first target.

Several times we repeated these maneuvers, the four Fokkers still wrangling among themselves about their formation. And all the time we were getting far-

ther back into Germany. I decided on one bold attack.

Watching my two adversaries closely, I suddenly found an opening between them. They were flying parallel to each other and not fifty yards apart. Dropping down in a sideslip until I had one machine between me and the other, I straightened out smartly and leveled my Spad. I began firing. The nearest German passed directly through my line of fire and just as I ceased firing I had the infinite satisfaction of seeing him gush forth flames. The Fokker escort came tearing up to the rescue. I put on the gas and *piquéd* for my own lines.

Pleased as I was over this doubleheader, the effect it might have on my pilots was far more gratifying to me....

Precisely at four o'clock [on 26 September 1918] I was awakened by my orderly who informed me that the weather was good. Hastily getting out of doors, I looked over the dark sky wondering as I did so how many of our boys it would claim before this day's work was done! For we had an important part in this day's operations. Headquarters had sent us orders to attack all the enemy observation balloons along that entire front throughout this morning and to continue the attacks until the infantry's operations were completed. Accordingly every fighting squadron had been assigned certain of these balloons for attack, and it was our duty to see that they were destroyed. The safety of thousands of our attacking soldiers depended on our success in eliminating these all-watching eyes of the enemy. Incidentally, it was the first balloon-strafing party that Squadron 94 had been given since I had been made its leader and I desired to make a good showing on this first expedition.

Just here it may be well to point out the difficulties of balloon strafing, which make this undertaking so unattractive to the new pilot. German "Archy" is terrifying at first acquaintance. Pilots affect a scorn for it, and indeed at high altitudes the probabilities of a hit are small. But when attacking a balloon that hangs only 1,500 feet above the guns (and this altitude is of course known precisely to the antiaircraft gunner), Archy becomes more dangerous.

So when a pilot begins his first balloon-attacking expeditions, he knows that he runs a gauntlet of fire that may be very deadly. His natural impulse is to make a nervous plunge into the zone of danger, fire his bullets, and get away. Few victories are won with this method of attack.

The experienced balloon strafers, particularly such daring airmen as Coolidge and Luke, do not consider the risks or terrors about them. They proceed in the attack as calmly as though they were sailing through a stormless sky. Regardless of flaming missiles from the ground, they pass through the defensive barrage of fire, and often return to attack the target, until it finally bursts into flame from their incendiary bullets.

The office charts informed me that the day would break this morning at six o'clock. Consequently, we must be ready to leave the ground in our machines at 5:20, permitting us thirty minutes in which to locate our individual balloons. For it is essential to strike at these well-defended targets just at the edge of dawn. As the balloons are just starting aloft, our attacking aeroplanes are but scantily visible from below.

I routed out five of my best pilots, Lieutenants [H. Weir] Cook, Chambers, Taylor, Coolidge, and [William W.] Palmer; as we gathered for an early breakfast, we went over again all the details of our prearranged plans. We had two balloons assigned to our squadron, and three of us were delegated to each balloon. Both lay along the Meuse between Brabant and Dun-sur-Meuse. Every one of us had noted down the exact location of this target on the evening before. It would be difficult perhaps to find them before daylight if they were still in their nests, but we were to hang about the vicinity until we did find them, if it took all day. With every man fully posted on his course and objective, we put on our coats and walked over to the hangars.

I was the last to leave the field, getting off the ground at exactly 5:20. It was still dark and we had to have the searchlights turned onto the field for a moment to see the ground while we took off. As soon as we lifted into the darkness, the lights were extinguished. And then I saw the most marvelous sight I have ever seen.

A terrific barrage of artillery fire was going on ahead of me. Through the darkness the whole western horizon was illumined with one mass of sudden flashes. The big guns were belching out their shells with such rapidity that there appeared to be millions of them shooting at the same time. Looking back I saw the same scene in my rear. From Lunéville on the east to Reims on the west there was not one spot of darkness along the whole front. The French were attacking along both our flanks at the same time with us in order to help demoralize the weakening enemy forces. The picture made me think of a giant switchboard that emitted thousands of electric flashes as invisible hands manipulated the plugs.

So fascinated did I become over this extraordinary fireworks display that I was startled on peering over the side of my machine to discover the city of Verdun below my aeroplane's wings. Fastening my course above the dim outline of the Meuse River, I followed its windings downstream, occasionally cutting across little peninsulas that I recognized along the way. Every inch of this route was as familiar to me as was the path around the corner of my old home. I knew exactly the point in the Meuse Valley where I would leave the river and turn left to strike the spot where my balloon lay last night. I did not know what course the other pilots had taken.

Just as these thoughts were going through my mind I saw directly ahead of me the long snaky flashes of enemy tracer bullets from the ground piercing the sky. There was die location of my balloon, and either Cook or Chambers was already attacking it. The enemy had discovered them and were putting up the usual hail of flaming projectiles around the balloon site. But even as the flaming bullets continued streaming upward, I saw a gigantic flame burst out in their midst!

Even before the glare of the first had died, I saw our second enemy balloon go up in flames. My pilots had succeeded beyond my fondest expectations. Undoubtedly the enemy would soon be swinging new balloons up in their places, but we must wait a while for that.... *

An Irish Airman Forsees His Death

1919

William Butler Yeats

I KNOW THAT I SHALL MEET MY FATE
Somewhere among the clouds above;
Those that I fight I do not hate,
Those that I guard I do not love;
My county is Kiltartan Cross,
My countrymen Kiltartan's poor;
No likely end could bring them loss
Or leave them happier than before.
Nor law, nor duty bade me fight,
Nor public men, nor cheering crowds,
A lonely impulse of delight
Drove to this tumult in the clouds;
I balanced all, brought all to mind,
The years to come seemed waste of breath,
A waste of breath the years behind,
In balance with this life, this death.

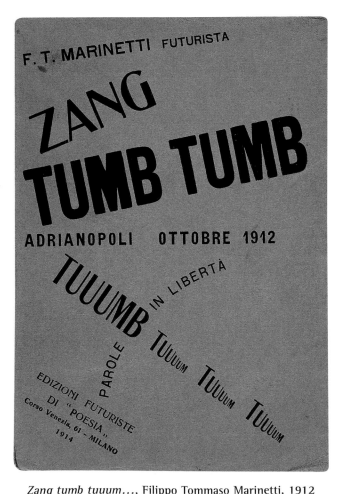

Zang tumb tuuum…, Filippo Tommaso Marinetti, 1912

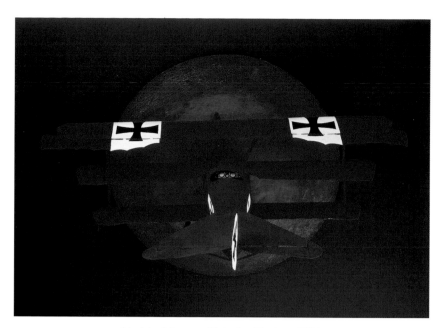

Flight of Icarus, Malcolm Morley, 1995

The Dawn Patrol

1917

Paul Bewsher

Sometimes I fly at dawn above the sea,
Where, underneath, the restless waters flow—
Silver, and cold, and slow.
Dim in the east there burns a new-born sun,
Whose rosy gleams along the ripples run,
Save where the mist droops low,
Hiding the level loneliness from me.

And now appears beneath the milk-white haze
A little fleet of anchored ships, which lie
In clustered company,
And seem as they are yet fast bound by sleep,
Although the day has long begun to peep,
With red-inflamèd eye,
Along the still, deserted ocean ways.

The fresh, cold wind of dawn blows on my face
As in the sun's raw heart I swiftly fly,
And watch the seas glide by.
Scarce human seem I, moving through the skies,
And far removed from warlike enterprise—

Like some great gull on high
Whose white and gleaming wings beat on through
space.

Then do I feel with God quite, quite alone,
High in the virgin morn, so white and still,
And free from human ill:
My prayers transcend my feeble earth-bound
plaints—
As though I sang among the happy Saints
With many a holy thrill—
As though the glowing sun were God's bright
Throne.

My flight is done. I cross the line of foam
That breaks around a town of grey and red,
Whose streets and squares lie dead
Beneath the silent dawn—then am I proud
That England's peace to guard I am allowed;
Then bow my humble head,
In thanks to Him Who brings me safely home.

PEANUTS © UFS, Inc.

Snoopy and the Red Baron, Charles Schulz, 1966

The End of the Red Baron

1958

John Norman Harris

THEN, OF COURSE, there was the end of Richtofen. The great German ace, conqueror or eighty British machines, and chief organizer of the large German formations which opposed the unceasing air offensive of the RFC, was finally killed, in April, 1918, by a bullet believed to have been fired by Captain Roy Brown, of Carleton Place, Ontario. Richtofen had aroused the admiration of friend and foe alike. He never showed any remorse or distaste for the killing of an enemy—he had the professional soldier's attitude to the grim task—but he had always treated the pilots who were taken prisoner with the strictest courtesy. He had fought with the greatest British airmen, with Bishop, with Collishaw, with Ball, with Hawker (whom he killed in combat) and they all spoke highly of his skill.

Richtofen's end came on a day when a young relative was being introduced to air fighting. Richtofen was keeping an eye on the new pilot, to steer safely through his first fight. On the same day a young Canadian pilot, later to become famous as Wop May, the pioneer bush pilot, was also experiencing his first combat. May was successful in getting on the tail of Richtofen's protégé, which brought the old master

down in a screaming dive to protect his kinsman. May was about to become Richtofen's eighty-first victim, when Captain Roy Brown saw his danger, and flew to his assistance. He fired a burst at Richtofen from the right-hand side, and a single bullet struck the great German pilot, penetrating his heart, and killing him instantly.

The red triplane was seen to crash behind the British lines, and Brown reported the victory, without having any idea who the enemy was. Late in the afternoon word came through that the Red Knight of Germany was dead. Two Australian machine-gun crews on the ground had fired at Richtofen, and they claimed to have shot him down, but a very careful examination proved that the bullet must have come from the air. The seat of Richtofen's triplane was brought to Canada, and is still a treasured relic in the Royal Canadian Military Institute in Toronto.

Though the British flying men were pleased to have eliminated this dangerous enemy, nevertheless they were generous in their tributes to him. "If only we could have taken him alive" was the common sentiment expressed about a skilful and courageous pilot. ✳

Totes Meer, Paul Nash, 1940–41

R.A.F.
(aged 18)

1919

Rudyard Kipling

LAUGHING THROUGH CLOUDS, HIS MILK-TEETH
still unshed,
Cities and men he smote from overhead.
His deaths delivered, he returned to play
Childlike, with childish things now put away.

Poem XXXVII

Elizabeth Daryush

Now that delight is seen for what she is,
A half-wit dancing while her home's afire,
Now that of doting hope the melodies
Are drowned in thunders, that simple desire Who spread her feast
On a volcano has decamped, scared like a beast,

Yes, now that every tenderness is naught
Whereby hard Nature won us to her will
Who has at last o'erreached herself, has wrought
The self-destroying bomb of human skill Unhallowed, how
Shall man's long soul be aided? Who shall save him now?

One only is there (though defiance too
Is mortal, though even stubborn pride must die)
One that with engined wings lifts to the blue
Of a bare heaven, whence (under its smoke-sky) Earth pales, is made
Merely a phantom background for his own firm shade.

The Aero, Marsden Hartley, 1914

Mustang Staffel, Gerhard Richter, 1964

SPIT FIRE

A2✪3

Roy E. La Grone 88 S.i.
TUSKEGEE AIRMEN

Dear Mom, This is a Hell of a Hole: An Ode to the Tuskegee Airmen

1991

Benjamin O. Davis, Jr.

IN THE EARLY 1940s it was unheard-of for blacks to be recognized as equally capable as whites in just about any field of endeavor, and for a long time the Army Air Corps did not believe that blacks trained by TAAF to fly military airplanes were generally within the same range of ability as white pilots trained at other Air Corps bases. In fact, the general belief within the Air Corps that blacks could fly to required standards did not develop until years after World War II. [Maj. Noel] Parrish's professional attitude toward the training of black pilots and his application of reason to the problem—his ability to overcome any prejudices he may have brought to Tuskegee by recognizing the abilities of black pilots—enabled him to support black military aviation at a time when its future hung in the balance. As director of training, he was in an influential position to advise those above him whether blacks could be trained to fly to Air Corps standards, so his goodwill was of major importance. Just as significant, his personality and his willingness to talk to blacks softened their reaction to the continued segregation and the complete control of all activities by white officers, from the commander down to the flying instructors.

It would be fair to say that most blacks at TAAF transferred their hatred of segregation to Colonel Kimble and the other white administrative officers in the command structure. Much of this hatred was based on what they considered the unfair utilization of black officers and discrimination in the promotion system.

Woody Driver...Black Birdman (Tuskegee Airman),
Roy LaGrone, 1988

Many black aviation cadets were also "washed out," that is, cut from the program—eight out of my class of thirteen trainees. Given that all the basic and advanced instructors were white, and given our collective experience of racial discrimination both inside and outside the military service, it was only human nature for some of those who were washed out to blame not their inability to fly, but rather racism.

Kimble's strict adherence to segregation as it was practiced in the Deep South roused further resentments. Black military police (MPs) from the airfield were frequently harassed by the white police of Tuskegee. Pat Evans, the town sheriff, complained to Colonel Kimble that black MPs were driving jeeps through Tuskegee with side arms strapped to their legs. The issue came to a head one night when a black airman was arrested by town police and held in the town jail. Following standard procedure, black MPs entered the jail and asked that the prisoner be released to them for transfer to the TAAF guardhouse. When one MP became belligerent, the town police reacted with their customary brutality and relieved the MPs of their weapons. Much to the dismay of Capt. George Webb, the commander of the guard squadron, Colonel Kimble acceded to the sheriff's demand that MPs not carry weapons in Tuskegee or anywhere else in Macon County. Captain Webb, who considered the entire situation degrading to him and his men, protested this action to Colonel Kimble, but to no avail.

The following poem written by Agatha is a valid description of life at TAAF and the attitudes of many of the men who trained there:

Dear Mom, This Is a Hell of a Hole

Dear Mom, this is a Hell of a hole,
To Tuskegee Army Flying School you are to report,
From Headquarters was the message they sent me, sweet and short.
At last I would go to the field that had been my first choice,
Again I could feel like a man, a real man with a voice.
"Goodbye and good luck," to me my old pals happily said.
They knew where I was going, Jim Crow would surely be dead.
I paid my debts, packed my bags, signed the book, and took my leave,
Glad to go to a good place, where no longer I would grieve.
"Chehaw," the conductor called from the rear of the car,
As the slow train came to a stop with an awful jar.
Much we had heard of this one and only Negro air post,
Here was one place of which officers and soldiers could boast.
"Reporting, sir," were the words I used as I entered camp,
And I had a strange feeling then that things were cold and damp.

Dear Mom, this is a Hell of a hole.
Well, it really didn't take very long for us all to see
That the morale and place were not what they're supposed to be.
The Air Corps officers seemed to be a mighty fine bunch,
I thought when I talked to a group of them after a light lunch.
The tales they told of the feeling of hate were sad but true;
In the South, they said, that was the lot that all black men drew.
It makes them ever so bitter, angry, and hateful, too,
Because about it, there's not a single thing they can do.
To tell of the awful treatment that the colored man took
Honestly would fill page after page and book after book.
He's neither man nor American in this State you know,
He's a nigger or a coon, a darky, or something low.
He has no rights, no peace, no voice, no, not even a vote.
The crackers in this area on the race issue dote.
In other words, their law says please do all and what you can
To make a Negro feel small, down, and much less of a man.

Dear Mom, this a Hell of a hole.
The blacks have their own mess and the whites have theirs.
They sort of look down on us like we're big, ugly black bears.
They don't seem to know we feel, we hope, we love, and we hate;
In some things our plans and our actions might well seal their fate.
They want us to appear unfit, weak, stupid and so lame
That at a superior rating, we dare not aim.
Tuskegee, the small town nearest the post, is really frail.
It started many years ago, but it is truly stale.

Prejudice and jealousy are the two things that have grown;
They have developed well ever since the day they were sown.
It's a crime for a Negro to walk on the street after ten.
The only place wide open is the vile city jail pen.
There they will throw you, beat you, fine you without any cause
If in this unjust southern village too long you should pause.

Dear Mom, this is a Hell of a hole.
It seems to me a great pity this old, old State should be
A place where Americans and Southerners can't agree.
They have rules, and their interpretations are fair to none;
And thus, true justice and fairness are ever on the run.
It's the whites against the blacks and the blacks against the whites,
One just fighting and the other fighting for his rights.
Neither can ever win as long as there is racial hate;
True religion in this area simply doesn't rate.
We are very thankful there are a few who are quite sane,
Who talk and think and even act like they might be humane.
They try to be fair and just and hear both sides of a tale,
Before they pass judgment on whom they are to send to jail.
I mean whites at the base when I say they, but let me see,
I don't believe if I tried very hard, I could find three.

Dear Mom, this is a Hell of a hole.
I've tried to tell you some things, Mom, of how this place is run.
You know there are always those, who out of life do take the fun.
In spite of all, we aim to prove to all the world at war,
That we of T.A.F.S., United States Army Air Corps,
Are doing a patriotic job on the side of right
In an effort to win the Double V for which we fight.
We hope that after war will come a fair and lasting peace
And all hostility between the blacks and whites will cease.
It always makes me glow to think of the day there will be
A world of brother-loving men, all men equal and free.
Hate and force will be gone and tolerance will take their place,
'Twill matter not if you belong to the black or white race,
A home where you want it and the right to vote if you choose,
A job you are fit for and no reason to sing the blues.
Until that glorious day, dear God, give me control,
So for my Mom's sweet sake, I can stand this Hell of a hole

Burning Plane, Vija Celmins, 1965

Flying/Spring of '44

1975

Marie-Lynn Hammond

HE HAD TWELVE DAYS LEAVE WHEN I MET HIM IN MONTREAL
We courted a week then got married
He wore his uniform
I wore my grey silk suit and a hat with a veil
My mother shook her head and said
You hardly know the boy

But it was the spring of '44
It was such a crazy time
And he seemed so brave
So full of glory
With his talk of planes and the sky
I remember him saying—

"Oh flying
Well the Hurricane is a damn fine plane
And I wish you could see all the boys and me
Doing loops and dives in tight formation
Chasing the wind
Like eagles in the sun"

It was spring again when I went to meet his train
They sent him home a hero
With medals and that look in his eyes
And a cane—
I hardly knew him
And most nights he'd wake up shaking and scared
But he'd never tell me what
He was seeing

But it was the spring of '45
It was such a hopeful time
When he was finally on the mend
We'd sit on the porch
And he'd watch the sky
Like he was looking for something

Oh flying
Sun on the silver wing
It's so silent out there
Like a blue cathedral
You can climb and climb
Till the earth falls away
And you're finally alone now
You've finally come home

Well the doctors told him he could never fly again
But a hero's a hero
And the air force takes care of its own
Oh they let him fly a desk for thirty years
And except for the drinking
Nothing much has changed
Ah he's still got his medals and his aches and pains
Still got his bad dreams

Ah he's still the same stranger I met
At the train

But there was a boy in '44
He always talked of flying
And one day his plane took off
And you know, they've never come down
They're still somewhere flying

Oh flying
Sun on the silver wing…

Twice as Fast as Sound

1956

Chuck Yeager

IN 1943 THE IDEA WAS CONCEIVED to design and build an airplane that would actually fly at speeds of a Mach number of one, or a little faster, to see what type of stresses and forces caused airplanes to buffet and shake and lose their tail surfaces.

The airplanes went the way of all airplanes, drawing up on paper, trying, and improving and finally it came out as a piece of hardware in 1946 in flyable condition. It was decided that this airplane, the X-1, since we had no jet engines that would drive an airplane as fast as we wanted this airplane to go, should be powered with rocket power. The most

common and the safest fuels were liquid oxygen and alcohol, so that was the type of propulsive fuels that we should use.

The X-1 was finished, they installed a motor and prior to the powered flights they thought maybe we had better drop this airplane from a B-29, because it carried only 288 gallons of liquid oxygen and 300 gallons of alcohol and this gave us enough fuel for only two and a half minutes of full power. If we took it off the ground, by the time we got up to altitude with it we wouldn't have enough fuel left to do any work with. So they modified a B-29 by cutting the

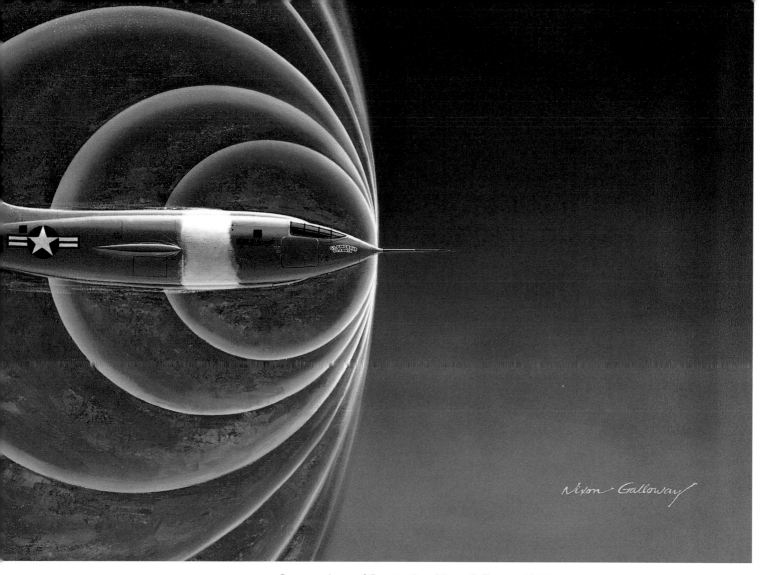

Compression and Penetration, Nixon Galloway, 1985

bomb bay out and fixed a plain B-7 bomb shackle in the bottom of the B-29. They put some hooks in the top of the X-1, and hoisted it up under the B-29, then decided to drag it upstairs and kick it out.

The aircraft, after being completed as any conventional type airplane would, had no rotary engines in it or any source of power to run a hydraulic pump or run big pumps to force the fuel back to the motor. We incorporated in the X-1 a pneumatic system which raised and lowered the gear, worked the flaps, pressurized the cockpit and ran the gyros for flight instruments, the same as electrical power or hydraulic power would in a normal airplane, The airplane so designed was made up of just fuselage, two straight wings, horizontal stabilizers and elevators and vertical stabilizer and rudder.

We went out to Edwards where we had the large dry lake bed that at the time was seven miles long and five miles wide, which we figured we could hit on any dead-stick landing we had to make....

The airplane was backed into a pit, the B-29 was pulled over it and they hoisted the X-1 up into the B-29. They pulled it up between the loading pits, filled the aft tank full of alcohol and water and the fore tank full of liquid oxygen and then pressurized the manifold up to 5,000 pounds.

On none of our take-offs with the X-1 under the B-29 did we take off with the pilot in the X-1 cockpit, because the climbing speed of the X-1 fully loaded, which it was at that time, was 240. m.p.h. so if you had an inadvertent failure of the bomb shackle or had a fire in the B-29 and wanted to get rid of the X-1 you would probably lose the X-1 pilot too because he would not be high enough to recover from resulting stall and spin that he would be in.

So at 7,000 feet above the ground these two big strong men would pull the X-1 pilot back to the cockpit. You would climb down on a ladder which they would lower into the slipstream. You had your parachute on of course. You would slide into the cockpit of the X-1 and get all squared around, they would slide the door down and you would hook it on from the inside and then you would get your helmet on and get all connected up with your oxygen and radio and check in with the B-29 pilot. All this would take a matter of three of four minutes and the bomber would get on up to about 10,000 feet. Then you would start around the cockpit, setting up all your domes, loading various stages, pressurizing your tanks and setting the airplane up for the actual flight. All this would take in the order of ten to fifteen minutes; by that time the B-29 would have climbed up to about 25,000 feet.

On the initial flight of the X-1 that I made in August, 1947, we flew the airplane without liquid oxygen or alcohol in it; it was completely empty; we just took it up and dropped it just to familiarize the pilot with the landing characteristics and stalling characteristics and the type of pattern you had set up to land, because it was a dead-stick landing. Your landing speed was in the order of 180 to 200 m.p.h. It was a little critical not to overshoot or undershoot, but we had a very long runway to aim at so fortunately we never did overshoot or undershoot.

The first drop was quite an experience for me. You are sitting there; it is quite dark, and the bomber pilot starts coming down. He says: "I'll give you a five-minute warning here and you can set up all your knobs the way they are supposed to be set up and set in and get a death grip on the stick." He gives you about a minute warning and then he starts counting down to 5 seconds and he says 5 seconds, 4, 3, 2, 1, drop, and about a minute later the copilot finally releases you....

My first powered flight, I wanted to feel out the engine. We climbed away as normally as you do prior to the drop, they drop you out and you turn on one chamber and you get a kick in the rear and since your thrust is instantaneous there is no build up. I tried out all four chambers by turning one chamber on and letting it run a few seconds and turning it off. Then I turned on three chambers,

climbed up to 40,000 feet, accelerated up to 0.87 Mach number, or 87 per cent of the speed of sound; shut everything off, jettisoned the remainder of the liquid oxygen and fuel, glided down and landed and crossed myself a couple of times....

On about the fourth flight we took the airplane up to 0.94 Mach number, 94 per cent of the speed of sound. At this speed I laid the airplane over and pulled back on the control column and the airplane did not turn, it went the way it was headed so I shut everything off and came down and had a heart to heart talk to the engineers. We looked at all our data and it showed that the shock wave that had formed on the horizontal stabilizers the same as on the wing, had moved back and attached itself to the trailing edge of the stabilizer just in front of where the elevator was hinged. So all the longhairs got together and talked and talked and talked and finally they came out with the next program. We would go up. Instead of turning with the elevator—the flippers on the airplane—we would change the angle of incidence on the horizontal stabilizer, or change the whole tail plane and make the airplane turn, starting at 0.86 Mach number where our elevators were very effective....

We made a total of some 80 flights on the X-1. We had a lot of fires in the rear end of it but fortunately it did not blow up on us, and we lost a lot of pieces off it, but fortunately they made some new ones....

On the first flight, in practicing for this type of the profile mission, they dropped me at 30,000 feet and I fired off three chambers, went up to 45,000 feet, fired off the fourth one and the airplane reacted exactly in the same way as the old X-1 did since it had the same wings, same tail, practically the same fuselage, only 7 feet longer. It reacted practically the same way by getting into buffeting at about 0.88 Mach number, getting wing roll and losing elevator effectiveness at about 0.94, but we used the stabilizer to increase our angle of climb or adjust our flight path. Then after you get up to about 1.1 your airplane smooths out, your buffeting drops away, your airplane trims up again, the wing will raise the one it dropped and you can get the elevator control back again, or it becomes not quite as effective as it was down around Mach 0.8, but much more effective than it was from 0.94 to 1.05. The airplane reacted the same as the initial X-1 as I ram it on up to about 1.3 Mach number on the first flight.

The second flight was at about 50,000 feet. The second flight was identical to the first right on through the steps, except that I took it up to 50,000 feet, let it sit till it got up to 1.5, shut it off and jettisoned the remainder of the Lox and fuel and came down and landed. We looked at our data and I pretty well had the flight plan down perfect which was the most important.

The third flight ran the profile, instead of going on upstairs on above 60,000 feet. I leveled out at around 60,000 feet held it straight and level and ran it up to 1.9 Mach number, which is about 1,200 m.p.h., shut it off and came down and landed.

The fourth and last flight actually was on December 12th; we beat our schedule a little ahead of time. We dropped the airplane out at 30,000 feet, ran through our mission right on up. At 45,000 feet we had them all four going; we went up to about 1.1 Mach number and started climbing; went through 50,000 feet at about 1.15; went through 60,000 feet at about 1.4 and I was supposed to start leveling out to pull zero g's or flight in a parabolic curve, starting at 61,000 or 62,000 feet, but due to the excited nature of the pilot I overshot. Actually I got to around 68,000 feet before I started pushing over, came level at 78,000 feet and was indicating about 1.9 Mach number at that altitude and I had a few seconds of fuel remaining. I held it there straight and level and the airplane was accelerating at the rate of 31 m.p.h., that is about a six-hundredth of a Mach number a second. You are really knocking it off in a burry. The airplane ran out of fuel at about 76,000 feet, and at a Mach number of a little better than 2.5. Our instrumentation is accurate to within about one half of one per cent at 2.51, or 2.52, give or take a half of a point there, we get a true air speed of a little better than 1,650 m.p.h. The indi-cated air speed, of course, as you know the air is so rare, it was only around 440 m.p.h.

Actually the X-1A, you might say, was not designed for that sort of flying. It was designed for Mach numbers of about 2. We overstepped our bounds a little bit, since the airplane does not have a flying tail on it, it does not have boosted controls. When a body or an airplane accelerates it has induced stability due to acceleration, you might say. When I shut off the power, or ran out of fuel, the airplane started decelerating and at that point we lost all stability, or rather the stability completely deteriorated on the airplane, and, having very little control of it, the airplane started more or less changing ends, so we had a moment of anxiety there. The airplane got up to some pretty high rates of roll and yaw and pitch angles. The airplane started rolling to the right to start with, so I put all the controls against the rolls, as they taught me in flying school, and it did not help so I put them with it and it did not help. I let them loose and started praying about them. The airplane had got some pretty high accelerations, high yaw angles—actually this took a lot longer to tell than it took to happen. The airplane was going 1,650 at about 76,000 feet and 51 seconds later settled at 25,000 feet and 170 m.p.h., so I had not got much time to fool around. The airplane evidently started becoming stable as it slowed back down to a range of a Mach number of 2. I had pulled the stabilizer down in trying to slow the airplane up and I did not know what part of the High Sierras I was going to hit into out there and was trying to get in a little closer to the lake. The airplane finally pulled about 11 g's upward, tried to stabilize itself and of course then started snapping and I was pretty well blacked out due to the high acceleration forces. Finally it did slow down to below Mach 1 and came down to 35,000 feet. I rolled the stabilizer in but overshot, and the airplane got into an inverted spin, so then I got my eyeballs caged and came back to neutral, put everything with the inverted spin and flipped into a normal spin and I recovered at 25,000 feet and glided on back to the lake and that was the last flight I made in the airplane. ✳

The Aging Poet,
on a Reading Trip to Dayton,
Visits the Air Force Museum
and Discovers There
a Plane He Once Flew

1977

Richard Snyder

THERE WAS IN DANGER DESPERATE DELIGHT
When I in that ship was a stowaway.
It was primitive, I its proselyte.

Remembering, I give myself a fright
And the plane a pat, which still is to say
There was in danger desperate delight.

Or is that now romantic second-sight?
Machined in deadly earnest, not for play,
It was primitive, I its proselyte.

But, oh, that detachment, that impolite
Aloofness when I was its protégé.
There was in danger desperate delight

Of high, blue pasture through which to excite
By joystick whip a racing runaway.
It was primitive, I its proselyte.

Grounded now, hangared here, she was my rite.
We are survivors to a duller day.
There was in danger desperate delight.
It was primitive, I its proselyte.

Bombing of The Haruna,
Peter Hurd

Angel of History, Anselm Kiefer, 1989

'A Lonely Impulse of Delight'—W. B. Yeats

1973

David K. Vaughan

(For David Risher, who died in Vietnam)

AN AIRMAN MUST BE IRISH, SLIGHTLY MAD
To take that certain step that cancels all
The firm construction of an earthly stair,
And step to tread the thinner edge of air,
Where nothing yields support except the call
Of spirit in its element; who had
His start, perhaps, beneath an August night,
When, having seen the sign of Scorpio fixed
Among such suns, he seldom looked to earth
Again, unless to gain perspective when
He led his wingman toward the sun and then
Bent back to earth, then up again, to birth
A new maneuver of delight, to mix
The thought of man with sun, whose thought is light.

Part 4 The Airplane as Transportation

Anne Collins Goodyear

PERHAPS NO ASPECT of flight's development over the course of the past century has impacted the general public as directly as commercial aviation. Taking its first fledgling steps in the years following World War I, the new industry was initially forced to demonstrate its usefulness. In the United States it competed first to replace trains as vehicles for long-distance mail delivery—and only secondarily for passengers—while in Europe wartime damage to the rails made flight's benefits for transportation more readily apparent. In the course of less than a century, commercial air travel has permitted those without specialized knowledge of aviation to become familiar with the sensation of the birds-eye view, with the changing scale of objects witnessed during the ascent and descent of a plane, and with the sight of clouds close at hand.

As with all industries, commercial aviation has been influenced as much by economics as by technology, particularly in the United States. During the 1920s, American companies competed for contracts to deliver the mail. Although European passenger airlines were developing in the meanwhile, it was not until the 1930s that a viable American market for personal transport developed. The DC-3 (Douglas Commercial 3) proved critical in this regard. Introduced in the mid-1930s, the plane revolutionized air travel not only because of the comforts it provided passengers, but also because it represented the first commercial aircraft designed to profit from passengers rather than airmail.

As civil aviation became more common, artists and writers responded to its technological accomplishments as well as the new experiences it produced. Pilots such as Antoine de Saint-Exupéry recounted their adventures flying the mail, while Anne Morrow Lindbergh testified to the careful preparations undertaken by those pioneering new routes for air travel. Charles Sheeler, an American artist interested in the new sleek shapes of the modern era, celebrated the powerful Wright Cyclone engine as well as Pan American Airlines's commanding lead in international travel in the years prior to World War II. The plane he depicted, the Yankee Clipper, pioneered important transatlantic routes in 1939.

Following the Second World War, with the German invention of the jet engine, air travel reached new levels of comfort and efficiency. The Boeing 707, painted by Ben Schonzeit, entered service in the mid-1950s with great success. During the 1960s, air travel boomed. The decade witnessed important innovations in the design of commercial aircraft, with the development of the Boeing 747, which inaugurated the era of the "jumbo jet," and the Concorde, co-developed by France and Great Britain.

The culture of travel—of time spent in airports and in the air—inspired writers and visual artists. John Salt's painting *Host*, of 1973, pictures preparations for airborne hospitality aboard an American Airlines Boeing 727. The painting forms an amusing counterpart to F.T. Marinetti and Fillia's 1932 account of "An Aeropictorial Dinner in a Cockpit" and to Joe Brainard's ruminations on a Bloody Mary sipped in the air. Georgia O'Keefe, long associated with paintings of flowers and the landscape of New Mexico, responded to her experience of flying in her series *Sky Above Clouds*.

Since the deregulation of the airlines in the 1970s, the world of commercial aviation has become more volatile, with many well-established airlines, such as Pan American and Eastern, totally disappearing. The dangers of air transportation have long faced

passengers, as Elizabeth Daryush's "Air Crash" suggests. However, little could prepare the public for the devastating abuse of commercial airlines by terrorists. Such violence escalated brutally on September 11, 2001, when four commercial planes were hijacked in the United States. Two of these jets collided with the twin towers of New York's World Trade Center, bringing them to the ground. A third flew into the Pentagon in Washington, DC, while the fourth crashed over Pennsylvania after rebellious passengers overtook their captors.

Despite the disturbing implications of recent threats to air travel, it seems unlikely that this mode of transportation will cease. But what may not soon be recovered is the peaceful and meditative character of flight described by John Travolta in *Propeller One-Way Night Coach*, the story of a child's first plane trip, or evoked by Yvonne Jacquette's rich depiction of the landscape viewed from above in *Oregon Valley, Overcast Day II*. Yet if the future of air travel promises to be indelibly marked by the challenges of the past, its development will also be inspired by the sheer thrill of flight and by the unprecedented opportunities offered by new technologies, still in the making or yet to be imagined.

Sky Above Clouds IV, Georgia O'Keeffe, 1965

Wind, Sand and Stars

1939

Antoine de Saint-Exupéry

...OFF TO BENGHAZI! We still have two hours of daylight. Before we crossed into Tripolitana I took off my glare glasses. The sands were golden under the slanting rays of the sun. How empty of life is this planet of ours! Once again it struck me that its rivers, its woods, its human habitations were the product of chance, of fortuitous conjunctions of circumstance. What a deal of the earth's surface is given over to rock and sand!

But all this was not my affair. My world was the world of flight. Already I could feel the oncoming night within which I should be enclosed as in the precincts of a temple—enclosed in the temple of night for the accomplishment of secret rites and absorption in inviolable contemplation.

Already this profane world was beginning to fade out: soon it would vanish altogether. This landscape was still laved in golden sunlight, but already something was evaporating out of it. I know nothing, nothing in the world, equal to the wonder of nightfall in the air.

Those who have been enthralled by the witchery of flying will know what I mean—and I do not speak of the men who, among other sports, enjoy taking a turn in a plane. I speak of those who fly professionally and have sacrificed much to their craft. Mermoz said once, "It's worth it, it's worth the final smash-up."

No question about it; but the reason is hard to formulate. A novice taking orders could appreciate

this ascension towards the essence of things, since his profession too is one of renunciation: he renounces the world; he renounces riches; he renounces the love of woman. And by renunciation he discovers his hidden god.

I, too, in this flight, am renouncing things. I am giving up the broad golden surfaces that would befriend me if my engines were to fail. I am giving up the landmarks by which I might be taking my bearings. I am giving up the profiles of mountains against the sky that would warn me of pitfalls. I am plunging into the night. I am navigating. I have on my side only the stars.

The diurnal death of the world is a slow death. It is only little by little that the divine beacon of daylight recedes from me. Earth and sky begin to merge into each other. The earth rises and seems to spread like a mist. The first stars tremble as if shimmering in green water. Hours must pass before their glimmer hardens into the frozen glitter of diamonds. I shall have a long wait before I witness the soundless frolic of the shooting stars. In the profound darkness of certain nights I have seen the sky streaked with so many trailing sparks that it seemed to me a great gale must be blowing through the outer heavens.

Prévot was testing the lamps in their sockets and the emergency torches. Round the bulbs he was wrapping red paper.

"Another layer."

He added another wrapping of paper and touched a switch. The dim light within the plane was still too bright. As in a photographer's darkroom, it veiled the pale picture of the external world. It hid that glowing phosphorescence which sometimes, at night, clings to the surface of things. Now night has fallen, but it is not yet true night. A crescent moon persists.

Prévot dove aft and came back with a sandwich. I nibbled a bunch of grapes. I was not hungry. I was neither hungry nor thirsty. I felt no weariness. It seemed to me that I could go on like this at the controls for ten years. I was happy. ✳

Yankee Clipper, Charles Sheeler, 1939

Preparation

1935

Anne Morrow Lindbergh

FLYING IMPLIES FREEDOM to most people. The average person who hears the drone of a motor and looks up from the walls of a city street to see an airplane boring its way through the clear trackless blue above—the average person, if he stops to use his imagination, may say to himself casually, "Free as a bird! What a way to travel! No roads—no traffic dust—no heat—just pick up and go!"

In that careless phrase he is apt to overlook what lies behind the word "free." He is apt to forget, or perhaps he never knew, the centuries of effort which have finally enabled man to be a bird, centuries of patient desiring, which, reach back at least as far as the Greek world of Icarus. For Icarus, trying to scale the skies with his waxen wings, was merely an early *expression* of man's desire to fly. How long before him the unexpressed wish wrestled in the minds of men, no one can tell.

And since flight is not a natural function of man; since it has been won by centuries of effort; since it has been climbed to arduously, not simply stumbled upon; since it has been slowly built, not suddenly discovered, it cannot be suspended as the word "freedom" is suspended in the mind. It rests, firmly supported, on a structure of laws, rules, principles—laws to which plane and man alike must conform. Rules of construction, of performance, of equipment, for one; rules of training, health, experience, skill, and judgment, for the other.

Not only must a man know how his plane is made, what it will do, how it must be cared for; but also—to mention only a few of the rules that govern him—what the ceiling of his plane is, whether it will go high enough to clear any elevation on the route; what the gas capacity is, how far it will carry him; what points he can reach for refueling; how to navigate through a signless sky; where he will land for the night; where he can get emergency repairs; what weather conditions he may meet on his way; and, keeping in mind the back stairs, what equipment he should carry in case of a forced landing. All this he must know before he can win that freedom of a bird, before he can follow that straight line he has drawn on the map, directly, without deviation, proverbially "as the crow flies."

The firm black lines which we ruled straight across Canada and Alaska, preparatory to our flight, implied a route, which, in its directness of purpose and its apparent obliviousness of outside forces, looked as unerring and resistless as the path of a comet. Those firm black lines implied freedom, actual enough, but dearly won. Months, and indeed years, of preparation made such freedom possible.

It is true that as air travelers we were free of many of the difficulties that had beset the early surface travelers in search of a Northwest passage. Our fast monoplane could carry us far above most of the dangers mentioned by Master George Best: "mountaines of yce in the frozen Sea...fiercenesse of wilde beastes and fishes, hugenesse of woods, dangerousnesse of Seas, dread of tempestes, feare of hidden rockes." But in any comparison between us

and the early navigators, there were disadvantages to offset advantages.

The early travelers, although confined to navigable waters, and restricted by slow speed, nevertheless were favored with a limitless fuel supply. Wherever they went and no matter how long they were gone, they could count on the wind for power. They might have difficulties in using it, now coaxing it, now fighting it; but they would never completely drain their supply. It was inexhaustible. Whereas we must plan and budget our fuel, arrange for its location along the route, sometimes sending it ahead of us by boat or train, sometimes using fuel already cached through the North.

And although they had to be prepared for longer time, we must be prepared for greater space—north and south, sea and land—and therefore more varied conditions. Our equipment had to be as complete as theirs, and our carrying capacity was far more limited in weight as well as space.

Our craft, the *Sirius*, with its six-hundred-horse-power cyclone engine, was equipped with gasoline tanks which would carry us for two thousand miles, and with pontoons that would enable us to land in Hudson Bay, on the many inland lakes throughout Canada, along the coast of Alaska and Siberia, and among the Japanese islands. The general equipment had to include, among other things, instruments for blind flying and night flying; radio and direction-finding apparatus; facilities for fueling and for anchoring. (We had a twenty-five-pound anchor and rope tucked into a small compartment in the pontoons.) Aside from the general equipment indispensable for our everyday flying, we must carry a large amount of emergency supplies: an adequate repair kit and repair materials; a rubber boat, a sail and oars; an extra crash-proof, waterproof radio set; parachutes; general camping equipment and food supplies; firearms and ammunition; a full medicine kit; warm flying suits and boots; and many other articles.

The contingencies to be provided for were many and varied. We must consider the possibility of a parachute jump, and carry in our flying-suit pockets the most concentrated food and the most compact first-aid kit. We must be prepared for a forced landing in the North, where we would need warm bedding and clothes; and in the South, where we ought to have an insect-proof tent; and on the ocean, where we would need, in addition to food, plenty of fresh water.

And we must not exceed our limited weight budget. Every object to be taken had to be weighed, mentally as well as physically. The weight in pounds must balance the value in usefulness. The floor of our room for weeks before our departure was covered with large untidy piles of equipment. All day, while my husband was supervising the work on the plane, the piles had "Please do not disturb" signs on them. Each night they were rearranged. The things we had decided to take were heaped against one wall: rubber boat, flying suits, gloves, helmets, and stockings, pell-mell on top of each other. In the middle of the room were the baby's white scales and a large mountain of not-yet-decided-upon equipment. A third pile—by far the most untidy—of discarded things lay on the hearth.

I sat in the middle of the cans and read a book on calories, commenting from time to time, "Now, tomatoes haven't much food value, but they keep you from getting beri-beri. Magellan's men all got beri-beri, do you remember?" or, "Few calories in hard-tack, but it will fill up the hole still left inside of you, after you've eaten your army rations for the day."…

"Of course, we'll have to use pontoons instead of wheels up there," he remarked, studying the map of Canada, early in our preparations.

"Pontoons over all that dry land?" I queried.

"Yes, you can usually get down on a lake in northern Canada. The Canadian pilots always use seaplanes. And coming down the coast of Siberia, we could probably find sheltered water to land on—in an emergency we might even land in open ocean."

(Raised eyebrows, the only reply.)

"And if the ship got badly banged up," continued my husband, "we have the rubber boat."

"If we came down in the middle of the Bering Sea, Charles," I insisted, "it would be quite a long row to Kamchatka!"

"We might sail to shore, but otherwise we wouldn't have much chance of being found without radio," he agreed, and then firmly, "We'll have to carry radio."

"Can you operate radio?" (I can see it coming, I thought, I can just see what's going to happen.)

"A little—I learned at Brooks," (Then turning to me.) "But you will have to be radio operator."

"Oh!" (There it is! I thought.) "Well—I'll see."

The next day he came home with a small practice set of buzzers and keys, connected to two dry cells.

When I pressed down the key, there was a little squeak which brought four dogs and the baby scrambling into my room. I went on boldly with the Morse code in front of me, and, like everyone with a new fountain-pen, spelling out my own name in dots and dashes: "Dit-darr, darr-dit, darr-dit, dit."

An experienced radio operator gave us practice in receiving in the evenings. It reminded me of French *dictées* in school, where, at first, I could copy all the words; then I stumbled over a hard one; finally, after struggling along, three or four words behind, I gave up in a panic, and let the dark torrent of language stream over me without trying to stem the tide.

In the meantime, my husband had been working with the experts of Pan American Airways over the installation of the radio equipment in the plane. We found that we would have to have a third-class license to operate other than emergency calls.

"Here it is," said my husband, reading out of a book of radio regulations, "Applicants…must pass a code test in transmission and reception at a speed of fifteen words per minute in Continental Morse Code…and a practical and theoretical examination consisting of comprehensive questions on the care and operation of vacuum tube apparatus and radio communication laws and regulations.'"

"Comprehensive questions on the care and operation of vacuum tube apparatus," I read over this shoulder.

"Now, Charles, you know perfectly well that I can't do that. I never passed an arithmetic examination in my life I had to be tutored to get through elementary physics in college. I never understood a

Fluid Dynamics, Tina York, 1995

thing about electricity from the moment that man started rubbing sealing wax and fur!"

"It's too bad you didn't take more," he said heartlessly, "but it's not too late; we'll start tonight. I don't know much about radio; we'll work on it together."

We sat in front of clean pads and newly sharpened pencils that night.

"We might as well start with the vacuum tube," said our instructor.

"We might as well," I echo, as one replies to the dentist's phrase, "We might as well start on that back wisdom tooth."

He began drawing hieroglyphic diagrams on the pad, and skipping through a rapid simple sketch of the theory. He was about to start on the second diagram.

"Just a moment," I said. "Before you leave that, *where* is the vacuum tube?"

The instructor's face wore an expression of incredulity, amazement, and then, simply, pity.

"Well, don't you see," he said very gently, as though talking to a child, "*this* is it," and then he started all over again.

"Oh, I see *now*," I said, elaborately emphatic, as though it were just a small detail he had cleared up.

We went on to the next diagram. I knew my role now. It had a familiar swing, so often had I played It; to sit silent, confused, listening to long explanations which one pretended to understand because one could echo the last phrase said—"This in turn sets up a magnetic field in the tickler coil." The only beam of light in my dark mind was, as always, the thought—"I'll get it all explained to me after class."

This scheme worked very well. With the help of all of the diagrams, my college textbooks, and my husband's explanations, I managed to walk in the examination room one very hot day. I walked out before my husband; but I did not go as fully into the "Theory of regeneration in the vacuum tube." He passed with higher marks.

The practical end was on the whole easier. Long hours of work on the buzzer set in the silence of my bedroom gave me a kind of false confidence. The metallic *tick, tick, tick* of the key, against a background of chintz, rugs, and sofa pillows, seemed quite crisp and professional. This quality, however, quickly faded in the austere setting of a hangar. On the day of the radio test, the antenna was reeled out and hung on a rafter. An unknown radio operator somewhere on Long Island had agreed to listen for us. I called him shakily, three times. My own sending hissed in the earphones. Would I forget the letters? No, they sprang instinctively from my fingers and I read from the notebook. "Who—is—at—the—key?" came back the answer. I had to write down the letters as fast as they came. Still a beginner, my mind heard only single letters, and could not retain whole words.

"Anne—Lindbergh—how—is—this—sending?" I scribbled on my pad and the tapped out. My fingers could not yet read directly from my mind, but only from the written word on the paper.

"Pretty—good—" the letters ran slowly into words as I copied, "but—a—little—heavy—on—the—dashes—" (It seemed intensely funny to me, this slow deliberate conversation with a strange person somewhere on Long Island.) "—just—like—my—wife's—sending."

I smiled in the cockpit. How strange to feel you knew an unknown man from a single phrase over the radio—"just like my wife's sending!" I could hear the tone of his voice, the inflection, the accent on the *my*, the somewhat querulous, somewhat weary, somewhat kindly and amused, somewhat supercilious, husbandly tone—"just like *my* wife's sending," Yes, decidedly, there was still a good deal for me to learn.

We thought we were rather well along in our preparations. My husband had been in contact with the State Department in Washington. Gasoline was located along the routes; the pontoons were completed; we had installed a radio of the type used on the South American routes of Pan American Airways; and we were third-class radio operators. But we realized how little we had done when, the morning after the announcement was made of our trip; the newspapers voluntarily flooded us with information. Our routes, stops distances, and fuel consumption were all accurately planned out for us. (Who, I thought sympathetically, did all that arithmetic in such a short time? I detest turning gas into RPM—revolutions per minute—and RPM into miles.) Someone had gleaned all the statistics for year about weather, winds, and flying conditions across the Arctic. Someone else had fettered out all known travelers, by foot, ship, train, or plane to Canada, Alaska, Siberia, Japan, and China, and gathered together all the information they had to give. Guidebooks, travelers' diaries, and encyclopedias must have been open long past midnight for that great body of tourist information. "What the Lindberghs will see." "What the Lindberghs should see." "What might interest them." Somebody must have spent sleepless nights for all this. I felt quite guilty as I sat down in a comfortable chair and read about "the hairy Ainus, wild inhabitant of the Chishima Islands" and "primitive Eskimos who suck the eyes out of raw fish."

It was just as well that I read about them—I never saw any. ✳

Air Crash

Elizabeth Daryush

WHAT HAPPENED IN THOSE MOMENTS, THOSE SHORT FEW
Seconds, that seemed to each so timeless-long,
(Eternity had touched them) when they knew—
The modish, prosperous passengers, the strong
Young unreflective pilot, crew—that here,
Fronting them, barring inescapably
Their road to life, was the all-conqueror—
That they together faced that none could flee?…

Each one of his slow words, his acts delayed
(That were in truth so hurried) heard and saw,
Powerless—some other being its soul obeyed,
Some stranger published loudly his life-law…

Each had but one companion—knew, alone,
Himself, that till this hour he had not known.

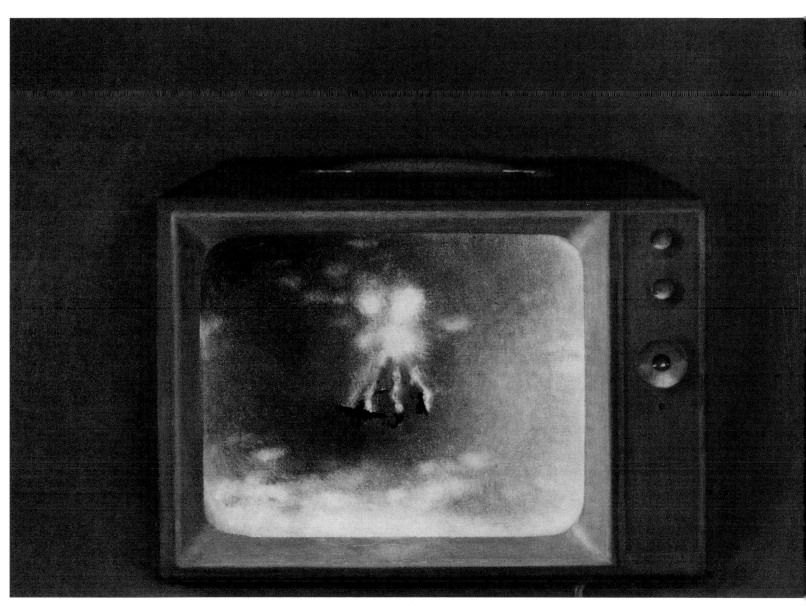

T.V., Vija Celmins, 1964

Aeropictorial Dinner in a Cockpit

1932

F.T. Marinetti and Fillia

INSIDE THE BIG COCKPIT of a great De Bernardi airship, flying through aeropaintings by the Futurists Marasco, Tato, Benedetta, Oriani and Munari, that hang on the peaks and clouds on the horizon; flying high at one thousand meters, the passengers free 5 lobsters from their shells and boil them electrically in sea water. They stuff them with a batter of egg-yolks, carrots, thyme, garlic, lemon peel, lobster eggs, livers and capers. Then they sprinkle curry powder and put them back inside their shells tinted here and there with a Mytilene blue.

Then the lobsters are confusedly arranged upon a great ceramic Tullio d'Albisola mattressed with twenty different salads: these geometrically set up like checkers.

The dining passengers, seizing ceramic steeples filled with Barolo wine mixed with Asti Spumante, eat thus villages factories and lowlands carried off at great speed. ✳

Manifestazione Interventista, Carlo Carra, 1914

Aerial Palette

1975

Trevor Winkfield

HERE, ONE MAN'S CABIN EGRESS IS SOME WOMAN'S PORTHOLE,
or the painted hull of a boat where eyes of lakes have
stellar bruises: night stares. Up there, greens look no
more than turf rafts sky-fished through cloud-rents
(though her greens are tethered kites, surely) with
yellows up to here: so many bleached haystacks worth
razing float in my blue hair blue. And grays? Grays
are reddish really (redder lacings later look like
path chains, cinder-hued, leading nowhere) with
propeller smell shed in the air, air worth razing.
This air we slip through. Or dip into, as roofs
flattened for warming slant among the lengthening
shadows of shortened days: a strange place. So let
us land here. Why falter? For on turf rafts elsewhere, other
doors in other rooms open slowly into other rooms:
an even stranger place.

Oregon Valley, Overcast Day II, Yvonne Jacquette, 1995

Aeroplane Synchromy in Yellow-Orange, Stanton Macdonald-Wright, 1920

London to Paris, by Air

Lord Gorell

I

THE DRONING ROAR IS QUICKENED, AND WE LIFT
On steady wing, like upward sweep of air,
Into the fleece-strewn heaven. The great plane
Draws to herself the leagues: onward we bear
In one resistless eddy towards the south
Over the English fields, trim-hedged and square,
And countless, winding lanes, a vast expanse
Of flattened green: huge shapes of shadow float
Inconsequent as bubbles. haunts of men
Stripped of their cherished privacy we note
And crawling multitudes within a town—
On all we rangers of the wind look down.

II

The coast-line swings to us: beneath our feet
The gray-green carpet of the sliding sea
Stretches afar, on it small, busy ships
Whose comet-tails in foamy whiteness flee:
We lift, and snowy cloudlets roam below,
Frail, wistful spirits of pure charity
Blessing the waters: like green marble veined,
The waves roll in upon the yellowing sand,
Then break to myriad, filmy curves of lace
Where they eternally caress the land:
Now low lies France—the kingdom of the breeze
Parts not the nations like the severing seas.

III

Down the wide river, jauntily outspread,
A fishing fleet comes seaward, to our eyes
Mere walnut shells with autumn leaves for sails:
And now a fellow-pilgrim of the skies,
Like a big insect droning past our flank,
Cruises to England home: before us lies
The rolling plain with its great, hedgeless strips
Of close-tilled fields, red roofs, and pointed trees,
The feathered arrows of the long French roads,
And all the stretch of quiet harmonies:
Then haven shows, and downward to earth's breast,
Like homing bird, we wheel and sink to rest.

Biplane

1966

Richard Bach

IT IS LIKE OPENING NIGHT on a new way of living, only it is opening day, and instead of velvet curtains drawing majestically aside there are hangar doors of corrugated tin, rumbling and scraping in concrete tracks and being more stubborn than majestic. Inside the hangar, wet still with darkness and with two wide pools of dark underwing and evaporating as the tall doors slide, the new way of living. An antique biplane.

I have arrived to do business, to trade. As simple as that. A simple old airplane trade, done every day. No slightest need to feel unsure.

Still, a crowd of misgivings rush toward me from the hangar. This is an old airplane. No matter how you took at it, this airplane was built in 1929 and this is today and if you're going to get the thing home to California you've got to fly it over twenty-seven hundred miles of America.

It is a handsome airplane, though. Dark red and dark yellow, an old barnstormer of a biplane, with great tall wheels, two open cockpits and a precise tictactoe of wires between the wings.

For shame. You have a fine airplane this moment. Have you forgotten the hours and the work and the money you poured into the rebuilding of the airplane you already own? That was only a year ago! A completely rebuilt 1946 Fairchild 24, as good as brand new! Better than brand new; you know every rib and frame and engine cylinder of the Fairchild, and you know that they're perfect. Can you say as much for this biplane? How do you know that ribs aren't broken beneath that fabric, or wingspars cracked?

How many thousand miles have you flown the Fairchild? Thousands over the Northeast, from that day you rolled her out of the hangar in Colt's Neck,

New Jersey. Then from Colt's Neck more thousands to Los Angeles, wife and children seeing the country at first hand as we moved to a new home. Have you forgotten that flight and the airplane that brought your country alive in rivers coursing and great craggy mountains and wheat tassels in the sun? You built this airplane so no weather could stop it, with full flight instruments and dual radios for communication and navigation and a closed cabin to keep out the wind and rain. And now this airplane has flown you across more thousands of miles, from Los Angeles to this little land of Lumberton, North Carolina.

This is good biplane country. March in Lumberton is like June is like August. But the way home is a different land. Remember the frozen lakes in Arizona, three days ago? The snow in Albuquerque? That's no place for an open-cockpit biplane! The biplane is in her proper place this moment. In Lumberton, with tobacco fields green about her airport, with other antique airplanes sheltered nearby, with her gentle owner taking time from his law practice to tend to her needs.

This biplane is not your airplane, your *kind* of airplane, even. She belongs and she should belong to Evander M. Britt, of Britt and Britt, attorneys at law. A man who loves old airplanes, with the time to come down and take care of their needs. He has no wild schemes, he hasn't the faintest desire to fly this airplane across the country. He knows his airplane and what it can do and what it can't do. Come to your senses. Just fly home in the Fairchild and forget this folly. His advertisement for a trade should find him his coveted low-wing Aeronca, and from some-place just down the road, not a brand new Fairchild 24 from Los Angeles, California. The biplane doesn't

Propeller Reflections, John Rummelhoff, 1973

even have a radio!

It is true. If I make this trade, I will be trading the known for the unknown. On the other side stands only one argument, the biplane itself. Without logic, without knowledge, without certainty. I haven't the right to take it from Mr. Britt. Secretary to the local chapter of the Antique Airplane Association, he should have a biplane. He needs a biplane. He is out of his mind to trade this way. This machine is his mark of belonging to an honored few.

But Evander Britt is a grown man and he knows what he is doing and I don't care why he wants the Fairchild or how much money I've put in the rebuilding or how far I've flown in it. I only know that I want that biplane. I want it because I want to travel through time and I want to fly a difficult airplane and I want to feel the wind when I fly and I want people to look, to see, to know that glory still exists. I want to be part of something big and glorious.

This can be a fair trade only because each airplane is worth the same amount of money. Money aside,

the two airplanes have absolutely nothing in common. And the biplane? I want it because I want it. I have brought sleeping bag and silk scarf for a biplane voyage home. My decision is made, and now, touching a dark wingtip, nothing can change it.

"Let's roll 'er out on the grass," Evander Britt says. "You call pull on that outboard wing strut, down near the bottom...."

In the sunlight, the darks of red and yellow go bright scarlet and blazing bright flame to become a glowing sunrise-biplane in four separate wing panels of cloth and wood and an engine of five black cylinders. Thirty-five years old, and this hangar could be the factory, and this air, 1929. I wonder if airplanes don't think of us as dogs and cats; for every year they age, we age fifteen or twenty. And as our pets share our household, so do we in turn share with airplanes the changing drifting sweeping household of the sky.

"...not really so hard to start, but you have to get the right combination. About four shots of prime, pull the prop through five or six times..."

It is all strange and different, this cockpit. A deep leather-trimmed wood-and-fabric hole, cables and wires skimming the wooden floorboards, three knobbed stalks of engine controls to the left, a fuel valve and more engine controls forward, six basic engine and flight instruments on a tiny black-painted instrument panel. No radio.

A four-piece windscreen, low in front of my eyes. If it rains now, this whole thing is going to fill with water.

"Give it a couple of slow pumps with the throttle."

"One…two. OK." Funny. You never hear of cockpits filling up with water, but what happens when it rains on one of these things?

"One more shot of prime, and make the switches hot."

Click-click on the instrument panel.

"CONTACT! And brakes."

One quick downward swing of the shining propeller and the engine is very suddenly running, catching its breath and choking and coughing hoarse in the morning chill. Silence runs terrified before it and hides in the far corners of the forests around. Clouds of blue smoke wreathe for a second and are whipped away and the silver blade becomes nothing more than a great wide fan, and it blows air back over me like a giant blowing on a dandelion and the sound of it over the engine sound is a deep westwind in the pines.

I can't see a thing ahead but airplane; a two-passenger front cockpit and a wide cowling and a silver blur that is the propeller. I let go the brakes and look out over the side of the cockpit into the big fan-wind giant-wind and touch the throttle forward. The propeller blur goes thinner and faster and the engine-sound goes deeper, all the while hollow and resonant, as though it were growling and roaring at the bottom of a thousand-gallon drum, lined in mirrors.

The old tall wheels begin to roll along the grass. The old grass, under the old wind, and bright old wings of another year and of this year, bound solidly together with angled old wires and forward-tilting old struts of wood, all a painted butterfly above the chill Carolina grass. Pressing on the rudder pedals,

I swing the nose slowly from one side to the other as we roll, making sure that the blind way ahead is clear.

What a very long way has come the dream of flight since 1929. None of the haughty proud business-like mien of the modern airplane hinted here. None of it. Just a slow leisurely taxi, with the constant S-turns to see ahead, pausing to sniff the breeze and inspect a flower in the grass and to listen to the sound of our engine. A quiet-seeming old biplane. Seeming, though, only seeming.

I have heard about these old airplanes, heard stories aplenty. Unreliable, these machines. You've always got to be ready for that engine to stop running. Quit on takeoff, usually, just when you need 'em most. And there's nothing you can do about it, that's just the way they are. If you do make it through the takeoff, look out for those old ones once they're in the air. Slow up just a little too much, boy, and they'll jerk the rug right out from under you and send you down in a spin. Like as not, you won't be able to recover from the spin, either. They'll just wrap up tighter and tighter and all you can do is bail out…. But worst of all are the landings. Biplanes have that narrow landing gear and not much rudder to work with; they'll get away from you before you can blink your eyes and suddenly you're rolling along the runway in a big ball of wires and splinters and shredded old fabric. Just plain vicious and that's the only word for 'em. Vicious.

But this airplane seems docile and as trim as a young lady earnestly seeking to make a good impression upon the world. Listen to that engine tick over. Smooth as a tuned racing engine, not a single cylinder left out of the song. "Unreliable," indeed.

A quick engine runup here on the grass before takeoff. Controls all free and working properly, oil pressure and temperature pointing as they should. Fuel valve is on, mixture is rich, all the levers are where they belong. Spark advance lever, even, and a booster magneto coil. Those haven't been built into airplanes for the last thirty years.

All right, airplane, let us see how you can fly. A discreet nudge on the throttle, a touch of left rudder to swing the nose around into the wind, facing a broad expanse of tall moist airport grass. Someone should have stamped out those rumors long ago.

Chinstrap fastened on leather helmet, dark goggles lowered.

Throttle coming full forward, and the giant blows hard twisting sound and fanned exhaust upon me. Certainly aren't very quiet, these engines.

Push forward on the control stick and instantly the tail is flying. Built for little grass fields, the biplanes. Weren't many airports around in 1929. That's why the big wheels, too. Roll over the ruts in a pasture, a racetrack, a country road. Built for shortfield takeoffs, because that's where the passengers were, short fields were where you made your money.

Grass fades into a green felt blur, and the biplane is already light on her wheels.

And suddenly the ground is no more. Smooth into the sky the bright wings climb, the engine thunders in its hollow drum, the tall wheels, still spinning, are lifted. Listen to that!... That screaming by my ears and that whipping of my scarf—the wind! It's here for me now just as it was here for the first pilots, that same wind that carried their mega-phoned words across the pastures of Illinois and the meadows of Iowa and the picnic grounds of Pennsylvania and the beaches of Florida. *"Five dol-lars, folks, for five minutes. Five minutes with the summer clouds, five minutes in the land of the angels. See your town from the air. You there, sir, how about taking the little lady for a joyride? Absolutely safe, perfectly harmless. Feel that fresh wind that blows where only birds and airplanes fly."* The same wind drumming on the same fabric and singing through the same wires and smashing into the same engine cylinders and sliced by the same sharp bright propeller and stirred and roiled by the same passage of the same machine that roiled it so many years ago.

If the wind and the sun and the mountains over the horizon do not change, a year that we make up in our heads and on our paper calendars is nothing. The farmhouse, there below. How call I tell that it is a farmhouse of today and not a farmhouse of 1931?

There's a modern car in the driveway. That's the only way I can tell the passing of time. It isn't the cal-endar makers who give us our time and our modern days, but the designers of automobiles and dishwashers and television sets and the current trends in fashion. Without a new car, then, time stands still. Find an old airplane and with a few pumps of prime and the swing of a shining propeller you can push time around as you will, mold it into a finer shape, give its features a more pleasant countenance. An escape machine, this. Climb in the cockpit and move the levers and turn the valves and start the engine and lift from the grass into the great unchanging ocean of air and you are master of your own time.

The personality of the biplane filters back to me as we fly. Elevator trim has to be almost full down to keep the nose from climbing when I take my hand from the control stick. Aileron forces are heavy, rudder and elevator forces are light. In a climb, I can push the throttle full forward and get no more than 1750 revolutions per minute from the shining propeller. The horizon is balanced, in level flight, just atop the Number Two and Five cylinder heads. The airplane stalls gently, and before it stalls there is a tapping in the stick, a warning that the nose is about to drop slowly down, even with the control stick pulled back. There's nothing at all vicious about this airplane. Windy, of course, when you move your head from behind the glass wind-screen, and not so quiet as modern airplanes. The wind goes quiet when the airplane is near its stalling speed; it shrieks warnings if it flies too fast. There is a great deal of airplane flying out ahead of the pilot. The forward windscreen clouds over with oil film and rocker-box grease after an hour in the air. When the throttle has been back for a moment, the engine misfires and chokes as it comes forward again. Certainly not a difficult airplane to fly. Certainly not a vicious one....

Another takeoff, another landing, another bit of knowing tucked away. Somehow, taxiing to the hangar, I'm surprised that it should be so easy to demolish the stories and the grim warnings. ✳

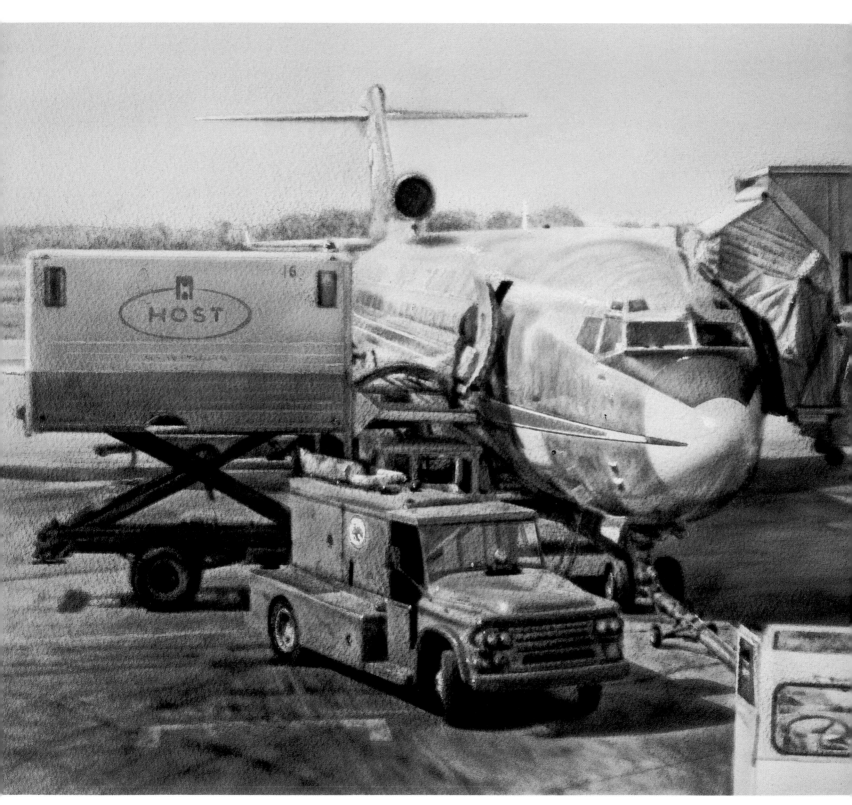

Host, John Salt, 1973

Tuesday
December 8, 1970

Joe Brainard

HERE I AM. Up in the air. Drinking a bloody mary. On my way to Chicago.

The great thing about flying is that for a while I can make myself realize that nothing really matters.

This is not a depressing thought. I love it. (Feeling this way.) I wish I could feel this way all the time. Because it's the truth (even if it isn't very practical) that *nothing really matters*!

Now I don't know if I really believe this or if I just *want* to believe this.

No, I *do* believe this.

Nothing really matters!

Propeller One-Way Night Coach

1992

John Travolta

It WAS LATE AT NIGHT and there was hardly anyone in the terminal. The voice over the P.A. system seemed so sophisticated, I imagined it belonged to someone really beautiful, more like an actress of some sort. "United Air Lines Flight 393 for Pittsburgh, Cleveland, and points west is now boarding at the West Arcade. All aboard please." The excitement ran through my body like nothing I had ever felt before. Knowing that within minutes I would be airborne for the first time was comparable to nothing, including playing doctor with the kids on the block, and that was saying a lot for an eight-year-old.

I remember everything about that night—the lights being dim in the terminal; the colors of every airline insignia as we rushed to the gate in the West Arcade. Even my mother seemed excited, but for totally different reasons, I'm sure. Probably something like the free drinks she could have, or the potential for meeting a handsome man on the plane. My mother was about forty-nine years old and quite attractive—blue eyes, black hair, and a good figure for her age, she told me....

As the engines started, one at a time, and I sat in what seemed a big, soft, comfortable chair, I could hardly hear them at all. The big propellers turned round as fire exited through the backside exhausts. I knew it was the "jet age," but there was something exciting about being in an aircraft that would take twice as long to get there as a jet would, especially my first time.

I had saved my coins in a floral-patterned ladies' purse that belonged to my mother. She told me that if I saved long enough we could go on a trip togeth-

er. She would match my money....

There were a total of about fifteen people on this first segment of the flight. I was wearing a hunter's cap that I forgot to remove, probably due to coming in from the cold....I could tell that my mother was excited for me, but for the moment was kind of impatiently waiting to be airborne, so she could have a cigarette and a drink. As we sped down the runway that surreal feeling came over me again. "I can't believe I'm flying," I told her. She smiled at me, and at that moment the aircraft left the ground. I'll always remember my mother that way. The take-off was much more gentle in feeling than I thought it would be. For some reason everything that happened thus far that night seemed perfect. For years after, no matter what negative experience I might have, from the time I would leave for the airport until the time I would arrive at my destination, life would seem safe and I would be happy.

My mother liked Manhattans. Just before we leveled off at our altitude, Liz [the flight attendant] showed up by the side of our seats and asked what we would like to drink. I immediately asked for a Coke and Mom asked for a Manhattan along with confirmation that she could smoke. Newport filter cigarettes. That turquoise box, that half-moon in the middle of it, would always bring to mind pleasurable memories. As she lights up and that first satisfying breath of smoke leaves here mouth, I would think "how festive." Smoke meant show business and good times. All of Mom's friends from the theater smoked. As a matter of fact, I don't remember an adult who didn't.

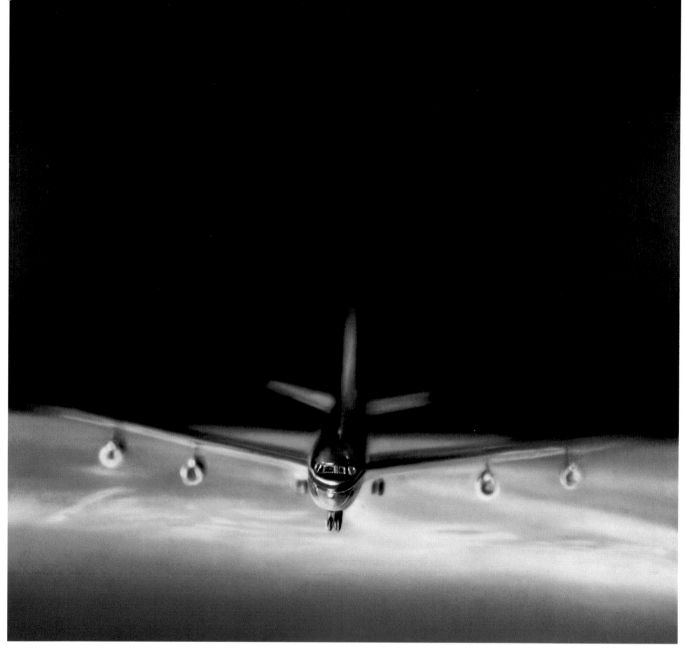

707, Ben Schonzeit, 1973

I could see every star in the night, or so it seemed as I looked out the window. This is so beautiful. "Why don't people just live in airplanes?" I started to reflect on how sometimes at home, late at night, I would lie in bed awake, listening to the drone of some airplane flying over my house, probably just having left Newark or La Guardia airport. And I would think "Where is that plane going this late at night? And who's on it, anyway? Are they sleeping? Are there beds on board?" And here I am, maybe even on that very same plane I had been pondering....

"Wow," I said to myself. This is fantastic, I thought. And it was. We were over the Colorado mountains before we knew it. The snowcapped mountains at sunset were unforgettable. As we leveled off in what seemed just minutes, I decided to roam the cabin. Maybe just for a minute I would break my pretense of being alone and visit mother. On the way to my mother's seat, I was walking in a very cocky manner, a way that only an eight-year-old could do when he knows he is doing something truly special. As I looked to the left, midway down the aisle, I saw a young kid there, older than me, about ten maybe. His face was buried in an airline schedule. It said "United, effective March, 1962." Is that the new one?" I asked him. The face of a redheaded braced-faced boy looked up at me, stared right into my eyes and said, "My dad gets them in the mail before anyone else does." I said, "God, you're so lucky." "That was the beginning of a beautiful friendship," to quote Humphrey Bogart. ✳

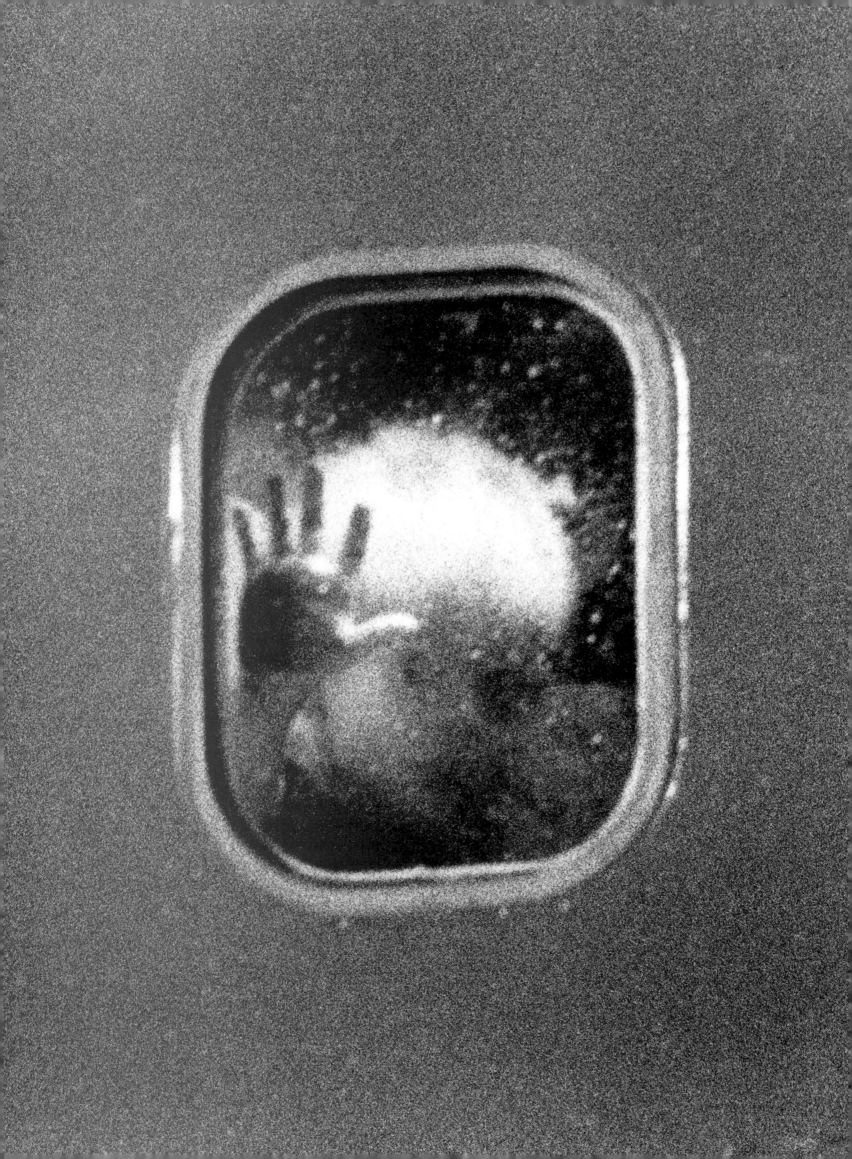

Sleeping on the Wing

Frank O'Hara

PERHAPS IT IS TO AVOID SOME GREAT SADNESS,
as in a Restoration tragedy the hero cries "Sleep!
O for a long sound sleep and so forget it!"
that one flies, soaring above the shoreless city,
veering upward from the pavement as a pigeon
does when a car honks or a door slams, the door
of dreams, life perpetuated in parti-colored loves
and beautiful lies all in different languages.

Fear drops away too, like the cement, and you
are over the Atlantic. Where is Spain? Where is
who? The Civil War was fought to free the slaves,
was it? A sudden down-draught reminds you of gravity
and your position in respect to human love. But
here is where the gods are, speculating, bemused.
Once you are helpless, you are free, can you believe
that? Never to waken to the sad struggle of a face?
to travel always over some impersonal vastness,
to be out of, forever, neither in nor for!

The eyes roll asleep as if turned by the wind
and the lids flutter open slightly like a wing.
The world is an iceberg, so much is invisible!
and was and is, and yet the form, it may be sleeping
too. Those features etched in the ice of someone
loved who died, you are a sculptor dreaming of space
and speed, your hand alone could have done this.

Curiosity, the passionate hand of desire. Dead,
or sleeping? Is there speed enough? And, swooping,
you relinquish all that you have made your own,
the kingdom of your self sailing, for you must awake
and breathe your warmth in this beloved image
whether it's dead or merely disappearing,
as space is disappearing and your singularity.

(Passenger #3-463),
John Schabel, 1994–95

Flight

B. P. Young

HOW CAN THEY KNOW THAT JOY TO BE ALIVE
Who have not flown?
To loop and spin and roll and climb and dive,
The very sky one's own,
The urge of power while engines race,
The sting of speed,
The rude winds' buffet on one's face,
To live indeed.

How can they know the grandeur of the sky,
The earth below,
The restless sea, and waves that break and die
With ceaseless ebb and flow;
The morning sun on drifting clouds
And rolling downs—
And valley mist that shrouds
The chimneyed towns?

So long has puny man to earth been chained
Who now is free,
And with the conquest of the air has gained
A glorious liberty.
How splendid is this gift He gave
On high to roam,
The sun a friend, the earth a slave,
The heavens home.

X-15, Stan Stokes, 1986

The Spirit of Flight Research, Robert T. McCall, 1977. On display at the Dryden Flight Research Center, Lancaster, CA.

Space Flight and the Human Imagination

Part 5

Roger D. Launius

HUMANITY HAS LONG EXPRESSED CURIOSITY about the universe and the other worlds of the Solar System. Prior to the twentieth century, however, they had little opportunity to explore the universe except in fiction and through astronomical observations. These early efforts led to the compilation of a body of knowledge that inspired and informed the efforts of scientists and engineers applying rocket technology to the challenge of space-flight in the early part of the twentieth century. The scientists and engineers engaged in research about the cosmos essentially became the first spaceflight pioneers, translating centuries of dreams and observations into a reality that matched in some measure the expectations of the public that watched, and the governments that supported their efforts.

All of these early enthusiasts believed humanity would soon go off to explore the Solar System. And many of them worked relentlessly to make that belief a reality. They successfully convinced everyone of space-flight's possibility. Through their constant public relations efforts during the decade following World War II, they engineered a sea change in perceptions, as most Americans went from skepticism about the probabilities of spaceflight to an acceptance of it as a near-term reality.

This is apparent in the public opinion polls of the era. In December 1949, Gallup pollsters found that only 15 percent of Americans believed humans would reach the Moon within fifty years, while 15 percent had no opinion, and a whopping 70 percent believed that it would not happen within that time. In October 1957, at the same time as the launching of Sputnik I, only 25 percent believed that it would take longer than twenty-five years for humanity to reach the Moon, while 41 percent believed firmly that it would happen within twenty-five years, and 34 percent were not sure. An important shift in perceptions had taken place, and it was largely the result of well-known advances in rocket technology—coupled with a public relations campaign—that emphasized the real possibilities of spaceflight.

From the defining event of Sputnik in 1957, four major themes have been used to justify a large-scale space exploration agenda:

- human destiny,
- national defense and military applications,
- scientific understanding about the universe,
- commercial applications and economic competitiveness.

Those themes have continued in American space policy from the very beginning of the space age to the present. Specific aspects of these four programs have fluctuated over time but remain within the boundaries of these general interests.

The first and most common rationale for human spaceflight is that an integral part of human nature is a voyage of discovery. With the Earth so well known, moreover, exploration and settlement of the Moon and Mars is the next logical step in human exploration. Humans must question and explore and discover or die, advocates for this position insist. It is the "final frontier," and Americans have always responded well to their frontiers.

From Captain James T. Kirk's soliloquy—"Space, the final frontier"—at the beginning of each Star Trek episode to President John F. Kennedy's 1962 speech about setting sail on "this new ocean" of space, the frontier allusion has been a critical component of space program promotion. Astronaut, then Senator John Glenn captured some of this tenor in 1983 when he summoned images of the American

heritage of pioneering and argued that the next great frontier challenge was in space. "It represents the modern frontier for national adventure. Our spirit as a nation is reflected in our willingness to explore the unknown for the benefit of all humanity, and space is a prime medium in which to test our mettle."

Quintessential American novelist James A. Michener also applied this frontier analogy to the space program. In two articles in Omni magazine in the early 1980s, he explicitly compared the space program to the Anglo-American westward movement of the nineteenth century. He described the American sense of pioneering and argued that the next great challenge in this arena is space. "A nation that loses its forward thrust is in danger," he commented. "The way to retain it is exploration." In an eloquent and moving way he argued for the American space program as the logical means of carrying out exploration. One of these articles had the ironic title of "Manifest Destiny," a blatant hearkening to the ideology of continental expansion that gained preeminence in the 1840s. Michener argued that it is the American destiny to explore and colonize, and space is the next logical place to do this. His statement presents an eloquent and moving defense of America's human space program in all its permutations.

A second rationale of national defense and military space activity has proceeded through several stages in development. From the beginning, national leaders sought to use space to ensure U.S. security from nuclear holocaust. For instance, in 1952 a popular conception of the U.S.-occupied space station showed it as a platform from which to observe the Soviet Union and the rest of the globe in the interest of national security. The U. S. military also argued for a human capability to fly in space for rapid deployment of troops to hot spots anywhere around the Earth. The human spaceflight enterprise also gained energy from cold war rivalries in the 1950s and 1960s, as international prestige—translated into American support from non-aligned nations—found an important place in the space policy agenda. Human spaceflight also had a strong military nature during the 1980s, when astronauts from the military services deployed reconnaissance satellites into Earth orbit from the Space Shuttle. A human military presence in space promises to remain a compelling aspect of spaceflight well into the twenty-first century.

The third rationale of scientific advancement is closely tied to the compelling vision of human destiny driving much of the human space exploration agenda. At one level, there exists the ideal of the pursuit of abstract scientific knowledge—learning more about the universe to expand the human mind. Indeed, to some Americans, from the 1960s to the present, space has represented prestige and the American image on the world stage. That certainly drove the effort to reach the Moon before the Soviet Union. To others, it has signified the quest for national security. To still others, space represents the pure science and exploration of the unknown. In the thinking and writing about space exploration, the first two views of American interest in space have eclipsed the third. Indeed, the history of space science is one of the largely neglected aspects in the evolution of the human space program.

Even so, science as a goal may have been clearly envisioned in the National Aeronautics and Space Act of 1958 that created the National Aeronautics and Space Administration (NASA), with its mandate for "the expansion of human knowledge of phenomena in the atmosphere and space." This idea has continually drawn verbal and fiscal support, but it has proven less important than the pursuit of knowledge that enables some practical social or economic payoff.

Even the Apollo missions to the Moon, certainly inaugurated as a cold war effort to best the Soviet Union and establish the United States as the preeminent world power, succeeded in enhancing scientific understanding. The scientific experiments placed on the Moon and the lunar soil samples returned through Project Apollo have provided grist for scientists' investigations of the Solar System ever since. The scientific return was significant, even though the Apollo program did not answer conclusively the age-old questions of lunar origins and evolution. In that case, and many others, a linkage between the spirit and need of scientific inquiry, and the spirit and need for exploration served as strong synergetic forces for human spaceflight. The performance of scientific experiments on the Space Shuttle and the science program envisioned for the ISS demonstrate the same linkages at the end of the twentieth century.

Indeed, NASA has developed a set of fundamental questions to be used in formulating its plans for the exploration of space. They invite serious consideration and inform the direction of future justifications of human spaceflight as a means of advancing human knowledge:

1. How did the universe, galaxies, stars and planets form and evolve? How can our exploration of the universe and our solar system revolutionize our understanding of physics, chemistry and biology?

2. Does life in any form, however simple or complex, carbon-based or other, exist elsewhere than on planet Earth? Are there Earth-like planets beyond our solar system?

3. How can we utilize the knowledge of the Sun, Earth and other planetary bodies to develop predictive environmental, climate, natural disaster and natural resource models to help ensure sustainable development and improve the quality of life on Earth?

4. What is the fundamental role of gravity and cosmic radiation in vital biological, physical and chemical systems in space, on other planetary bodies and on Earth; and how do we apply this fundamental knowledge to the establishment of permanent human presence in space to improve life on Earth?

5. How can we enable revolutionary technological advances to provide air and space travel for anyone, anytime and anywhere—more safely, more affordably, and with less impact on the environment—and in a way that improves business opportunities and global security?

6. What cutting-edge technologies, processes and techniques, and engineering capabilities must we develop to enable our research agenda in the most productive, economical and timely manner? How can we most effectively transfer the knowledge we gain from our research and discoveries to commercial ventures in the air, in space and on Earth?

Finally, concerns over commercial applications and economic competitiveness have provided a rationale for the human exploration of space. Space technologies—especially the complex human spaceflight component—demand a skilled and well-trained work force, whose talents are disseminated to the larger technological and economic base of the nation. The Apollo program, for example, served explicitly as an economic engine fueling the southern states' economic growth. In recent years, the economic rationale has become stronger and even more explicit, as space applications especially communications satellites become increasingly central for maintaining the United States' global economic competitiveness. President Ronald Reagan's administration, in particular, emphasized enlarging the role of the private sector, and its priorities have remained in place thereafter. One of the key initiatives in this effort for human spaceflight is tourism, a major aspect of which envisions hotels in Earth orbit and lunar vacation packages. While this has yet to find realization, it remains a tantalizing possibility for the twenty-first century.

The literary and artistic pieces that follow explore the longstanding excitement of spaceflight in the twentieth century. They show the mystical nature of the desire to travel to other worlds. At a fundamental level, these dreams tap into the strong utopian impulse so prevalent in American intellectual thought and political tradition. Twenty-first century space advocates continue to dream about winged spaceships, rotating space stations, lunar bases and colonies on Mars in an effort to remake society. Some of these visions will come true. To a large extent, however, the motivating vision draws its force from nostalgic memories of a past that to a great extent never existed.

Space exploration continues to provide a window on the universe from which fantastic new discoveries may be made. Humans may well discover extraterrestrial life. They may set their eyes on the image of an Earth-like planet around a nearby star. They may discover some fantastic material that can only be made in a gravity-free realm. Perhaps they may discover some heretofore unknown principle of physics. Perhaps they will capture an image of the creation.

That is the true excitement of the endeavor.

From *From the Earth to the Moon*

Fire!
A Fictional Launch to the Moon

1866

Jules Verne

THE FIRST OF DECEMBER HAD ARRIVED! the fatal day! · for, if the projectile were not discharged that very night at 10h. 46m. 40s. P.M., more than eighteen years must roll by before the moon would again present herself under the same conditions of zenith and perigee.

The weather was magnificent. Despite the approach of winter, the sun shone brightly, and bathed in its radiant light that earth which three of its denizens were about to abandon for a new world.

How many persons lost their rest on the night which preceded this long-expected day! All hearts beat with disquietude, save only the heart of Michel Ardan. That imperturbable personage came and went with his habitual business-like air, while nothing whatever denoted that any unusual matter pre-occupied his mind.

After dawn, an innumerable multitude covered the prairie which extends as far as the eye can reach, round Stones Hill. Every quarter of an hour the railway brought fresh accessions of sightseers; and, according to the statement of the Tampa Town *Observer*, not less than five millions of spectators thronged the soil of Florida. For a whole month previously, the mass of these persons had bivouacked round the enclosure, and laid the foundations for a town which was afterward called "Ardan's Town."

The whole plain was covered with huts, cottages, and tents. Every nation under the sun was represented there; and every language might be heard spoken at the same time. It was a perfect Babel reenacted. All the various classes of American society were mingled together in terms of absolute equality. Bankers, farmers, sailors, cotton-planters, brokers, merchants, watermen, magistrates, elbowed each other in the most free-and-easy way. Louisiana Creoles fraternized with farmers from Indiana; Kentucky and Tennessee gentlemen and haughty Virginians conversed with trappers and the half-savages of the lakes and butchers from Cincinnati. Broad-brimmed white hats and Panamas, blue cotton trousers, light-colored stockings, cambric frills, were all here displayed; while upon shirt-fronts, wristbands, and neckties, upon every finger, even upon the very ears, they wore an assortment of rings, shirt-pins, brooches, and trinkets, of which the value only equaled the execrable taste. Women, children, and servants, in equally expensive dress, surrounded their husbands, fathers, or masters, who resembled the patriarchs of tribes in the midst of their immense households.

At meal-times all fell to work upon the dishes peculiar to the Southern States, and consumed with an appetite that threatened speedy exhaustion of the victualing powers of Florida, fricasseed frogs, stuffed monkey, fish chowder, underdone 'possum, and raccoon steaks. And as for the liquors which accompanied this indigestible repast! The shouts, the vociferations that resounded through the bars and taverns decorated with glasses, tankards, and bottles of marvelous shape, mortars for pounding sugar, and bundles of straws! "Mint-julep!" roars one of the barmen; "Claret sangaree!" shouts another; "Cocktail!"

"Brandy-smash!" "Real mint-julep in the new style!" All these cries intermingled produced a bewildering and deafening hubbub.

But on this day, 1st of December, such sounds were rare. No one thought of eating or drinking, and at four P.M. there were vast numbers of spectators who had not even taken their customary lunch! And, a still more significant fact, even the national passion for play seemed quelled for the time under the general excitement of the hour.

Up till nightfall, a dull, noiseless agitation, such as precedes great catastrophes, ran through the anxious multitude. An indescribable uneasiness pervaded all minds, an indefinable sensation which oppressed the heart. Every one wished it was over.

However, about seven o'clock, the heavy silence was dissipated. The moon rose above the horizon. Millions of hurrahs hailed her appearance. She was punctual to the rendezvous, and shouts of welcome greeted her on all sides, as her pale beams shone gracefully in the clear heavens. At this moment the three intrepid travelers appeared. This was the signal for renewed cries of still greater intensity. Instantly the vast assemblage, as with one accord, struck up the national hymn of the United States, and "Yankee Doodle," sung by five million of hearty throats, rose like a roaring tempest to the farthest units of the atmosphere. Then a profound silence reigned throughout the crowd.

The Frenchman and the two Americans had by this time entered the enclosure reserved in the center of the multitude. They were accompanied by the members of the Gun Club, and by deputations sent from all the European Observatories. Barbicane, cool and collected, was giving his final directions.

Nicholl, with compressed lips, his arms crossed behind his back, walked with a firm and measured step. Michel Ardan, always easy, dressed in thorough traveler's costume, leathern gaiters on his legs, pouch by his side, in loose velvet suit, cigar in mouth, was full of inexhaustible gayety, laughing, joking, playing pranks with J. T. Maston. In one word, he was the thorough "Frenchman" (and worse, a "Parisian") to the last moment.

Ten o'clock struck! The moment had arrived for taking their places in the projectile! The necessary operations for the descent, and the subsequent removal of the cranes and scaffolding that inclined over the mouth of the Columbiad, required a certain period of time.

Barbicane had regulated his chronometer to the tenth part of a second by that of Murchison the engineer, who was charged with the duty of firing the gun by means of an electric spark. Thus the travelers enclosed within the projectile were enabled to follow with their eyes the impassive needle which marked the precise moment of their departure.

The moment had arrived for saying "good-by!" The scene was a touching one. Despite his feverish gayety, even Michel Ardan was touched. J. T. Maston had found in his own dry eyes one ancient tear, which he had doubtless reserved for the occasion. He dropped it on the forehead of his dear president.

"Can I not go?" he said, "there is still time!"

"Impossible, old fellow!" replied Barbicane. A few moments later, the three fellow-travelers had ensconced themselves in the projectile, and screwed down the plate which covered the entrance-aperture. The mouth of the Columbiad, now completely dis-encumbered, was open entirely to the sky.

The moon advanced upward in a heaven of the purest clearness, outshining in her passage the twinkling light of the stars. She passed over the constellation of the Twins, and was now nearing the halfway point between the horizon and the zenith. A terrible silence weighed upon the entire scene! Not a breath of wind upon the earth! not a sound of breathing from the countless chests of the spectators! Their hearts seemed afraid to beat! All eyes were

View of Earth, Dennis Davidson, 1992

fixed upon the yawning mouth of the Columbiad.

Murchison followed with his eye the hand of his chronometer. It wanted scarce forty seconds to the moment of departure, but each second seemed to last an age! At the twentieth there was a general shudder, as it occurred to the minds of that vast assemblage that the bold travelers shut up within the projectile were also counting those terrible seconds. Some few cries here and there escaped the crowd. "Thirty-five!—thirty-six!—thirty-seven!—thirty-eight!—thirty-nine!—forty! FIRE!!!"

Instantly Murchison pressed with his finger the key of the electric battery, restored the current of the fluid, and discharged the spark into the breech of the Columbiad.

An appalling, unearthly report followed instantly, such as can be compared to nothing whatever known, not even to the roar of thunder, or the blast of volcanic explosions! No words can convey the slightest idea of the terrific sound! An immense spout of fire shot up from the bowels of the earth as from a crater. The earth heaved up, and with great difficulty some few spectators obtained a momentary glimpse of the projectile victoriously cleaving the air in the midst of the fiery vapors! ✳

Robert Shore

On the Beaches
of the Moon

1966

Archibald MacLeish

ON THE BEACHES OF THE MOON
No wind ever blows, no air
Stirs the snow upon the dune
Moves the frozen water there

On the beaches of the moon
No wave breaks nor any sound
Comes but only noon to noon
Shadows of the rocks creep round

Only in the cloudless sky
Moves by day the sun; by night
Slow among the stars the white
Silence of the Earth goes by

. . . . .

To the beaches of the moon
Comes across the night no cry,
No faint singing down the sky,
No words whisper on the dune

Lunar Confrontation (with Jules Verne), Robert Shore, 1970

Can We Get to Mars?

1954

Wernher von Braun with Cornelius Ryan

THE FIRST MAN WHO SET OUT FOR MARS had better make sure they leave everything at home in apple-pie order. They won't get back to earth for more than two and a half years.

The difficulties of a trip to Mars are formidable. The outbound journey, following a huge arc 255,000,000 miles long, will take eight months—even with rocket ships that travel many thousands of miles an hour. For more than a year, the explorers will have to live on the great red planet, waiting for it to swing into a favorable position for the return trip. Another eight months will pass before the 70 members of the pioneer expedition set foot on earth again. All during that time, they will be exposed to a multitude of dangers and strains, some of them impossible to foresee on the basis of today's knowledge.

Will man ever go to Mars? I am sure he will—but it will be a century or more before he's ready. In that time scientists and engineers will learn more about the physical and mental rigors of interplanetary flight—and about the known dangers of life on another planet. Some of that information may become available within the next 25 years or so, through the erection of a space station above the earth (where telescope viewings will not be blurred by the earth's atmosphere) and through the subsequent exploration of the moon, as described in previous issues of *Collier's*.

Even now science can detail the technical requirements of a Mars expedition down to the last ton of fuel. Our knowledge of the laws governing the solar system—so accurate that astronomers can predict an eclipse of the sun to within a fraction of a second—enables scientists to determine exactly the speed a space ship must have to reach Mars, the course that will intercept the planet's orbit at exactly the right moment, the methods to be used for the landing, take-off and other maneuvering. We know, from these calculations, that we already have chemical rocket fuels adequate for the trip.

Better propellants are almost certain to emerge during the next 100 years. In fact, scientific advances will undoubtedly make obsolete many of the engineering concepts on which this article, and the accompanying illustrations, are based. Nevertheless, it's possible to discuss the problems of a flight to Mars in terms of what is known today. We can assume, for example, that such an expedition will involve about 70 scientists and crew members. A force that size would require a flotilla of 10 massive space ships, each weighing more than 4,000 tons—not only because there's safety in numbers, but because of the tons of fuel, scientific equipment, rations, oxygen, water and the like necessary for the trip and for a stay of about 31 months away from earth.

All that information can be computed scientifically. But science can't apply a slide rule to man; he's the unknown quantity, the weak spot that makes a Mars expedition a project for the far distant, rather than the immediate, future. The 70 explorers will endure hazards and stresses the like of which no men before them have ever known. Some of these hardships must be eased—or at least better understood—before the long voyage becomes practical.

Imagine yourself in a space ship millions of miles from earth. You see the same people every day. The earth, with all it means to you, is just another bright star in the heavens; you aren't sure you'll ever get back to it. Every noise about the rocket ship sug-

Mars Part 1, Russell Crotty, 2000

gests a breakdown, every crash a meteor collision. If somebody does crack, you can't call off the expedition and return to earth. You'll have to take him with you.

The psychological problem probably will be at its worst during the two eight-month travel periods. On Mars, there will be plenty to do, plenty to see. To be sure, there will be certain problems on the planet, too. There will be considerable confinement. The scenery is likely to be grindingly monotonous. The threat of danger from some unknown source will hang over the explorers constantly. So will the knowledge that an extremely complicated process, subject to possible breakdown, will be required to get

them started on their way back home. Still, Columbus's crew at sea faced much the same problems the explorers will face on Mars: the fifteenth-century sailors felt the psychological tension, but no one went mad.

But Columbus traveled only ten weeks to reach America; certainly his men would never have stood an eight-month voyage. The travelers to Mars will have to, and psychologists undoubtedly will make careful plans to keep up the morale of the voyagers.

The fleet will be in constant radio communication with the earth (there probably will be no television transmission, owing to the great distance). Radio programs will help relieve the boredom, but it's

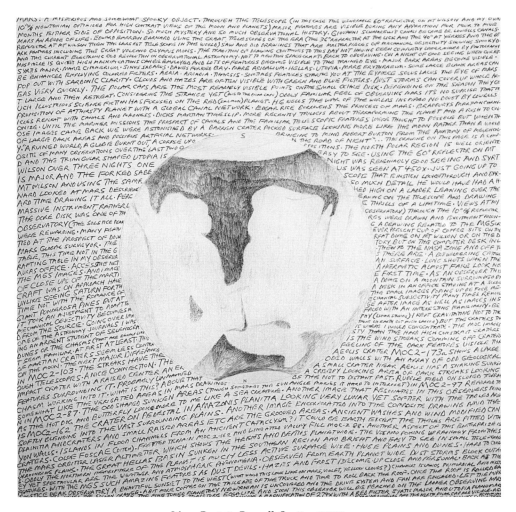

Mars Part 2, Russell Crotty, 2000

possible that the broadcasts will be censored before transmission; there's no way of telling how a man might react, say, to the news that his home town was the center of a flood disaster. Knowing would do him no good-and it might cause him to crack.

Besides radio broadcasts, each ship will be able to receive (and send) radio pictures. There also will be films which can be circulated among the space ships. Reading matter will probably be carried in the form of microfilms to save space. These activities— —plus frequent intership visiting, lectures and crew rotations—will help to relieve the monotony.

There is another possibility, seemingly fantastic but worth mentioning briefly because experimentation already has indicated it may be practical. The non-working members of a Mars expedition may actually hibernate during part of the long voyage. French doctors have induced a kind of artificial hibernation

in certain patients for short periods in connection with operations for which they will need all their strength (*Collier's* December 11, 1953—Medicine's New Offensive Against Shock, by J.D. Ratcliff). The process involves a lowering of the body temperature, and the subsequent slowing down of all normal physical processes. On a Mars expedition, such a procedure, over a longer period, would solve much of the psychological problem, would cut sharply into the amount of food required for the trip, and would, if successful, leave the expedition members in superb physical condition for the ordeal of exploring the planet.

Certainly if a Mars expedition were planned for the next 10 or 15 years, no one would seriously consider hibernation as a solution for any of the problems of the trip. But we're talking of a voyage to be made 100 years from now; I believe that if the

French experiments bear fruit, hibernation may actually be considered at that time.

Finally, there has been one engineering development which may also simplify both the psychological and physical problems of a Mars voyage. Scientists are on the track of a new fuel, useful only in the vacuum of space, which would be so economical that it would make possible far greater speeds for space journeys. It could be used to shorten the travel time, or to lighten the load of each space ship, or both. Obviously, a four- or six-month Mars flight would create far fewer psychological hazards than a trip lasting eight months.

In any case, it seems certain that members of an expedition to Mars will have to be selected with great care. Scientists estimate that only one person in every 6,000 will be qualified, physically, mentally and emotionally, for routine space flight. But can 70 men be found who will have those qualities—and also the scientific background necessary to explore Mars? I'm sure of it.

One day a century or so from now, a fleet of rocket ships will take off for Mars. The trip could be made with 10 ships launched from an orbit 1,000 miles out in space, that girdles our globe at its equator. (It would take tremendous power and vast quantities of fuel to leave directly from the earth. Launching a Mars voyage from an orbit about 1,000 miles out, far from the earth's gravitational pull, will require relatively little fuel.) The Mars-bound vehicles, assembled in the orbit, will look like bulky bundles of girders, with propellant tanks hung on the outside and great passenger cabins perched on top. Three of them will have torpedo-shaped noses and massive wings—dismantled, but strapped to their sides for future use. Those bullet noses will be detached and will serve as landing craft, the only vehicles that will actually land on the neighbor planet. When the 10 ships are 5,700 miles from the earth, they will cut off their rocket motors; from there on, they will coast unpowered toward Mars.

After eight months they will swing into an orbit around Mars, about 600 miles up, and adjust speed to keep from hurtling into space again. The expedition will take this intermediate step, instead of preceding directly to Mars, for two main reasons: first, the ships (except for the three detachable torpedo-shaped noses) will lack the streamlining required for flight in the Martian atmosphere; second, it will be more economical to avoid carrying all the fuel needed for the return to earth (which now comprises the bulk of the cargo) all the way down to Mars and then back up again.

Upon reaching the 600-mile orbit—and after some exploratory probings of Mars's atmosphere with unmanned rockets—the first of the three landing craft will be assembled. The torpedo nose will be unhooked, to become the fuselage of a rocket plane. The wings and set of landing skis will be attached, and the plane launched toward the surface of Mars.

The landing of the first plane will be made on the planet's snow covered polar cap—the only spot where there is any reasonable certainty of finding a smooth surface. Once down, the pioneer landing party will unload its tractors and supplies, inflate its balloon-like living quarters, and start on a 4,000 mile overland journey to the Martian equator, where the expedition's Main base will be set up (it is the most livable part of the planet—well within the area that scientists want most to investigate). At the equator, the advance party will construct a landing strip for the other two rocket planes. (The first landing craft will be abandoned at the pole.)

In all, the expedition will remain on the planet 15 months. That's a long time—but it still will be too short to learn all that science would like to know about Mars.

When, at last, Mars and the earth begin to swing toward each other in the heavens, and it's time to go back, the two ships that landed on the equator will be stripped of their wings and landing gear, set on their tails and, at the proper moment, rocketed back to the 600-mile orbit on the flat leg of the return journey.

What curious information will these first explorers carry back from Mars? Nobody knows—and its extremely doubtful that anyone now living will ever know. All that can be said with certainty today is this: the trip can be made, and will be made...someday. ✳

View From Mimas, Ron Miller, 1981

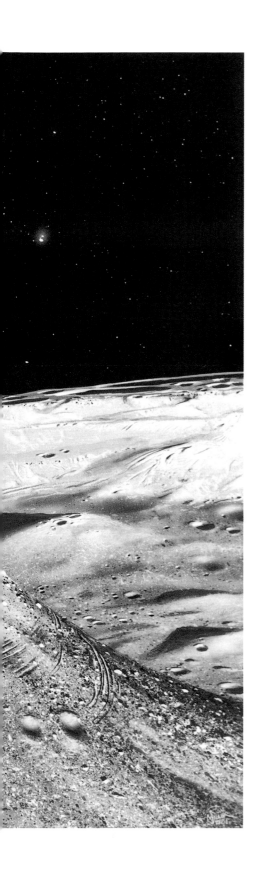

The Rockets That Reached Saturn

Vachel Lindsay

On the Fourth of July sky rockets went up
Over the church and the tress and the town,
Stripes and stars, riding red cars.
Each rocket wore a red-white-and-blue gown,
And I did not see one rocket come down.

Next day on the hill I found dead sticks,
Scorched like blown-out candle-wicks.

But where are the rockets? Up in the sky.
As for the sticks, let them lie.
Dead sticks are not the Fourth of July.

In Saturn they grow like wonderful weeds,
In some ways like weeds of ours,
Twisted and beautiful, straight and awry.
But nodding all day to the heavenly powers.
The stalks are smoke,
And the blossoms green light,
And crystalline fireworks flowers.

2001: Space Station Operations, Robert McCall, 1968

The Shores of Infinity

1970

Arthur C. Clarke

THE STORY OF MAN has been one of expanding horizons; even today, there are a few Stone Age cultures where the limits of the unknown are only a dozen miles away.

First by land, thanks to conquerors and travelers like Alexander the Great and Marco Polo, the world widened. Yet not until the development of the sailing ship, and the arts of navigation, did Columbus, Magellan and their successors reveal the true lineaments of the globe. The fantastic cosmographies of the Dark Ages, with their mythical realms and monsters, lost their power over the minds of men. For the last four hundred years, every educated person has lived in essentially the world our parents knew.

But not the world we know. In one brief decade, our imaginations have had to encompass the moon. We can pinpoint the very moment when it ceased to be a heavenly body and became a place; it was November 23, 1966, when Lunar Orbiter 2 radioed back to earth the historic photograph of the Copernicus crater—and for the first time we looked not upon, but across, the landscape of another world.

In a few more years, we will experience the same revelation with Mars, Mercury, Venus.... Before the end of this century, the entire solar system will have become the background of our lives, as robot probes penetrate to its farthest reaches, and men prepare to follow them. Human thought will undergo another change of scale, comparable to that which occurred during the first Age of Discovery, half a millennium ago.

But for all the obvious parallels, there will be a profound difference between these two eras. Columbus and his fellow navigators were filling in the details of a world which, though large, they knew to be finite. The men of the twenty-first century will always be aware that, far beyond their widest voyaging, the stars and galaxies are scattered across a volume of space which is unimaginably large, and may indeed be infinite.

There is a familiar household object which gives a good idea of the scale of the solar system, and of the gulfs beyond. Take an ordinary twelve-inch LP record, and imagine that the hole in the center is the earth's orbit—180,000,000 miles wide. Then Pluto lies on the rim, and all the outer planets are scattered across the disc; Saturn is at the edge of the label.

As yet, we have just started to explore the hole in the middle, which contains the sun, Mercury and Venus, and have sent a few probes a tenth of an inch outwards toward Mars. The remainder is still unknown, though already within our reach if we are prepared to spend years in silent coasting through space.

On this scale, the very nearest of the stars—and therefore the closest possible system of other planets— is three-quarters of a mile away. Our sun is a barely visible speck of dust, one of a hundred thousand million which on the average are about a mile apart. The whole collection of suns (the Galaxy) forms a disc about five times the diameter of earth. Even with this drastic reduction, our model has got a little out of hand....

It is not surprising, therefore, that we do not know if there are any other solar systems besides our own. Across gulfs which shrink the sun itself to a feeble star, even a giant planet like Jupiter is utterly invisible. Nevertheless, there is indirect evidence that a few of the neighbor stars do have dark, planet-sized companions, and today most astronomers think it likely that the majority of suns possess solar systems. From this, it is an easy step to assume that planets bearing life—and intelligence—are common-place throughout the universe.

This is probable; the alternative—that this tiny earth is the only inhabited planet in a cosmos of at least 10,000,000,000,000,000,000,000 suns—seems the wildest fantasy one can imagine. But at this stage of our knowledge there is no proof whatsoever that any life, or any intelligence, exists beyond the solar system. Some scientists, rashly ignoring the lessons of the past, have denied that such proof will ever be obtained; they feel that the distances involved present an insuperable barrier to knowledge. And they ridicule the idea that living creatures—men or other beings, should they exist—can ever span the abyss between the stars.

The development of space flight itself shows how dangerous it is to make such negative predic-

tions. Moreover, in this case they can be shown to be false, at least to a high degree of probability. There may indeed be absolute bars to interstellar *travel*—but if so, they must be based on factors not yet known. What is already certain is that there are no serious difficulties in establishing interstellar *communication*—always assuming, of course, that there is someone to talk to at the other end....

The quite amazing development of radio astronomy during the last thirty years has given us all the technology required. The gigantic antennas designed to catch faint, natural signals from the depths of space, and the sensitive receivers to amplify them, are the very tools needed for this task. In barely more than half a century since Marconi flashed his first signals across the Atlantic (a feat then widely declared to be impossible!) we have developed equipment with which we can talk to the stars.

No one has yet tried to do this, though there have been limited attempts to listen for intelligent messages from space. If these are ever discovered, it is likely to be as a by-product of some radio-astronomical investigation, because no one is going to tie up millions of dollars' worth of equipment on a random search that may last for decades—or centuries—with no certainty that it will ever meet with success. The detection of the extraordinary pulsars occurred in just such a fashion; at first, their trains of accurately timed radio pulses appeared to fit exactly the specifications of intelligent signals. Now it seems that they can be explained as a natural, though very surprising, phenomenon; the sharply defined pulses may be produced by spinning "neutron stars"—dense bodies only a few miles in diameter, yet weighing as much as the sun.

To be quite certain that we are receiving intelligent signals, we must prove that they carry some kind of message, even if it is not one that we can interpret. So far, there is no indication that the pulsars—or any other sources of radiation in space—are doing this.

That discovery might come at any moment, and would have a shattering impact upon human philosophy, religion and perhaps even politics. The mere knowledge that another intelligence existed somewhere else in the universe would affect our thoughts and our behavior in a myriad subtle ways. At the very least, it might cause our quarrelsome species to close its ranks.

Beyond this, the possibilities are so numerous that speculation is limited only by the laws of logic. Just a few of the questions that might arise are: does the message contain any useful information? (It would be possible to transmit a cosmic encyclopaedia, and an advanced, benevolent civilization might do so.) Should we attempt to answer? (It might not be worth it; if the message came from the Andromeda galaxy, it would have been on its way since the first ape men experimented with clubs. On the other hand, if it came from one of the nearer stars, our reply could be received in a decade or so.) And perhaps most interesting of all: is the source approaching? ("We shall be landing on the White House Lawn/Red Square in thirty minutes…")

The theme of cosmic confrontation is, of course, the classic stand-by of the science fiction writers, but it is now time that we took it seriously. (In the past it has sometimes been taken too seriously, as in 1938 when Orson Welles's War of the Worlds radio play spread panic across the eastern U.S. seaboard.) Some writers have expressed perhaps premature thanks for the existence of "God's quarantine regulations," which may allow us to communicate across the interstellar distances, but which will prohibit any form of physical contact.

It is true that the distances involved in flight to the stars are about a million times greater than those which must be crossed to reach the planets; but this does not imply a proportionate increase in difficulty. It is a surprising fact that a Saturn V could send a payload of many tons clear out of the solar system—to reach, for example, Sirius. But it would take a few hundred thousand years to get there.

However, this is at the very beginning—the log-canoe stage—of our space technology, which will advance beyond recognition in the centuries to come. There is no theoretical reason why speeds which are a substantial fraction of the velocity of light may not be ultimately achieved, at least by

robot probes on one-way missions. This would make the closer stars perhaps twenty years away, and it would be surprising if, during the next few centuries, we do not attempt to send successors of today's Mariners and Voyagers to the nearest stellar systems.…

It is possible that even interstellar travel may not be particularly time consuming—at least, from the viewpoint of the travelers themselves. As is widely known, though imperfectly understood, Einstein's theory of relativity predicts that as velocities approach that of light (186,000 miles a second, or 670,000,000 miles an hour) time itself appears to slow down.

This prediction has been experimentally verified with high-speed atomic particles, and has fascinating consequences for space travelers. It means (in theory at least) that journeys of any distance are possible during the span of a human life, and indeed in as short a period of time as may be desired, if there is enough power to give the necessary speed, and the crew can withstand the acceleration involved.…

Whether we shall be setting forth into a universe which is still unbearably empty, or one which is already full of life, is a riddle which the coming centuries will unfold. Those who described the first landing on the moon as man's greatest adventure are right; but how great that adventure will really be we may not know for a thousand years.…

It is not merely an adventure of the body, but of the mind and spirit, and no one can say where it will end. We may discover that our place in the universe is humble indeed; we should not shrink from the knowledge, if it turns out that we are far nearer the apes than the angels.

Even if this is true, a future of infinite promise lies ahead. We may yet have a splendid and inspiring role to play, on a stage wider and more marvelous than ever dreamed of by any poet or dramatist of the past. For it may be that the old astrologers had the truth exactly reversed, when they believed that the stars controlled the destinies of men.

The time may come when men control the destinies of stars. ✳

Chesley Bonestell

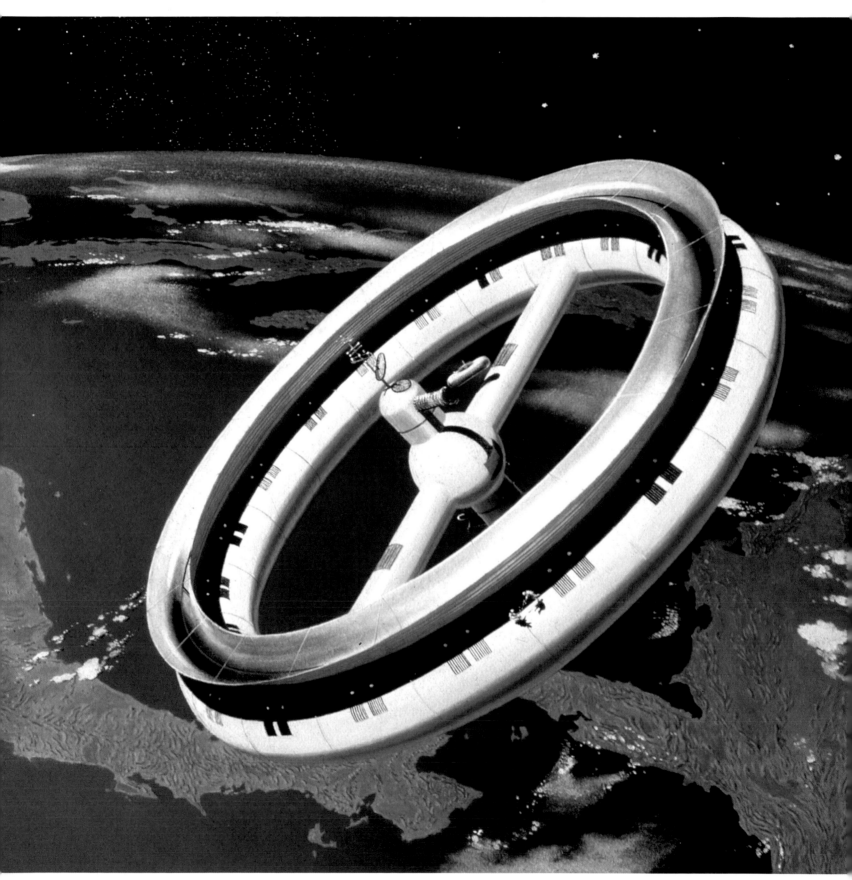

Space Station over Yucatan, Chesley Bonestell, 1952

Two Roads

1976

James Michener

WHEN I WAS A LITTLE BOY in a small town in Pennsylvania, past my door ran a remarkable road. To the east it went a quarter of a mile and stopped dead. To the west it was limitless. It went all the way to the Pacific, and from there to Asia and the entire world. As a child I looked at that road and understood its two directions—limited and unlimited— and thought how craven it would be for a human being to devote his life to the exploration of the eastern portion, which could be exhausted in an afternoon, and how commendable to turn westward and thus enter upon a road and a complexity of roads that would lead to the very ends of the Earth. I chose the western road.

Four years ago, when I was 65, I drew up a memorandum of work still to be done and I remarked upon the fact that I had been fortunate in being able to visit every place on Earth that I had wanted to see except three. I had never been to Peking, which my fellow Asian experts told me was the greatest city of the world, particularly in the old days when it captivated the imagination. Nor had I ever seen the Amazon River. Nor had I been to the South Pole. And I reflected then that perhaps it was proper for a man who had seen so much to leave three unsatisfied targets.

And then, within two weeks of my having written that memorandum, I was by the sheerest accident possible at the Amazon, and a week later in Peking. That leaves the South Pole. I still feel as I did. It is proper that there should always remain one target over the horizon.

I was in Christchurch two weeks ago and went to pay my homage to that marvelous monument to Robert Falcon Scott, the great explorer who raced Amundsen to the South Pole. Amundsen went south to the Pole almost as if he were on a weekend picnic. Everything went right; he got there first; he left his flag; he returned without incident.

But Scott and his crew struggled south with everything conceivable going wrong, and on the way back, as you remember, they perished one by one. Scott, by some miracle, was the last left alive— certainly not because he shied away from the ultimate tests, but maybe because he was in superb psychological condition. And as he lay freezing to death, he wrote that remarkable letter to James Barrie in which he recounts what it is like to be an explorer at the moment of defeat, when everything has gone against you and the other man has got there first and you watch your companions die off one by one. Again, there is no finer statement concerning the nature of exploration than Scott's letter to Barrie. I commend it most highly.

I think, however, that when one deals with exploration, one has got to be aware that in every generation one field of exploration ends. We have done it. We have exhausted the possible. With Darwin we explored the beginning of life and the characteristics which modify it.

As that epoch ends, we start something new. We are always at the end of something, always at the beginning of something else. This is true not only of societies, not only of total culture, but also of individuals. If we have no accomplishment, if we never know success, we lead embittered lives. But if we stop with one success and do not recognize that it stands merely as a threshold to something greater, more complex, more infinite, then I think we do only half our job. Tonight, as we contemplate Mars, I feel as if I were standing on a threshold of immense dimension. All my life I have followed the explorations of Mars intellectually, philosophically, imaginatively. It is a planet which has special connotations. I cannot recall anyone ever having been as interested as we are in Jupiter or Saturn or Pluto. Mars has played a special role in our lives, because of the literary and philosophical speculations that have centered upon it. I have always known Mars.

But to be here tonight, to have seen that remarkable series of photographs which has come from that remote planet, and to realize what a weight of information they are bringing, what a freight of imagination and possible solution, is a moment of such excitement for me that I can hardly describe it. If the photographs I have seen do indeed show riverine action—I mean those marks which look like possible river terracing or the benchmarks customarily made by rivers—then I, for one, will have to admit that a major segment of my inherited knowledge has been shattered. Much of what I have believed about space will have to be revised, for we will now have in Mars a planet which once had a liquid component, which means that it had a substantial atmosphere, which means that it once had illimitable possibilities. Imagine living the days when a discovery of such fundamental significance is possible!

The Moon never caused me much trouble. I had to revise few of my concepts. After all, getting there was merely a technical problem. Scientists had already taught me as much about the Moon as I needed to know. It was a minor appendage attached to Earth; it was egocentric. But when you move out to a planet which is a creation comparable to our own and which has similar propensities and possibilities, then you are moving into a whole new orbit of speculation. The realization that in these very days, we are getting information from the threshold of our particular galaxy, an information which we can then apply to the billionth galaxy in farthest space, is to me an overwhelming experience. If subsequent photographs do produce evidences of riverine action, then we are faced with the question: Why did the water leave? What caused the great change? Is such change inevitable in all such successions? What does such evidence mean concerning life on other comparable planets, the billions upon billions of other stars that are in this galaxy alone and the billions of galaxies beyond them?

It is this kind of threshold that has always made the explorer's life exciting. And it is only one of the small number of thresholds that we live on right now: What are the ultimate capacities of the mind? How do cells operate? Which organizations of society are better than the ones we sponsor? I am much like the old man of Belem, apprehensive about the explorations, yet absolutely certain that they will go forward and that the triumphs and defeats that go with them will form a basic characteristic of man, and one of the best characteristics. As a one-time explorer I wish I could conform to Tennyson's statement in his poem "Ulysses." He was an older man when he wrote this, and he spoke of Ulysses, an older explorer:

"COME, MY FRIENDS,
'Tis not too late to seek a newer world.
Push off, and sitting well in order smite
The sounding furrows; for my purpose holds
To sail beyond the sunset, and the baths
Of all the western stars, until I die.
It may be that the gulfs will wash us down;
It may be we shall touch the Happy Isles,
And see the great Achilles, whom we knew.
Tho' much is taken, much abides; and tho'
We are not now that strength which in old days
Moved earth and heaven, that which we are,
we are—
One equal temper of heroic hearts.
Made weak by time and fate, but strong in will
To strive, to seek, to find, and not to yield."

Othello's Occupations
A Poetic Meditation on Shakespeare and Saturn V

1976

Ray Bradbury

OTHELLO'S OCCUPATIONS, HERE THEY LIE
In countries where the space men flow in fire
And much desire the Moon and reach for Mars
And teach the fiery atoms how to sing
And bring intemperate blood to God-lost lands
To warm his snow-frost lunar sands
And never ask To Be or Not To Be
For here All is
And is again at our behest.
Man's quest makes footfall here
for transfer across space
To lift mankind. Here blind
We catwalk breadths and heights,
Fix sights in rare assembly shops
As vast as Shakespeare's mind
And think that Melville once drowsed here
And dreamt the Beach awake,
Pumped Lox for blood
And with one quake of God's triumphant voice
Made rocket blast
Thus rousing lunar whales to swim in star tides vast.
But this too solid flesh will fall,
Resolve itself into a dew.
No, ask this solid flesh to rise,
Resolve itself into a fire,
Conspire to see and know and build and try,
For if God's dead
Then Man will surely die. But all being one—
It is, it is! God, Man, Ghost takes as bride,
Entire cornet Universe, to yoke with pride.

Lift Off From The Moon, Norman Rockwell, 1965

Put out the light
And then put out the light?
No, No, rekindle night!
And then rekindle night.
Othello unemployed, now reemployed
To summon racial memory from Jung and Freud
And in genetics marrow.
Seek God's Will, to find lost man
And send him up the hill of stars
To change the dreadful dates of 1984 and
send them up with shouts
To make a score man could not dream or hope or
care to do.
Make Orwell laugh in year 2002.
Grand Things To Come? Yes. Cabell stands here,
the towering son of Wells, who saw a sea of
wheeling orbs and sparks and cried,
'Which Shall it be,'
Sink back to dust and tomb, to worms and grave,
Or onward to lost Mars and mankind save?
And star-blown winds then echo endlessly,
Which shall it be?
Oh wandering man, which shall, which shall it be?

I tread this place and read his time and dream,
his corridors of night,
His islands lost in him. His thunders, rumors,
Questionings of self
To be or not to be on Saturn's shelf.
I measure our vast journeys in his head
And find alive what was considered dead.
From ear to ear tread halls of fire blood
Where room in room like chambered Nautilus lost
man makes neighborhood
Of Kennedy-Canaveral—Avon's birthing place.
Not lost? No no, not lost in dust
Or rain or falling down of years.
From Yorick's skull, God's manifesto peers.
From graveyard dirt he shapes a striding man
To jig the stars and go where none else can.
What pulls him there in aeroflights of ships?
A birth of sons that fall from Shakespeare's lips.
Not dumb dull TV news inspires lost man
But will,
Who turned in sleep earthquakes are plan
And answers Job
Whose agonies and sulks ask why.
This fragile flesh is thrust forth cold
To sink and die

'Not so!' says Pleiades for tongue,
'Not so, not so!'
From Stratford's fortress-mind we build and go
And strut-work catwalk stars across Abyss
And to small wondering seedbed souls do promise this:
To Be is best
and Not To Be far worse
And Will says What?
Stand here, grow tall, rehearse.
Be God-grown-man,
Act out the Universe!

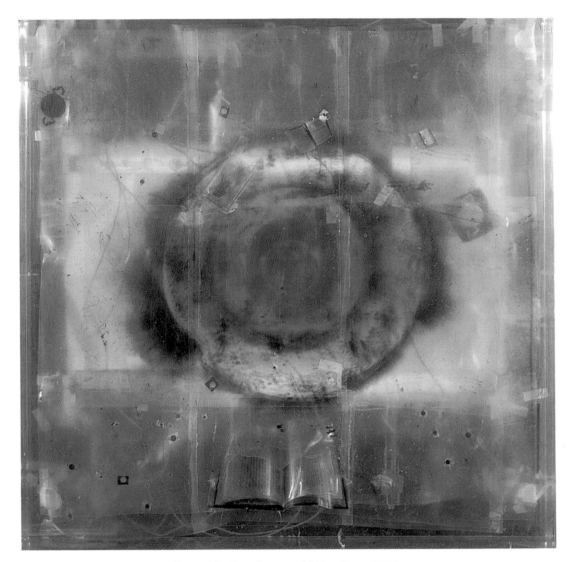

Burned Retina, Doug and Mike Starn, 2000

To the Sky

1994

Carl Sagan

THE MOON WAS WHERE the tree of immortality grew in ancient Chinese myth. The tree of longevity if not of immortality, it seems, indeed grows on other worlds. If we were up there among the planets, if there were self-sufficient human communities on many worlds, our species would be insulated from catastrophe. The depletion of the ultraviolet-absorbing shield on one world would, if anything, be a warning to take special care of the shield on another. A cataclysmic impact on one world would likely leave all the others untouched. The more of us beyond the Earth, the greater the diversity of worlds we inhabit, the more varied the planetary engineering, the greater the range of societal standards and values— then the safer the human species will be.

If you grow up living underground in a world with a hundredth of an Earth gravity and black skies through the portals, you have a very different set of perceptions, interests, prejudices, and predispositions than someone who lives on the surface of the home planet. Likewise if you live on the surface of Mars in the throes of terraforming, or Venus, or Titan. This strategy—breaking up into many smaller self-propagating groups, each with somewhat different strengths and concerns, but all marked by local pride—has been widely employed in the evolution of life on Earth, and by our own ancestors in particular. It may, in fact, be key to understanding why we humans are the way we are. This is the second of the missing justifications for a permanent human presence in space: to improve our chances of surviving, not just the catastrophes we can foresee, but also the ones we cannot. Gott also argues that establishing human communities on other worlds may offer us our best chance of beating the odds.

To take out this insurance policy is not very expensive, not on the scale on which we do things on Earth. It would not even require doubling the space budgets of the present spacefaring nations (which, in all cases, are only a small fraction of the military budgets and many voluntary expenditures that might be considered marginal or even frivolous). We could soon be setting humans down on near-Earth asteroids and establishing bases on Mars. We know how to do it, even with present technology, in less than a human lifetime. And the technologies will quickly improve. We will get better at going into space.

A serious effort to send humans to other worlds is relatively so inexpensive on a *per annum* basis that it cannot seriously compete with urgent social agendas on Earth. If we take this path, streams of images from other worlds will be pouring down on Earth at the speed of light. Virtual reality will make the adventure accessible to millions of stay-on-Earths. Vicarious participation will be much more real than at any earlier age of exploration and discovery. And the more cultures and people it inspires and excites, the more likely it will happen.

But by what right, we might ask ourselves, do we inhabit, alter, and conquer other worlds? If any-one else were living in the Solar System, this would be an important question. If, though, there's no one else in this system but us, don't we have a right to settle it?

Of course, our exploration and homesteading should be enlightened by a respect for planetary environments and the scientific knowledge they hold. This is simple prudence. Of course, exploration and settlement ought to be done equitably and transnationally, by representatives of the entire human species. Our past colonial history is not encouraging in these regards; but this time we are not motivated by gold or spices or slaves or a zeal to convert the heathen to the One True Faith, as were the European explorers of the fifteenth and sixteenth centuries. Indeed, this is one of the chief reasons we're experiencing such intermittent progress, so many fits and starts in the manned space programs of all nations.

Despite all the provincialisms I complained about…, here I find myself an unapologetic human chauvinist. If there were other life in this solar sys-tem, it would be in imminent danger because the humans are coming. In such a case, I might even be persuaded that safeguarding our species by settling certain other worlds is offset, in part at least, by the danger we would pose to everybody else. But as nearly as we can tell, so far at least, there is no other life in this system, not one microbe. There's only Earth life.

In that case, on behalf of Earthlife, I urge that, with full knowledge of our limitations, we vastly increase our knowledge of the Solar System and then begin to settle other worlds.

These are the missing practical arguments: safe-guarding the Earth from otherwise inevitable catastrophic impacts and hedging our bets on the many other threats, known and unknown, to the environment that sustains us. Without these argu-ments, a compelling case for sending humans to Mars and elsewhere might be lacking. But with them—and the buttressing arguments involving sci-ence, education, perspective, and hope—I think a strong case can be made. If our long-term survival is at stake, we have a basic responsibility to our species to venture to other worlds.

Sailors on a becalmed sea, we sense the stirring of a breeze. ✳

Bing of the Ferro Lusto X, by Panamarenko, 1997
OVERLEAF: *Biosphere (Primates)*, Alexis Rockman, 1993

The Search for Life in the Universe

Reflections on the scientific and cultural implications of finding life in the cosmos

2002

Neil de Grasse Tyson

If the person on next to me on a long airplane flight ever finds out that I am an astrophysicist, nine times out of ten they ask, with wide eyes, about life in the universe. And only later do they ask me about the big bang and black holes. I know of no other discipline that triggers such a consistent and reliable reaction in public sentiment. This phenomenon is not limited to Americans. The time-honored question: "What is our place in the universe" might just be genetically encoded in our species. All known cultures across all of time have attempted to answer that question. Today we ask the same question, but with fewer words: "Are we alone?"

Ordinarily, there is no riskier step that a scientist (or anyone) can take than to make sweeping generalizations from just one example. At the moment, life on Earth is the only known life in the universe, but there are compelling arguments to suggest we are not alone. Indeed, most astrophysicists accept a high probability of there being life elsewhere in the universe, if not on other planets or on moons within our own solar system. The numbers are, well, astronomical: If the count of planets in our solar system is not unusual, then there are more planets in the universe than the sum of all sounds and words ever uttered by every human who has ever lived. To declare that Earth must be the only planet in the cosmos with life would be inexcusably egocentric of us.

Many generations of thinkers, both religious and scientific, have been led astray by anthropic assumptions, while others were simply led astray by ignorance. In the absence of dogma and data, history tells us that it's prudent to be guided by the notion that we are not special, which is generally known as the Copernican principle, named for the Polish astronomer Nicholas Copernicus who, in the mid 1500s, put the Sun back in the middle of our solar system where it belongs. In spite of a third century B.C. account of a sun-centered universe proposed by the Greek philosopher Aristarchus, the Earth-centered universe was by far the most popular view for most of the last 2000 years. Codified by the teachings of Aristotle and Ptolemy, and by the preachings of the Roman Catholic Church, people generally accepted

Earth as the center of all motion. It was self-evident: the universe not only looked that way, but God surely made it so. The sixteenth-century Italian monk Giordano Bruno suggested publicly that an infinite universe was filled with planets that harbor life. For these thoughts he was burned upside down and naked at the stake. Fortunately, today we live in somewhat more tolerant times.

While there is no guarantee that the Copernican principle will guide us correctly for all scientific discoveries to come, it has humbled our egos with the realization that not only is Earth not in the center of the solar system, but the solar system is not in the center of the Milky Way galaxy, and the Milky Way galaxy is not in the center of the universe. And in case you are one of those people who thinks that the edge may be a special place, then we are not at the edge of anything either.

A wise contemporary posture would be to assume that life on Earth is not immune to the Copernican principle. If so, then how can the appearance or the chemistry of life on Earth provide clues to what life might be like elsewhere in the universe?

I do not know whether biologists walk around every day awestruck by the diversity of life. I certainly do. On this single planet called Earth, there co-exist (among countless other life forms), algae, beetles, sponges, jellyfish, snakes, condors, and giant sequoias. Imagine these seven living organisms lined up next to each other in size-place. If you didn't know better, you would be hardpressed to believe that they all came from the same universe, much less the same planet. Try describing a snake to somebody who has never seen one: "You gotta believe me. There is this animal on Earth that 1) can stalk its prey with infrared detectors, 2) swallows whole live animals up to five times bigger than its head, 3) has no arms or legs or any other appendage, yet 4) can slide along level ground at a speed of two feet per second!"

Given the diversity of life on Earth, one might expect a diversity of life exhibited among Hollywood aliens. But I am consistently amazed by the film industry's lack of creativity. With a few notable exceptions such as life forms in *The Blob* (1958) and

in *2001: A Space Odyssey* (1968), Hollywood aliens look remarkably humanoid. No matter how ugly (or cute) they are, nearly all of them have two eyes, a nose, a mouth, two ears, a head, a neck, shoulders, arms, hands, fingers, a torso, two legs, two feet—and they can walk. From an anatomical view, these creatures are practically indistinguishable from humans, yet they are supposed to have come from another planet. If anything is certain, it is that life elsewhere in the universe, intelligent or otherwise, will look at least as exotic as some of Earth's own life forms.

The chemical composition of Earth-based life is primarily derived from a select few ingredients. The elements hydrogen, oxygen, and carbon account for over 95% of the atoms in the human body and in all known life. Of the three, the chemical structure of the carbon atom allows it to bond readily and strongly with itself and with many other elements in many different ways, which is how we came to be carbon-based life, and which is why the study of molecules that contain carbon is generally known as "organic" chemistry. The study of life elsewhere in the universe is known as exobiology, which is one of the few disciplines that, at the moment, attempts to function in the complete absence of firsthand data.

Is life chemically special? The Copernican principle suggests that it probably isn't. Aliens need not look like us to resemble us in more fundamental ways. Consider that the four most common elements in the universe are hydrogen, helium, carbon, and oxygen. Helium is inert. So the three most abundant, chemically active ingredients in the cosmos are also the top three ingredients in life on Earth. For this reason, you can bet that if life is found on another planet, it will be made of a similar mix of elements. Conversely, if life on Earth were composed primarily of, for example, molybdenum, bismuth, and plutonium, then we would have excellent reason to suspect that we were something special in the universe.

Appealing once again to the Copernican principle, we can assume that the size of an alien organism is not likely to be ridiculously large compared with life as we know it. There are cogent structural reasons why you would not expect to find a life the size of the Empire State Building strutting around a planet. But if we ignore these engineering limitations of biological matter we approach another, more fundamental limit. If we assume that an alien has control of its own appendages, or more generally, if we assume the organism functions coherently as a system, then its size would ultimately be constrained by its ability to send signals within itself at the speed of light—the fastest allowable speed in the universe. For an admittedly extreme example, if an organism were as big as the entire solar system (about 10 light-hours across), and if it wanted to scratch its head, then this simple act would take no less than 10 hours to accomplish. Sub-slothlike behavior such as this would be evolutionarily self-limiting because the time since the beginning of the universe may be insufficient for the creature to have evolved from smaller forms of life over many generations.

How about intelligence? Since there is still debate on how to define it and measure it in people, I wonder what the question even means when applied to extraterrestrials. Hollywood has tried, but I give them mixed reviews. I know of some aliens that should have been embarrassed at their stupidity. What about all those aliens that manage to traverse thousands of light years through interstellar space, yet bungle their arrival by crash-landing on Earth?

Then there were the aliens in the 1977 film Close Encounters of the Third Kind, who, in advance of their arrival, beamed to Earth a mysterious sequence of repeated digits that were eventually decoded to be the latitude and longitude of their upcoming landing site. But Earth longitude has a completely arbitrary starting point—the prime meridian—which passes through Greenwich, England by international agreement. And both longitude and latitude are measured in peculiar unnatural units we call degrees, 360 of which are in a circle. Armed with this much knowledge of human culture, it seems to me that the aliens could have just learned English and beamed the message, "We're going to land a little bit to the side of Devil's Tower National Monument in Wyoming. And since we're coming in a flying saucer we won't need the runway lights."

The award for dumbest creature of all time must go to the alien from the original 1983 film *Star Trek, The Motion Picture*. V-ger, as it called itself (pronounced vee-jer) was an ancient mechanical space probe that was on a mission to explore and discover and report back its findings. The probe was "rescued" from the depths of space by a civilization of mechanical aliens and reconfigured so that it could actually accomplish this mission for the entire universe. Eventually, the probe did acquire all knowledge and, in so doing, achieved consciousness. The Star Trek crew came upon this now-sprawling monstrous collection of cosmic information at a time when the alien was searching for its original creator and the meaning of life. The stenciled letters on the side of the original probe revealed the characters V and ger. Shortly thereafter, Captain Kirk discovers that the probe was Voyager 6, which had been launched by humans on Earth in the late twentieth century. Apparently, the oya that fits between the V and the ger had been badly tarnished and was unreadable. Okay. But I have always wondered how V-ger could have acquired all knowledge of the universe and achieve consciousness yet not know that its real name was Voyager.

Regardless of how Hollywood aliens are portrayed, or how good or bad the films are, we must not stand in denial of the public's interest in the subject. Let us assume, for the sake of argument, that humans are the only species in the history of life on Earth to evolve high-level intelligence. (I mean no disrespect to other big-brained mammals. While most of them cannot do astrophysics, my conclusions are not substantially altered if you wish to include them.) If life on Earth offers any measure of life elsewhere in the universe, then intelligence must be rare. By some estimates, there have been more than ten billion species in the history of life on Earth. It follows that among all extraterrestrial life forms we might expect no better than about one in ten billion to be as intelligent as we are, not to mention the odds against the intelligent life having an advanced technology and a desire to communicate through the

vast distances of interstellar space.

On the chance that such a civilization exists, radio waves would be the communication band of choice because of their ability to traverse the galaxy unimpeded by interstellar gas and dust clouds. But humans on Earth have only understood the electromagnetic spectrum for less than a century. More depressingly put, for most of human history, had aliens tried to send radio signals to earthlings we would have been incapable of receiving them. For all we know, the aliens have already done this and unwittingly concluded that there was no intelligent life on Earth. They would now be looking elsewhere. A more humbling possibility would be if aliens had become aware of the technologically proficient species that now inhabits Earth, yet they had drawn the same conclusion.

Our life-on-Earth bias, intelligent or otherwise, requires us to hold the existence of liquid water as a prerequisite to life elsewhere. A planet's orbit should not be too close to its host star, otherwise the temperature would be too high and the planet's water content would vaporize. The orbit should not be too far away either, or else the temperature would be too low and the planet's water content would freeze. In other words, conditions on the planet must allow the temperature to stay within the range for liquid water. As in the three-bowls-of-food scene in the fairy tale Goldilocks and the Three Bears, the temperature has to be just right. When I was interviewed about this subject recently on a syndicated radio talk show, the host commented, "Clearly, what you should be looking for is a planet made of porridge!"

While distance from the host planet is an important factor for the existence of life as we know it, other factors matter too, such as a planet's ability to trap stellar radiation. Venus is a textbook example of this "greenhouse" phenomenon. Visible sunlight that manages to pass through its thick atmosphere of carbon dioxide gets absorbed by Venus's surface and then re-radiated in the infrared part of the spectrum. The infrared, in turn, gets trapped by the atmosphere. The unpleasant consequence is an air temperature

that hovers at about 900 degrees Fahrenheit, which is much hotter than we would expect knowing Venus's distance to the Sun. At this temperature, zinc would swiftly become molten and a 16" pepperoni pizza will cook in nine seconds.

The discovery of simple, unintelligent life forms elsewhere in the universe (or evidence that they once existed) would be far more likely and, for me, only slightly less exciting than the discovery of intelligent life. Two excellent nearby places to look are the dried riverbeds of Mars, were there may be fossil evidence of life from when waters once flowed, and the subsurface oceans that are theorized to exist under the frozen ice layers of Jupiter's moon Europa. Once again, the promise of liquid water defines our targets of search.

If we consider the possibility that we may rank as primitive among the universe's technologically competent life forms—however rare they may be— then the best we can do is keep alert for signals sent by others because it is far more expensive to send rather than receive them. Presumably, an advanced civilization would have easy-access to an abundant source of energy such as its host star. These are the civilizations that would be more likely to send rather than receive. The search for extraterrestrial intelligence (affectionately known by its acronym "SETI") has taken many forms. The most advanced efforts today uses a cleverly designed electronic detector that monitors, in its latest version, billions of radio channels in search of a signal that might rise above the cosmic noise.

The discovery of extraterrestrial intelligence, if and when it happens, will impart a change in human self-perception that may be impossible to anticipate. If we don't soon find life elsewhere, what will matter most is that we had not stopped looking. Our species demands that we keep looking. Deep in our soul of curiosity we are intellectual nomads—in search of other places, in search of other life forms because we derive almost as much fulfillment from the search as we do from the discovery. ✳

Strange Encounter for the First Time, Clayton Pond, 1981

Dragonfly above Io, Yvonne Jacquette, 2000

Way Up There

2002

Tena R. Clark

Way up there
Where peace remains
Where silence thunders
And angels sing

Imagination
And amazing grace
Bring us closer
To our home in space

The stars all gather and illuminate
To lead us safely through heaven's gate

We look behind us at the wonder of the earth
Only to remind us where God gave birth

(Repeat Chorus)

Like a shooting star through endless time
We say a prayer for all mankind

If we could all see through that tiny window
We would all be reborn and we would know

(Chorus)
Way up there
Peace remains
Silence thunders
Angels sing

Imagination
And amazing grace
Bring us closer
To our home in space

(Bridge)
We are all one
Created with the stars, moon and sun
Every woman, child and man
Will one day take each other's hand

Reaching for the Stars

Part 6

Anne Collins Goodyear

THE ACHIEVEMENT OF HUMAN SPACE FLIGHT in the 1960s, culminating with the realization of President John F. Kennedy's goal of placing astronauts on the moon, represented the fulfillment of longstanding human dreams and aspirations. Initially motivated by political tensions between the United States and the Soviet Union, each of whom sought to prove their superiority in the eyes of the world, space flight has evolved in the past four decades into a new arena for international cooperation and scientific research. Although commercial airliners have not yet taken on the responsibility of space flight, as predicted by Stanley Kubrick and Arthur C. Clarke, who collaborated to create the 1968 film *2001: A Space Odyssey*, the Space Shuttle, combining the technologies of rockets and airplanes, has indeed served as an important mode of space transport.

The Space Age opened in dramatic fashion when the Soviet Union sent Sputnik into orbit on October 4, 1957. Any suspicion that the Soviets had simply benefited from a lucky fluke with the 183-pound satellite vanished when the Soviets launched the 1,120 pound Sputnik II—which carried the dog Laika—less than a month later. As initial American attempts to match Soviet accomplishments floundered, the competition between the two global superpowers intensified, and the U.S. established NASA—almost exactly a year following Sputnik's appearance—to battle the Soviet Union for control of the skies. Witnessing yet another Soviet first on April 12, 1961, when Yuri Gargarin became the first man to enter space and orbit the earth, President Kennedy implored Vice President Lyndon Johnson, "Do we have any chance of beating the Soviets by putting a laboratory in space, or by a trip around the moon, or by a rocket to land on the moon, or by a rocket to go to the moon and back with a man? Is there any other space program which promises dramatic results in which we could win?" Shortly thereafter, Kennedy persuaded the country to follow his dream of sending astronauts to the moon.

Throughout the 1960s, the United States and the Soviet Union continued to race neck and neck, with the Soviets completing the first successful space walk, or EVA (Extravehicular Activity) in 1965. However the balance shifted in 1968, as the United States succeeded in sending Apollo 8 around the moon, making its crew the first people to orbit the moon. On July 16, 1969, American astronauts Neil Armstrong and Edwin (Buzz) Aldrin became the first men to walk on the moon, an accomplishment Armstrong famously characterized as "One small step for man; one giant leap for mankind."

Although the era of lunar exploration proved to be short-lived, coming to a conclusion in December 1972 only three years later, the 1970s witnessed important milestones. In May 1971, even before the last American moonwalk was completed, the Soviet Union put Salyut 1, the first space station, into orbit. Several more Salyut—meaning "salute"—space stations would follow during the ensuing decade. In 1973, with the launch of Skylab, American crews occupied their own extraterrestrial outpost, which permitted research that could not be conducted on earth. During this decade new international alliances were formed, making space an arena for transcending terrestrial rivalries. Perhaps most significant was the cooperation between the U.S. and the U.S.S.R, as American and Soviet crews docked and broke bread together on July 15, 1975, during the Apollo-Soyuz test project.

The 1980s marked an important era for space exploration, with new technological achievements and the expansion of the ranks of astronauts and cosmonauts. In 1981, the launch of the Space Shuttle Columbia marked the first use of a reusable space vehicle, promising to revolutionize space exploration by reducing costs and waste. But although the shuttle reenergized the American space program, with the flight of the first American woman, Sally K. Ride, and the first African-American astronaut, Guion S. Bluford, Jr., in 1983, the shuttle was not free of difficulties. A tragic setback to the program occurred in 1986, when Challenger, which carried Christa McAuliffe, the first teacher in space, and six other crew members, exploded less than two minutes after take-off.

Despite this great loss, significant accomplishments continued. In the month after the Challenger disaster, the Soviet Union sent aloft the central component of a new space station Mir, meaning "peace." Over the course of more than a decade, the space station—occupied by both American and Soviet crew members—would achieve a longevity as of yet unsurpassed. In 1996, flying aboard Mir, Shannon Lucid became the first American woman to crew the space station.

During the course of the past decade, the goals and accomplishments of space exploration have grown still further, with new robotic spacecraft flying to different planets and the first phases of construction of the International Space Station. The risks of space flight, however, have not disappeared. The break-up of the Space Shuttle Columbia, carrying an international crew, shortly before concluding its mission on February 1, 2003, provided a somber reminder of the extraordinary courage and dedication demanded by space exploration. Even in the face of such challenges, it is difficult to imagine that the lure of the cosmos will ever cease to inspire those on Earth.

Retroactive I, Robert Rauschenberg, 1963

We Choose to Go to the Moon

1962

President John F. Kennedy

....THOSE WHO CAME BEFORE US made certain that this country rode the first waves of the industrial revolutions, the first waves of modern invention, and the first wave of nuclear power, and this generation does not intend to founder in the backwash of the coming age of space. We mean to be a part of it—we mean to lead it. For the eyes of the world now look into space, to the moon and to the planets beyond, and we have vowed that we shall not see it governed by a hostile flag of conquest, but by a banner of freedom and peace. We have vowed that we shall not see space filled with weapons of mass destruction, but with instruments of knowledge and understanding.

Yet the vows of this Nation can only be fulfilled if we in this Nation are first, and, therefore, we intend to be first. In short, our leadership in science and in industry, our hopes for peace and security, our obligations to ourselves as well as others, all require us to make this effort, to solve these mysteries, to solve them for the good of all men, and to become the world's leading spacefaring nation.

We set sail on this new sea because there is new knowledge to be gained, and new rights to be won, and they must be won and used for the progress of all people. For space science, like nuclear science and all technology, has no conscience of its own. Whether it will become a force for good or ill depends on man, and only if the United States occupies a position of preeminence can we help decide whether this new ocean will be a sea of peace or a new terrifying theater of war. I do not say that we should or will go unprotected against the hostile misuse of space any more than we go unprotected against the hostile use of land or sea, but I do say that space can be explored and mastered without feeding the fires of war, without repeating the mistakes that man has made in extending his writ around this globe of ours.

There is no strife, no prejudice, no national conflict in outer space as yet. Its hazards are hostile to us all. Its conquest deserves the best of all mankind, and its opportunity for peaceful coopera-

tion many never come again. But why, some say, the moon? Why choose this as our goal? And they may well ask why climb the highest mountain? Why, 35 years ago, fly the Atlantic? Why does Rice play Texas?

We choose to go to the moon. We choose to go to the moon in this decade and do the other things, not because they are easy, but because they are hard, because that goal will serve to organize and measure the best of our energies and skills, because that challenge is one that we are willing to accept, one we are unwilling to postpone, and one which we intend to win, and the others, too.

It is for these reasons that I regard the decision last year to shift our efforts in space from low to high gear as among the most important decisions that will be made during my incumbency in the office of the Presidency.

In the last 24 hours we have seen facilities now being created for the greatest and most complex exploration in man's history. We have felt the ground shake and the air shattered by the testing of a Saturn C-1 booster rocket, many times as powerful as the Atlas which launched John Glenn, generating power equivalent to 10,000 automobiles with their accelerators on the floor. We have seen the site where five F-1 rocket engines, each one as powerful as all eight engines of the Saturn combined, will be clustered together to make the advanced Saturn missile, assembled in a new building to be built at Cape Canaveral as tall as a 48 story structure, as wide as a city block, and as long as two lengths of this field....

Many years ago the great British explorer George Mallory, who was to die on Mount Everest, was asked why did he want to climb it. He said, "Because it is there."

Well, space is there, and we're going to climb it, and the moon and the planets are there, and new hopes for knowledge and peace are there. And, therefore, as we set sail we ask God's blessing on the most hazardous and dangerous and greatest adventure on which man has ever embarked. ✳

Carrying The Fire

1974

Michael Collins

"APOLLO 11, APOLLO 11, good morning from the Black Team." Could they be talking to me? It takes me twenty seconds to fumble for the microphone button and answer groggily, "Good morning, Houston....You guys wake up early." "Yes...looks like you were really sawing them away." They can tell when we are in a deep sleep by monitoring our heart rates, which dip down to forty or so when we are really zonked. "You're right," I tell them, and then inquire about my machine. "How are all the CSM systems looking? "Looks like the command module is in good shape. Black Team has been watching it real closely for you." "...appreciate that, because I sure haven't." I guess I have only been asleep five hours or so; I had a tough time getting to sleep, and now I'm having trouble waking up. Neil, Buzz, and I all putter about fixing breakfast and getting various items of equipment ready for transfer into the LM.

Houston adds to the confusion by keeping up a steady chatter on the radio, reading us the day's news. "Among the large headlines concerning Apollo this morning, there's one asking that you watch out for a lovely girl with a big rabbit. An ancient legend says a beautiful Chinese girl called Chang-O has been living there for four thousand years. It seems she was banished to the moon because she stole the pill of immortality from her husband. You might also look for her companion, a large Chinese rabbit, who is easy to spot since he is always standing on his hind feet in the shade of a cinnamon tree." Jesus Christ,

am I imagining all this? Here I am, half asleep, trying to fix a tube full of coffee, about to watch two good friends depart for the crater fields of the moon, there to join a Chinese rabbit under a cinnamon tree! There are just too many things going this morning, and I have to force myself to stick with the activities of the fight plan." "A three-ring circus. I got a fuel-cell purge in progress and am trying to set up camera and brackets, watch an auto maneuver..." I grump groggily.

Now it is time for Neil and Buzz to get dressed, and they begin by pulling their lunar underwear out of storage bins. These garments are *liquid*-cooled, with hundreds of thin, flexible plastic tubes sewn into a fishnet fabric. The back pack they will wear on the lunar surface will pump water through these tubes, cooling their bodies much more efficiently than could be done simply by blowing cool oxygen over them. I don't need water cooled underwear because I don't have any back pack, and because hopefully I won't be working that hard, but I do require a pressure suit, so all three of us struggle into them, helping each other with inaccessible zippers and generally checking the condition of each other's equipment. What would we do if, for example, Neil's zipper broke, or his helmet somehow refused to lock on to his neck ring? He couldn't venture out onto the lunar surface that way, that's for sure, nor could be allow Buzz to, because he would perish as soon as the LM door was opened to the vacuum of space. He couldn't stay in the CM and let Buzz land by himself, because the LM requires simultaneous

Moonwalk 1, Andy Warhol, 1987

manipulation by two people. I couldn't take his place because I was not trained to fly the LM. Perhaps he and I could switch suits, but I doubt that he could fit into mine, and mine can't accommodate a back pack. From such fabric are nightmares woven. Fortunately, everything seems to fit together, and I stuff Neil and Buzz into the LM along with an armload of equipment.

Now I have to do the tunnel bit again, closing hatches, installing drogue and probe, and disconnecting the electrical umbilical running into the LM.

I am supposed to rig the TV camera to shoot out one of my windows to show the departure of the LM, but I decide I am too busy preparing for undocking to fool with it. I inform Houston, "There will be no television of the undocking, I have all available windows either full of heads or cameras, and I'm busy with other things." Generally one discusses these things with Houston and follows their advice, but this time I'm *telling* them, not asking them, and they must sense this, because they immediately reply, "We concur."

I am on the radio constantly now, running through an elaborate series of joint checks with *Eagle*. In one of them, I use my control system to hold both vehicles steady while they calibrate some of their guidance equipment. I check my progress with Buzz. "I have five minutes and fifteen seconds since we started. Attitude is holding very well." Roger, Mike. Just hold it a little bit longer." "No sweat, I can hold it all day. Take your sweet time. How's the czar over there? He's so quiet." Neil chimes in, "Just hanging on—and punching." Punching those computer buttons, I guess he means. "All I can say is, beware the revolution," and then, getting no answer, I formally bid them goodbye. "You cats take it easy on the lunar surface; if I hear you huffing and puffing, I'm going to start bitching at you." "O.K., Mike," Buzz answers cheerily, and I throw the switch which releases them. With my nose against the glass of window 2 and the movie camera churning away over in window 4, I watch them go. When they are safely clear of me, I inform Neil, and he begins a slow pirouette in place, allowing me a look at his outlandish machine and its four extended legs. "The *Eagle* has wings!" Buzz exults.

It doesn't look like any eagle I have ever seen. It is the weirdest-looking contraption ever to invade the sky, floating there with its legs awkwardly jutting out above a body which has neither symmetry nor grace. Everything seems to be stuck on at the wrong angle, which I suppose is what happens when you turn aeronautical engineers loose designing a vehicle which always flies in a vacuum and hence requires no streamlining. I make sure all four landing gear are down and locked, report that fact, and then lie a little, "I think you've got a fine-looking flying machine there, *Eagle*, despite the fact you're upside down." "Somebody's upside down," Neil retorts. "O.K., *Eagle*. One minute…you guys take care." Neil answers, "See you later." I hope so. When the one-minute is up, I fire my thrusters precisely as planned and we begin to separate, checking distances and velocities as we go. This burn is a very small one, just to give *Eagle* some breathing room. From now on it's up to them, and they will make two

separate burns in reaching the lunar surface. The first one, called descent orbit insertion (DOI, for short), will take place behind the moon and will serve to drop *Eagle*'s perilune to fifty thousand feet at a point 16 degrees east of the landing site. Then, when they reach this spot over the eastern edge of the Sea of Tranquility, *Eagle*'s descent engine will be fired up for the second and last time (power descent initiation, or PDI), and *Eagle* will lazily arc over into a twelve-minute, computer-controlled descent to some point at which Neil will take over a manual landing.

After DOI, the LM swoops down farther below me, picking up speed as it goes, so that at the time of PDI it will be about 120 miles in front of me. After PDI, the situation changes very swiftly. As *Eagle* slows down, I will start gaining on it and will whiz by overhead, so that I will be about two hundred miles ahead of it at the instant of touchdown. I will try to keep them in sight as long as possible, because if they have to abort, it would be nice for me to know where they have gone, helping to determine which one of my eighteen rendezvous cases applies.

As we swing around the right edge of the moon after DOI, I regain contact with Houston before *Eagle* does, as I am considerably higher now. I have to remember that I am *Columbia* for the next twenty-four hours, and I should stop calling myself Apollo 11. "Houston, *Columbia*. Reading you loud and clear." "Roger, Mike. How did it go?" They want to know about DOI, naturally enough. "Listen, babe, everything's going just swimmingly. Beautiful." I am wide-awake now and have lost this morning's feeling of being rushed. Things feel good, with the CSM shipshape and the LM also apparently in good condition. "Great," responds the ground. "We're standing by for *Eagle*." "O.K. he's coming along."

My navigational equipment is really working well, which adds to my confidence. On my last two platform alignments, I got five balls and four balls one, which is always nice, and I have been using my sextant to track a lunar landmark and the LM. All this work has been going extremely well, almost effortlessly, and the marks made on the LM in particular give me confidence about tomorrow's rendezvous. I don't really need to be able to make accurate marks on the LM today, but the fact I can do so (and old Colossus IIA confirms the fact) bodes well for tomorrow. As *Eagle* approaches PDI, I am still hanging in there, peering out through the sextant at a minuscule dot. The LM is nearly invisible and looks like any one of a thousand tiny craters, except that it is moving. Finally, as if passes the hundred-mile mark, I lose it. I rub my eyes in relief at the end of this practice session. I have been sighting with my right eye, my left being covered by a small black plastic patch held on by an elastic string I find that the muscles in my left eyelid get weary squinting shut, so I have used an eye patch since Gemini days.

The best thing I can do now is to keep quiet, as Houston and *Eagle* have lots to discuss as power descent initiation arrives and the final descent begins. At the beginning of the burn, Neil and Buzz are pointed heads up, feet forward, and see nothing but black sky. This awkward position is necessary to get the best communications with the earth and to confirm the accuracy of their trajectory; after that they will roll over and start checking the parade of familiar landmarks past their window. Then it's up to Neil to find a spot smooth enough to put it down. At five minutes into the burn, when I am nearly directly overhead, *Eagle* voices its first concern. "Program Alarm," barks Neil, "it's a 1202." A 1202? What the hell is that? I don't have all the alarm numbers memorized for my own computer, much less for the LM's, so I don't have the foggiest notion how bad it is in terms of continuing the descent. I jerk my own checklist out of my suit pocket and start thumbing through it, but before I can find 1202, Houston says, "Roger, we're GO on that alarm." No problem, in other words. My checklist says 1202 is an "executive overflow," meaning simply that the computer has been called upon to do too many things at once and is forced to postpone some of them. I guess it means the same thing for the LM, and M.I.T. has designed both computer programs. A little farther along, at just three thousand feet above the surface, the computer flashes 1201, another overflow condition, and

again the ground is super quick to respond with reassurances. Good work on someone's part.

Now it begins to sound like a ground-controlled approach into fog, as Buzz calls out altitude and velocity to Neil, who has his eyes glued on the scene out the window. "Six hundred feet, down at nineteen [feet per second]." "Four hundred feet, down at nine." "Three hundred feet…watch your shadow out there." "Two hundred feet, 4½ down." "One hundred feet, 3½ down, nine forward. Five percent [fuel remaining]." "Forty feet, down 2½, kicking up some dust." That sounds good, just a bit of dust at forty feet. "Thirty seconds," says Houston. That's how much fuel they have left. Better get it on the ground, Neil. "Contact light," sings out Buzz, and then a bunch of gibberish concerning shutting down their engine. They have arrived! "We copy you down, *Eagle*," says Houston, half answer. Neil makes it official. "Houston, Tranquility Base here, the *Eagle* has landed." Whew! I re-establish radio contact with Houston and they inform me of the landing. "Yes, I heard the whole thing…Fantastic!" Neil explains why he nearly ran out of gas. "The auto targeting was taking us right into a football-field size…crater…with a large number of big boulders…It required…flying manually over the rock field to find a reasonably good area." Christ, I don't care if the landed on top of a gigantic anthill, just as long as they are down in one piece.

My command module chores now include an extra task: finding the LM on the surface. If I can see it through my sextant, center my cross hairs on it, and mark the instant of superposition, then my computer will know something it doesn't know now: where the LM actually is, instead of where it is supposed to be. This is a valuable—not vital, but valuable—piece of information for "Hal" to have, especially as a starting reference point for the sequence of rendezvous maneuvers which will come tomorrow (or sooner?). Of course, the ground can take its measurements as well, but it really has no way of judging where the LM came down, except by competing Neil and Buzz's description of their surrounding terrain with the rather crude maps which Houston has. But I am far past the landing site now, about to swing around behind the left edge of the moon, so it will be awhile before I get my first crack at looking for the LM. It takes me two hours to circle the moon once.

Meanwhile, the command module is purring along in grand shape. I have turned the lights up bright, and the cockpit reflects a cheeriness, which I want very much to share. My concerns are exterior ones, having to do with the vicissitudes of my two friends on the moon and their uncertain return path to me, but inside, all is well, as this familiar machine and I circle and watch and wait. I have removed the center couch and stored it underneath the left one, and this gives the place an entirely different aspect, It opens up a central aisle between the main instrument panel and the lower equipment bay, a pathway which allows me to zip from upper hatch window to lower sextant and return. The main reason for removing the couch is to provide adequate access for Neil and Buzz to enter the command module through the side hatch, in the event that the probe and drogue mechanism cannot be cleared from the tunnel. If such is the case, we would have to open the hatch to the vacuum of space, and Neil and Buzz would have to make an extravehicular transfer from the LM, dragging their rock boxes behind them. All three of us would be in bulky pressurized suits, requiring a tremendous amount of space and a wide path into the lower equipment bay. In addition to providing more room, these preparations give me the feeling of being proprietor of a small resort hotel, about to receive the onrush of skiers coming in out of the cold. Everything is prepared for them; it is a happy place, and I couldn't make them more welcome unless I had a fireplace. I know from pre-flight press questions that I will be described as a lonely man ("Not since Adam has any man experienced such loneliness"), and I guess that the TV commentators must be reveling in my solitude and deriving all sorts of phony philosophy from it, but I hope not. Far from feeling lonely or abandoned, I feel very much a part of what is taking place on the lunar surface. I know that I would be a liar or a fool if I said that I have

the best of the three Apollo 11 seats, nut I can say with truth and equanimity that I am perfectly satisfied with the one I have. This venture has been structured for three men, and I consider my third to be as necessary as either of the other two.

I don't mean to deny a feeling of solitude. It is there, reinforced by the fact that radio contact with the earth abruptly cuts off at the instant I disappear behind the moon. I am alone now, truly alone, and absolutely isolated from any known life, I am it. If a count were taken, the score would be three billion plus two over on the other side of the moon, and one plus God only knows what on this side. I feel this powerfully—not as fear or loneliness—but as awareness, anticipation, satisfaction, confidence, almost exultation. I like the feeling. Outside my window I can see stars—and that is all. Where I know the moon to be, there is simply a black void; the moon's presence is defined solely by the absence of stars. To compare the sensation with something terrestrial, perhaps being alone in a skiff in the middle of the Pacific Ocean on a pitch-black night would most nearly approximate my situation. In a skiff, one would see bright stars above and black sea below; I see the same stars, minus the twinkling, of course, and absolutely nothing below. In each case, time and distance are extremely important factors. In terms of distance, I am much more remote, but in terms of time, lunar orbit is much closer to civilized conversation than is the mid-Pacific. Although I may be nearly a quarter of a million miles away, I am cut off from human voices for only forty-eight minutes out of each two hours, while the man in the skiff— grazing the very surface for the planet—is not so privileged, or burdened. Of the two quantities, time and distance, time tends to be a much more personal one, so that I feel simultaneously closer to, and farther away from, Houston than I would if I were on some remote spot on earth which would deny me conversation with other humans for months on end.

My windows suddenly flash full of sunlight, as *Columbia* swings around into the dawn. The moon reappears quickly, dark gray and craggy, its surface lightening and smoothing gradually as the sun angle increases. My clock tells me that the earth is about to pop into view, and I prepare for it by positioning my parabolic antenna so that it points at the proper angle. Sure enough, here comes the earth on schedule, rising swiftly above the horizon, and shortly thereafter I can tell from one of my many gauges that the antenna has locked onto its signal and conversation should be possible. The three big antennas on earth are located at Honeysuckle Creek in eastern Australia; near Madrid, Spain; and at Goldstone Lake in the Mojave Desert, not too far from Las Vegas. As the earth turns, Houston shifts its control from one to the other, the hand-off being based on which one is pointing most directly at the moon. Since they are nearly evenly spaced around the globe, one antenna is always in excellent position. I don't know which one I may be talking through, although I suppose I could tell either by looking at my flight plan or by carefully examining that blue and white pea out there, but the fact is I really don't care. I call them all Houston, which simplifies it. "Houston, *Columbia*. How's it going?" "Roger…we estimate he landed about four miles downrange…we'll have a map location momentarily. Over." Now they send me up a bunch of numbers which I punch into my computer. Colossus IIA knows how to use this ground estimate to point my sextant, but as I whiz by overhead, I can't see a darn thing but craters. Big craters, little craters, rounded ones, sharp ones, but no LM anywhere among them. The sextant is a powerful optical instrument, magnifying everything it sees twenty-eight times, but the price it pays for this magnification is a very narrow field of view, only 1.8 degrees wide, so that it is almost like looking down a gun barrel. The LM might be close by, and I swing the sextant back and forth in a frantic search for it, but in the very limited time I have, it is possible to study only a square mile or so of lunar surface, and this time it is the wrong mile.

I am sixty nautical miles above Tranquility Base, traveling at about thirty-seven hundred miles per hour. If Neil or Buzz were able to see me, they would find that I would come up over their eastern horizon, pass almost directly overhead, and disappear below their western horizon. The entire pass takes thirteen minutes, but most of that interval is not available to me, because I need to be looking down through my sextant at a steep angle. If I consider 45 degrees as the minimum acceptable angle, then I have only two minutes and twelve seconds of useful time, as I swing from 45 degrees on one side of the LM to 45 degrees on the other. A busy two minutes indeed. During the thirteen minutes, I can talk directly to the LM. At other times, when I am on the front side of the moon (but out of sigh of the LM), I can talk to them via earth, if Houston's switches are set properly to relay our conversation. At 186,000 miles per second (the speed of light), it takes about one and one quarter seconds for the radio waves to reach the earth and an equal time for them to be relayed back to the moon. This delay can have some interesting side effects, as, for example, in the seconds following the LM's touchdown, when Houston told Neil, "Be advised there's lots of smiling faces in this room and all over the world. Over." Neil responds, "Well, there are two of them up here." It takes two and a half seconds for me to hear this; as soon as I do, I say, "And don't forget one in the command module"; but in the meantime Houston has heard Neil and has answered him, "Roger. That was a beautiful job, you guys." I was more than a little embarrassed to hear their message coming in as I was mouthing mine. It sounded like I was asking them not to forget to compliment me for doing a beautiful job in the command module, instead of merely adding my smiling face to the list.

Although I can't see the LM, I *can* listen, as Neil and Buzz describe what no men have seen before— the view from the surface of another planet. I can't help interrupting. "Sounds like it looks a lot better than it did yesterday at that very low sun angle. It looked rough as a cob then." "It really was rough, Mike." Neil replies. "Over the targeted landing area, it was extremely rough, cratered, and large numbers of rocks that were…larger than five or ten feet in size." "When in doubt, land long," I say, using the pilot's cliché about never landing short of the runway. "So we did," he replies simply…. ✳

Part of Sabine D Region of the Moon, Southwest Mare Tranquilitatis, Nancy Graves, 1972

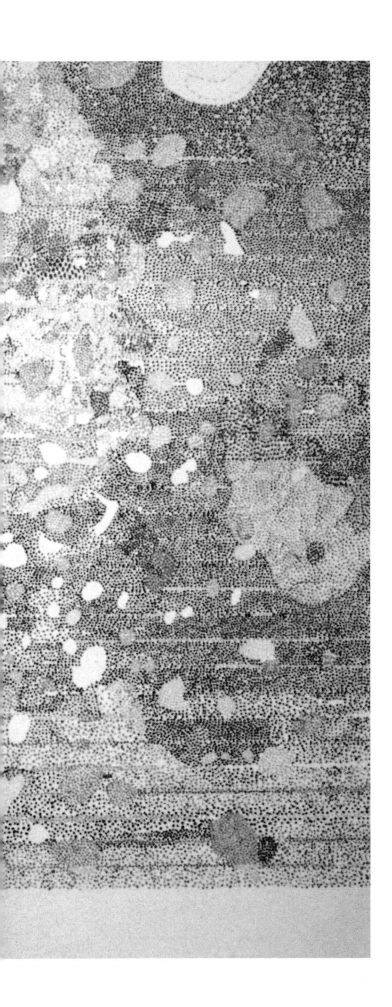

Voyage to the Moon

1969

Archibald MacLeish

WANDERER IN OUR SKIES,
dazzle of silver in our leaves and on our
waters silver, O
silver evasion in our farthest thought—
"the visiting moon," "the glimpses of the moon,"

and we have found her.

From the first of time,
before the first of time, before the
first men tasted time, we thought of her.
She was a wonder to us, unattainable,
a longing past the reach of longing,
a light beyond our light, our lives—perhaps
a meaning to us—O, a meaning!

Now we have found her in her nest of night.

Three days and three nights we journeyed,
steered by farthest stars, climbed outward,
crossed the invisible tide-rip where the floating dust
falls one way or the other in the void between,
followed that other down, encountered
cold, faced death, unfathomable emptiness.

Now, the fourth day evening, we descend,
make fast, set foot at last upon her beaches,
stand in her silence, lift our heads and see
above her, wanderer in her sky,
a wonder to us past the reach of wonder,
a light beyond our lights, our lives, the rising

Whose Earth?

1980

Russell Schweickart

Up there you go around every hour and a half, time after time after time. You wake up usually in the mornings. And just the way that the track of your orbits go, you wake up over the Mideast, over North Africa. As you eat breakfast you look out the window as you're going past and there's the Mediterranean area, and Greece, and Rome, and North Africa, and the Sinai, the whole area. And you realize that in one glance that what you're seeing is what was the whole history of man for years—the cradle of civilization. And you think of all that history that you can imagine, looking at that scene.

And you go around down across North Africa and out over the Indian Ocean, and look up at that great sub-continent of India pointed down toward you as you go past it. And Ceylon off to the side, Burma, Southeast Asia, out over the Philippines, and up across that monstrous Pacific Ocean, vast body of water—you've never realized how big that it before.

And you finally come up across the coast of California and look for those friendly things: Los Angeles, and Phoenix, and on across El Paso and there's Houston, there's home, and you look and sure enough there's the Astrodome. And you identify with that, you know—it's an attachment.

And down across New Orleans and then looking down to the south and there's the whole peninsula

of Florida laid out. And all the hundreds of hours you spent flying across the route, down in the atmosphere, all that is friendly again. And you go out across the Atlantic Ocean and back across Africa.

And that identity—that you identify with Houston, then you identify with Los Angeles, and Phoenix and New Orleans and everything. And the next thing you recognize in yourself, is you're identifying with North Africa. You look forward to that, you anticipate it. And there it is. That whole process begins to shift of what it is you identify with. When you go around it in an hour and a half you begin to recognize that your identity is with that whole thing. And that makes a change.

You look down there and you can't imagine how many borders and boundaries you crossed again and again and again And you don't even see 'em. At that wake-up scene—the Mideast—you know there are hundreds of people killing each other over some imaginary line that you can't see. From where you see it, the thing is a whole, and it's so beautiful. And you wish you could take one from each side in hand and say, "Look at it from this perspective. Look at that. What's important?"

And so a little later on, your friend, again those same neighbors, another astronaut, the person next to you goes out to the Moon. And now he looks back and he sees the Earth not as something big, where he can see the beautiful details, but he sees the Earth as small thing out there. And now that contrast between that bright blue and white Christmas tree ornament and that black sky, that infinite universe, really comes through.

The size of it, the significance of it—it becomes both things, it becomes so small and so fragile, and such a precious little spot in the universe, that you can block it out with your thumb, and you realize that on that small spot, that little blue and white thing is everything that means anything to you. All of history and music and poetry and art and war and death and birth and love, tears, joy, games, all of it is on that little spot out there that you can cover with your thumb.

And you realize that that perspective…that you've changed, that there's something new there. That relationship is no longer what it was. And then you look back on the time when you were outside on that EVA and those few moments that you had the time because the camera malfunctioned, that you had the time to think about what was happening. And you recall staring out there at the spectacle that went before your eyes. Because now you're no longer inside something with a window looking out at a picture, but now you're out there and what you've got around your head is a goldfish bowl and there are no limits here. There are no frames, there are no boundaries. You're really out there, over it, floating, going 25,000 mph, ripping through space, a vacuum, and there's not a sound. There's a silence the depth of which you've never experienced before, and that silence contrasts so markedly with the scenery, with what you're seeing, and the speed with which you know you're going. That contrast, the mix of those two things, really comes through.

And you think about what you're experiencing and why. Do you deserve this? This fantastic experience? Have you earned this in some way? Are you separated out to be touched by God to have some special experience here that other men cannot have? You know the answer to that is No. There's nothing that you've done that deserves that, that earned that.

It's not a special thing for you. You know very well at that moment, and it comes through to you so powerfully, that you're the sensing element for man.

You look down and see the surface of that globe that you've lived on all this time and you know all those people down there. They are like you, they are you, and somehow you represent them when you are up there—a sensing element, that point out on the end, and that's a humbling feeling. It's a feeling that says you have a responsibility. It's not for yourself.

The eye that doesn't see does not do justice to the body. That's why it's there, that's why you're out there. And somehow you recognize that you're a piece of this total life. You're out on that forefront and you have to bring that back, somehow. And that becomes a rather special responsibility. It tells you something about your relationship with this thing we call life. And so that's a change, that's something new.

And when you come back, there's a difference in that world now, there's a difference in that relationship between you and that planet, and you and all those other forms of life on that planet, because you've had that kind of experience. It's a difference, and it's so precious. And all through this I've used the word *you* because it's not me, it's not Dave Scott, it's not Dick Gordon, Pete Conrad, John Glenn, it's you, it's us, it's we, it's life. It's had that experience. And it's not just *my* problem to integrate, it's not my challenge to integrate, my joy to integrate—it's yours, it's everybody's!

I guess that's really about all I'd like to say, except that—I don't even know why, but to me it means a lot—I'd like to close this with a poem by e.e. cummings that has just become a part of me, somehow out of all this, and I'm not really sure how.

> He says, that
>> i thank You God for most this amazing
>> day; for the leaping greenly spirits of trees
>> and a blue true dream of sky; and for every-
>> thing which is natural which is infinite
>> which is yes

Thank you. ✳

Astronauts on the Moon, Red Grooms, Mimi Gross, 1972
OVERLEAF: *Grissom and Young Suiting Up*, Norman Rockwell, 1965

Why Do They Become Astronauts?

1969–70

Norman Mailer

T ....THEY WORKED LONG HOURS, perhaps an average of fifty hours a week, and hardly knew when they would have their first space flight, or once up, whether they would ever have a space flight again. They were the best pilots in their profession, but now they flew only for practice, and they could not know for certain whether they would ever be able to practice their new profession. (It is as if Truman Capote gave literature because he wished to write opera and suddenly could not find out whether any of his music would ever be sung.) All the while the astronauts were obliged to live in intense competition with one another, yet had to exhibit every face of good spirit and teamwork to the world. Stories were common at the Manned Spacecraft Center of astronauts who had shared the same flight yet hardly spoke to each other in the months before, so intense was their mutual dislike. Still they kept their animosity private for fear they could lose their seat on the flight. Then all of them had had to swallow the wrath they might have felt for the contractors connected to the fire which killed Grissom, Chaffee, and White. Say it worse. Eight of them altogether had already been killed. Besides the fire, four had gone in fatal crashes of the T-38, and one in an auto accident. (Astronauts were quietly famous for driving their cars a foot apart at a hundred miles an hour). One could say that the demand for order, hard work, and propriety in such competitive near-violent men had produced their deaths, as if the very tension of their existence as in a game of musical chairs had pushed the escape from death of one man over into a higher potentiality for accident of another. Being an astronaut was perhaps the most honored profession in the nation, but of sixty-six astronauts accepted since the program began, eight were dead and eight had resigned. Since seventeen of the original sixty-six were scientist-astronauts, and only three of them had separated from NASA, it meant that thirteen of the forty-nine flying astronauts were no longer present. The resignation and mortality rates are not so close in other honored professions. Of course, most of the astronauts work for only thirteen thousand dollars a year in base pay. Not much for an honored profession. There are, of course, increments and insurance policies and collective benefits from the *Life* magazine contract, but few earn more than twenty thousand dollars a year.

So we are obliged to consider why a man would divorce himself from his true talent—which is to test a new jet or rocket plane—and live instead in propriety, order, competition, and tension for twenty thousand dollars a year, knowing he could make three to five times that much in private life, and not be afraid to utter a resounding opinion, get drunk in public, yell at his children before strangers, or be paralyzed by scandal or divorce. Can it be that any

man who takes up such a life for thirteen thousand dollars base pay a year is either running for President, patriotic to the point of mania, or off on a mission whose root is the field of the magnet in the iron of the stars?

Some may have been running for President. John Glenn had been campaigning for senator before his accident in the tub, Bothan was now close to Nixon, Schirra was a television commentator (a holding position) and Collins was yet to enter the State Department. And there were bound to be others. If an astronaut had political ambitions he did not necessarily announce them.

Then there were men for whom a celebrity as astronaut was preferable to the professional anonymity of the test pilot. And some were patriots. There is no need to diminish the power of this motive. Once, in a meeting of astronauts, NASA executives and scientist-astronauts, the NASA administrator, then James Webb, had told them there had told them there would be a hiatus in the Space Program during the early 1970s due to budget cutting. The scientist-astronauts were gloomy. Last to arrive in the program, unscheduled for flights, they saw a delay of a decade or more before they could even go up. Scientific examination of the moon and space by experts such as themselves would be again and again delayed. One of the scientist-astronauts said, "Mr. Webb, this hiatus you've been referring to—how would you say that the scientific community—"

"To *hell* with the scientific community," Frank Borman cut in. The astronauts laughed. The attitude was clear. They were not in astronautics to solve the mysteries of the moon, they were astronauts to save America.

Nonetheless, if two-thirds of the astronauts were politicians and patriots, the remainder might still be priests of a religion not yet defined nor even discovered. One met future space men whose manner was friendly and whose talk was small, but it was possible they had a mission. Like Armstrong or Aldrin they were far from the talk at hand. If they followed the line of a conversation, they still seemed more in communion with some silence in the unheard echoes of space. ✳

-153:45

norman rockwell

Outward

1956

Louis Simpson

THE STAFF SLIPS FROM THE HAND
Hissing and swims on the polished floor.
It glides away to the desert.

It floats like a bird or Lilly
On the waves, to the ones who are arriving.
And if no god arrives,

Then everything yearns outward.
The honeycomb cell brims over
And the atom is broken in light.

Machines have made their god. They walk or fly.
The towers bend like Magi, mountains weep,
Needles go mad, and metal sheds a tear.

The astronaut is lifted
Away from the world, and drifts.
How easy it is to be there!

How easy to be anyone, anyone but oneself!
The metal of the plane is breathing;
Sinuously it swims through the Stars

First Steps, Mitchell Jamieson, 1967

The Heron and the Astronaut

1969

Anne Morrow Lindbergh

The Setting

IT WAS CALLED CAPE CANAVERAL when we first camped there with our children, over 20 years ago, behind the dunes in low palmettos and sprawling sea grape, only a few feet from the roar of the sea and the long white empty beach. Across the Indian River causeway was a sleepy Florida town, a row of stores, a hotel, a few well-kept palm trees flanking the post office, some outlying orange groves and stands of Australian pine, and leisurely traffic en route to more famous resorts, Miami or Palm Beach.

We had bumped over dusty single-track roads to the flat deserted Cape, a sharp elbow in the Atlantic. Threading our way through stretches of scrub oak, slash pine and palmetto, skirting around mangrove swamps, we found a camping site in the lee of grass-covered dunes. There were a few paths worn by surf fishermen, hot sandy spills one climbed over to reach the broad hard beach beyond. In the distance, a black-and-white-striped lighthouse stood guard over the Cape. Heavy winged pelicans sailed down-wind in formation and schools of sandpipers danced in unison on the iridescent foam path of retreating waves. On still days we saw white herons ankle-deep in the tideline, and found footprints of raccoon on the morning beach.

Local Means (Stoned Moon Series), Robert Rauschenberg, 1970

This time we have come down to watch the Apollo 8 launching, and as our wheels touch the Florida landing field, we wonder if anything will be left of the wilderness we knew. Nothing looks the same. Now the town has spread over broad highways, splashed with motels, ice cream drive-ins, gas stations, sprawling supermarkets, hotels and gaudily lit restaurants. The Cape itself, after one crosses the causeway, is now named Cape Kennedy, the great air and space center: NASA. The roads are straight and paved, the jungle bulldozed back from them, and the grass on each side is neatly cut. The flat spit of land jutting out to sea is lined with rocket launching towers, curious skyscrapers of scaffolding, over 30 of them, standing like sentinels at intervals along the shore, dwarfing our old striped lighthouse, which remains like a child's toy, relic from a forgotten past....

For some time we have been seeing the mammoth Vehicle Assembly Building in the distance. In the morning mist the VAB seems to hang on the horizon like a big gray-and-white cubist poster. As we approach, it takes on four dimensions, an enormous square mass surrounded by streets, smaller buildings and parking lots filled with hundreds of pygmy cars. A city in itself—a city for giants. Inside, one is overwhelmed not only by size but by the tremendous complication. Four cavernous wells, or vertical hangars, yawn upward. Here the rockets are assembled by giant cranes and tested by men who work on different parts from countless levels.

Apollo 8 is on its launching pad, near the beach. We peer at it through the low fog but it is barely visible, obscured by two service structures which enclose it like two halves of a shell.

Next to the mammoth VAB is a moderate-size building, about as large as a major air terminal, the Launch Control Center which houses the telemetry. Through glass walls we observe rows of TV consoles with technical experts behind them watching and checking final pre-launch details. Already on the wall a panel is flashing the countdown to tomorrow morning's takeoff. As I watch, it winks disconcertingly from 20:23 to 20:22....

I feel overwhelmed and rather oppressed by the complexity, weight and detail of what the astronauts lightly call the "hardware" of rocketry....

The Morning of Launching
WE WAKE TO THE ALARM AT 4:30, and leave our Cocoa Beach motel at 5:15. As we approach the Cape we see again the rocket and its launching tower from far off over the lagoon. It is still illumined with searchlights, but last night's vision has vanished. It is no longer tender or biological, but simply a machine, the newest and most perfected creation of a scientific age—hard, weighty metal.

We watch the launching with some of the astronauts and their families, from a site near the Vehicle Assembly Building. Our cars are parked on a slight rise of ground. People get out, walk about restlessly, set up cameras and adjust their binoculars. The launch pad is about three miles away from us, near the beach. We look across Florida marsh grass and palmettos. A cabbage palm stands up black against a shadowy sky, just left of the rocket and its launching tower. As dawn flushes the horizon, an egret rises and lazily glides across the flats between us and the pad. It is a still morning. Ducks call from nearby inlets. Vapor trails of a high-flying plane turn pink in an almost cloudless sky. Stars pale in the blue.

With the morning light, Apollo 8 and its launching tower become clearer, harder and more defined. On can see the details of installation. The dark sections on the smooth sides of the rocket, markings its stages, cut up the single fluid line. Vapor steams furiously off its side. No longer stark and simple, this morning the rocket is complicated, mechanical, earthbound. Too weighty for flight, one feels.

People stop talking, stand in front of their cars and raise binoculars to their eyes. We peer nervously at the launch site and then our wrist watches. Radio voices blare unnaturally loud from car windows. "Now only 30 minutes to launch time…15 minutes… 6 minutes…30 seconds to go…20. T minus 15, 14, 13, 12, 11, 10, 9…*Ignition*!"

A jet of steam shoots from the pad below the rocket. "Ahhh." The crowd gasps, almost in unison. Now great flames spurt, leap, belch out across the horizon. Clouds of smoke billow up on either side of the rocket, completely hiding its base. From the midst of this holocaust, the rocket begins to rise— slowly, as in a dream, so slowly it seems to hang suspended on the cloud of fire and smoke. It's impossible—it can't rise. Yes, it rises, but heavily, as if the giant weight is pulled by an invisible hand out of the atmosphere, like the lead on a plumb line from the depths of the sea. Slowly it rises and— because of our distance—silently, like a dream.

Suddenly the noise breaks, jumps across our three separating miles—a shattering roar of explosions, a trip-hammer over one's head, Under one's feet, through one's body. The earth shakes; cars rattle; vibrations beat in the chest. A roll of thunder, prolonged, prolonged, prolonged.

I drop the binoculars and put my hands to my ears, hold my head to keep steady, eyes still fixed on the rocket, mesmerized by its slow ascent.

The foreground is now full of birds; a great flock of ducks, herons, small birds rises pell-mell from the marshes at the noise. Fluttering in alarm and confusion, they scatter in all directions as if it were the end of the world. In the second, I take to look at them, the rocket has left the tower.

It is up and away, a comet boring through the

sky, no longer the vulnerable untried child, no longer the earth-bound machine, or the weight at the end of a line, but sheer terrifying force, blasting upward on its own titanic power.

It has gone miles into the sky. It is blurred by a cloud. No, it has made its own cloud—a huge vapor trail, which hides it. Out of the cloud something falls, cartwheeling down, smoking. "The first-stage cutoff," someone says. Where is the rocket itself?

There, above the cloud now, reappears the rocket, only a very bright star, diminishing every second. Soon out of sight, off to lunar space.

One looks earthward again. It is curiously still and empty. A cold of brown smoke hangs motionless on the horizon. Its long shadow reaches us across the grass. The launch pad is empty. The abandoned launching tower is being sprayed with jets of water to cool it down. It steams in the bright morning air. Still dazed, people stumble into cars and start the slow, jammed trek back to town. The monotone of radio voices continues. One clings to this last thread of contact with something incredibly beautiful that has vanished.

"Where are they—where are they now?" In 11 minutes we get word. They are in earth orbit. They "look good" in the laconic space talk that comes down from over a hundred miles above earth. And one realizes again that it is the men above all that matter, the individuals who man the machine, give it heart, sight, speech, intelligence and direction; and the men on earth who ate backing them up, monitoring their every move, even to their heart-beats. This is not sheer power, it is power under control of man.

We drive slowly back to town. Above us the white vapor trail of the rocket is being scattered by wind into feathery shapes of heron's wings—the only mark in the sky of the morning's launching…. ✳

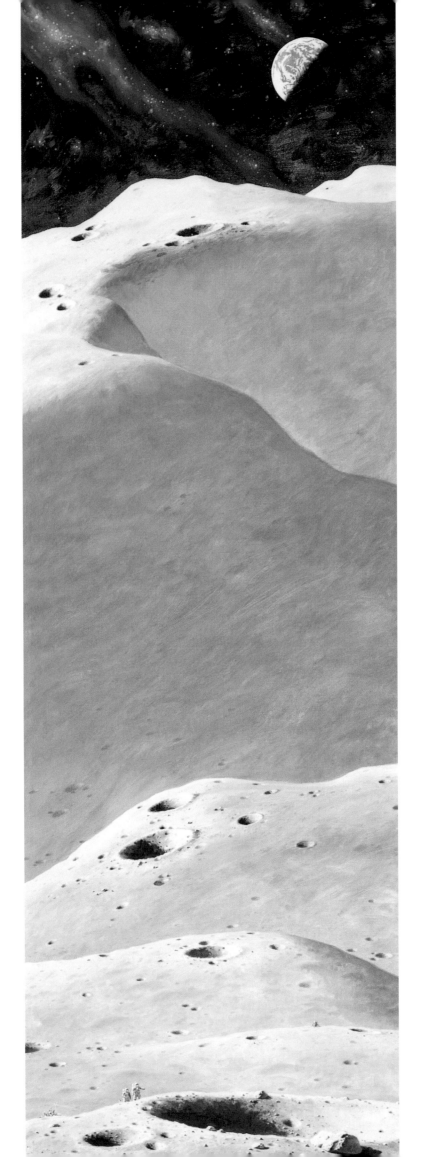

Astronauts Explore the Moon, Pierre Mion, 1979

The Last Man on the Moon

1999

Eugene Cernan and Don Davis

....Back at [the lunar lander] *Challenger*, we dusted each other off, loaded our final boxes of rocks, then Jack [Schweikart] climbed the ladder and disappeared into the hatch. By then, we had stayed longer and traveled further on the surface of the Moon than any other crew. We had covered about nineteen miles and collected more than 220 pounds of rock samples and, even before we were aboard, scientists in Houston were crowing that this had been the most meaningful lunar exploration ever. We were living proof that the Apollo program had paid dividends.

While Jack cleaned up inside, I drove the Rover about a mile away from the LM and parked it carefully so the television camera could photograph our takeoff the next day....

Alone on the surface, I hopped and skipped my way back to *Challenger*, my thoughts racing wildly as I sought to encompass this experience. Just being there was a triumph of science to be celebrated for ages, but it was more than a personal dream come true, fort I felt that I represented all humanity.

There was a sense of eternity about Apollo. Sir Isaac Newton once said, "If I have been able to see farther than others, it was because I stood on the shoulders of giants." Every man and woman who put in long hours to get us to the Moon now stood with me beside the lunar lander in that odd Sun-washed darkness. Every astronaut who had gone into space, who made it possible for me to fly a little higher, stay a little longer, was at my side. These were the giants upon whose shoulders I stood as I reached for the stars. I could almost feel the presence of Roger [Chaffee], Gus [Grissom], Ed [White], and all other astronauts and cosmonauts who died in the pursuit of the Moon. We had carried on in their names.

I took the last unfiltered look at the Earth and was enveloped by a sense of selfishness, for I was unable to adequately share what I felt. I wanted everyone on my home planet to experience this magnificent feeling of actually being on the Moon. That was not technologically possible, and I knew it, but there was a bit of guilt at being the Chosen One. I put a foot on the pad and grabbed the ladder. I knew that I had changed in the past three days, and that I no longer belonged solely to the Earth. Forever more, I would belong to the universe. With everyone back home listening, I ignored the notes on my cuff checklist and spontaneously spoke from my heart.

"As we leave the Moon and Taurus-Littrow, we leave as we came, and God willing, as we shall return, with peace and hope for all mankind." I lifted my boot from the lunar dust, adding, "As I take these last steps from the surface for some time to come, I'd just like to record that America's challenge of today has forged man's destiny of tomorrow." As I turned, I again saw the small sign pasted beneath the ladder by some unknown well-wishing worker, a phrase that I repeated every time I entered or left the *Challenger*. "Godspeed the crew of *Apollo Seventeen*," I said, and climbed on board.

Mine would be man's last footstep on the Moon for too many years to come.... ✳

Columbia Launch Fantasy, Andreas Nottebohm, 1982

Our Phenomenal First Flight

SPACE SHUTTLE COLUMBIA, APRIL 1981

John W. Young and Robert Crippen

Young: We had a complex flight plan, detailing what we were to do almost minute by minute. After we finished the first day's chores, Crip fixed us dinner. Mission Control told us it was bedtime and signed off for the next eight hours. Neither one of us slept well that first night. For one thing it was light out much of the time and far too beautiful looking down at earth.

I had taken along a 70-mm Hasselblad camera. Before launching, some geologists, oceanographers, and meteorologists I know had told me things they would like to see from space. Things like dune patterns, evidence of internal waves moving below the ocean surface, sediments off mouths of rivers, and clouds forming near coastlines and islands. 'Most of the time we were too busy to take pictures on this mission, but it was so easy to do after working hours....

Crippen: The shuttle has those wraparound windows up front. But the best views are from the flight deck windows, looking out through the payload bay when you are flying upside down with the doors open, which we were doing most of the time. You see the whole earth going by beneath you.

I remember one time glancing out and there were the Himalayas, rugged, snow covered, and stark. They are usually obscured by clouds, but this day was clear and the atmosphere so thin around them that we could see incredible detail and vivid color contrast. The human eye gives you a 3-D effect no camera can. Sights like the Himalayas and thunderstorms, which we later saw billowing high above the Amazon, are especially dramatic....

We had gorgeous views of Gibraltar, the Sahara, and the Bay of Naples. We could see Mount Etna smoking. Whenever the sun was setting, the sun glint on the water let us see ships on the surface hundreds of miles away. Perhaps the most stunning sight, however, was Dasht-e Kavir, a salt desert in Iran. It looked more like Jupiter with the great swirls of reds and browns and whites, the brilliant residues of generation after generation of evaporated salt lakes.

Young: I really liked the Bahamas. They glowed like emeralds. Unfortunately the pictures could not capture their shimmering beauty. The human eye is so much better for seeing colors and contrasts. The human being, with the detail he can pick out, will prove to be very useful in space.

I would like to get together with our photographic guys and touch up the colors in our pictures. That would probably not be cricket, but it is disappointing to look at Eleuthera and not see that emerald glowing.

I wasn't ready to go to bed that first night at quitting time even though we had been up for eighteen hours. I slept only three or four hours. Crip did a bit better. When we did turn in, we just fastened our lap belts and folded our arms. We could have gone down to the middeck and just floated around, but I like

some support. Any way you do it, sleeping in zero G is delightful. It is like being on a water bed in three dimensions.

Crippen: We were busy most of our second day, April 13, doing burns with the reaction control jets, going into different attitudes and performing maneuvers. We needed to understand how well the computer autopilot can control the vehicle. Could we make fine maneuvers? Houston wanted to see how well the crew could coordinate with the ground in positioning the orbiter.

Young: I just kept feeling better and better about that vehicle. After we launched and got it into orbit, I had said to myself, "Well, that went pretty good." Then the vehicle worked so well the first day I had said, "We'd better take it back before it breaks." The second day it worked even better and so I thought, "Man, this thing is really good. We'd better stay up here some more to get more data." But Mission Control made us come back the next day.

Crippen: We both slept soundly that second night. I was really sawing the z's when an alarm started going off in my ears. I didn't know where I was, who I was, or what I was doing for the longest time. I could hear John saying, "Crip, what's that?" It was a minor problem, fortunately. A heater control in one of our auxiliary power units quit working. We just switched on an alternate heater and went back to sleep.

It was about 2:30 A.M. Houston time when flight control greeted us with a bugle call and some rousing music. John fixed breakfast that morning, although usually I took care of the chow. Then we checked out the flight control system one last time and stowed everything away for reentry. We strapped on bio-medical sensors to keep the doctors happy, and got back into our pressure suits. We programmed the computers for reentry and closed the payload bay doors.

The first step toward getting home was to deorbit. We had tested all our engines and were very confident they were working. We were really looking forward to flying reentry. Bringing a winged vehicle down from almost twenty-five times the speed of sound would be a thrill for any pilot.

We were orbiting tail first and upside down. We fired the OMS engines enough to feel a nice little push that slowed us down by a little less than 300 feet per second. That is not dramatic, but it did change our orbit back to an ellipse whose low point would be close to the surface of the earth.

When we finished the OMS burn, John pitched the vehicle over so it was in the 40-degree nose-up angle that would let our insulated underbelly meet the reentry heat of the atmosphere.

Young: We hit the atmosphere at the equivalent of about Mach 24.5 after passing Guam. About the same time we lost radio contact with Houston. There were no tracking stations in that part of the Pacific. Also, the heat of reentry would block radio communications for the next sixteen minutes.

Just before losing contact, we noticed a slight crackling on the radio. Then, out of the sides of our eyes, we saw little blips of orange. We knew we had met the atmosphere. Those blips were the reaction control jets firing. In space we never noticed those rear jets because there were no molecules to reflect their light forward. Those blips told us that *Columbia* was coming through air—and hence plenty of molecules to reflect the thrusters' fire.

That air was also creating friction and heating *Columbia*'s exterior. About five minutes after we lost contact with Houston, at the beginning of reentry heating, when we were still flying at Mach 24.5, we noticed the reddish pink glow. Bob and I put our visors down. That sealed our pressure suits so that they would automatically inflate if somehow reentry heating burned through the cabin and let the air out. Other than the pink glow, however, we had no sense of going through a hot phase.

Crippen: *Columbia* was flying smoother than any airliner. Not a ripple!

As we approached the coast of northern California, we were doing Mach 7, and I could pick out Monterey Bay. We were about to enter the most uncertain part of our flight. Up to this point, *Columbia*'s course was controlled largely by firings of its reaction control thrusters. But as the atmosphere grew denser, the thrusters became less effective. *Columbia*'s aerodynamic controls, such as its elevons and rudder, began to take over.

We had more and more air building up on the vehicle, and we were going far faster than a winged vehicle had ever flown. Moreover, the thrusters were still firing. It was an approach with a lot of unknowns. Wind tunnels just cannot test such complex aerodynamics well. That was the main reason John took control of the flight from the automated system at a little under Mach 5. We had been doing rolls, using them a little like a skier uses turns to slow and control descent down a mountain. The flight plan called for John to fly the last two rolls manually. He would fly them more smoothly than the automatic system, helping to avoid excessive sideslipping and ensuring that we would not lose control as we came down the middle of our approach corridor.

Young: It turned out to be totally unnecessary for me to manually fly those last two roll reversals. *Columbia* had been flying like a champ. It has all those sensors: platforms for attitude control, gyroscopes, and accelerometers. Its computers take all the data, assimilate it instantly, and use it to fire thrusters, drive elevons, or do anything needed to fly the vehicle. They are much faster at this than any man. The orbiter is a joy to fly. It does what you tell it to, even in very unstable regions. All I had to do was say, "I want to roll right," or "Put my nose here," and it did it. The vehicle went where I wanted it, and it stayed there until I moved the control stick to put it somewhere else.

Crippen: Flying down the San Joaquin Valley exhilarated me. What a way to come to California! Visibility was perfect. Given some airspeed and altitude information, we could have landed visually.

John did his last roll reversal at Mach 2.6. The thrusters had stopped firing by then, and we shifted into an all-aerodynamic mode. We found out later that we had made a double sonic boom as we slowed below the speed of sound. We made a gliding circle over our landing site, Runway 23 on Rogers Dry Lake at Edwards Air Force Base.

On final approach I was reading out the airspeeds to John so he wouldn't have to scan the instruments as closely. *Columbia* almost floated in. John only had to make minor adjustments in pitch. We were targeted to touch down at 185 knots, and the very moment I called out 185, I felt us touch down. I have never been in any flying vehicle that landed more smoothly. If you can imagine the smoothest landing you've ever had in an airliner, ours was at least that good. John really greased it in.

"Welcome home, *Columbia*," said Houston. "Beautiful, Beautiful." ✳

Challenger, Edwards Air Force Base, Ron Cobb, 1982
OVERLEAF: *From the Seeds of Change…a Discovery*, Robert A.M. Stephens, 1984

Flight out of Time, Susan Kaprov, 1980

To Space and Back

1986

Sally Ride with Susan Okie

LAUNCH MORNING.

6 ... 5 ... 4 ...

The alarm clock counts down.

3 ... 2 ... 1 ...

Rrring! 3:15 A.M. *Launch minus four hours*. Time to get up.

It's pitch black outside. In four hours a space shuttle launch will light up the sky

Nine miles from the launch pad, in the astronaut crew quarters, we put on our flight suits, get some

last-minute information, and eat a light breakfast.

Launch minus three hours. It's still dark. We leave the crew quarters, climb into the astronaut van, and head for the launch pad.

The space shuttle stands with its nose pointed toward the sky, attached to the big orange fuel tank and two white rockets that will lift it—and us—into space.

The spotlights shining on the space shuttle light the last part of our route. Although we're alone, we know that thousands of people are watching us now, during the final part of the countdown.

When we step out onto the pad, we're dwarfed by the thirty-story-high space shuttle. Our space-plane looked peaceful from the road, hut now we can hear it hissing and gurgling as though it's alive.

The long elevator ride up the launch tower takes us to a level near the nose of the space shuttle, 195 feet above the ground. Trying hard not to look down at the pad far below, we walk out onto an access arm and into the "white room." The white room, a small white chamber at the end of the movable walkway, fits right next to the space shuttle's hatch. The only other people on the launch pad—in fact, the only other people for miles—are the six technicians waiting for us in the white room. They help us put on our escape harnesses and launch helmets and help us climb through the hatch. Then they strap us into our seats.

Because the space shuttle is standing on its tail, we are lying on our backs as we face the nose. It's awkward to twist around to look out the windows. The commander has a good view of the launch tower, and the pilot has a good view of the Atlantic Ocean, but no one else can see much outside.

Launch minus one hour. We check to make sure that we are strapped in properly, that oxygen will flow into our helmets, that our radio communication with Mission Control is working, and that our pencils and our books—the procedure manuals and check-lists we'll need during liftoff—are attached to something to keep them from shaking loose. Then we wait.

The technicians close the hatch and then head for safety three miles away. We're all alone on the launch pad.

Launch minus seven minutes. The walkway with the white room at the end slowly pulls away. Far below us the power units start whirring, sending a shudder through the shuttle. We close the visors on our helmets and begin to breathe from the oxygen supply. Then the space shuttle quivers again as its launch engines slowly move into position for blast-off.

Launch minus 10 seconds . . . 9 . . . 8 . . . 7 . . . The three launch engines light. The shuttle shakes and strains at the bolts holding it to the launch pad. The computers check the engines. It isn't up to us any-more—the computers will decide whether we launch.

3 . . . 2 . . . 1 . . . The rockets light! The shuttle leaps off the launch pad in a cloud of steam and a trail of fire. Inside, the ride is rough and loud. Our heads are rattling around inside our helmets. We can barely hear the voices from Mission Control in our headsets above the thunder of the rockets and engines. For an instant I wonder if everything is working right. But there's no more time to wonder, and no time to be scared.

In only a few seconds we zoom past the clouds. Two minutes later the rockets burn out, and with a brilliant whitish-orange flash, they fall away from the shuttle as it streaks on toward space. Suddenly the ride becomes very, very smooth and quiet. The shuttle is still attached to the big tank, and the launch engines are pushing us out of Earth's atmosphere. The sky is black. All we can see of the trail of fire behind us is a faint, pulsating glow through the top window.

Launch plus six minutes. The force pushing us against the backs of our seats steadily increases. We can barely move because we're being held in place by a force of 3 g's—three times the force of gravity we feel on Earth. At first we don't mind it—we've all felt much more than that when we've done acrobatics in our jet training airplanes. But that lasted only a few seconds, and this seems to go on forever. After a couple of minutes of 3 g's, we're uncomfortable, straining to hold our books on our laps and craning our necks against the force to read the instruments. I find myself wishing we'd hurry up and get into orbit.

Launch plus eight and one-half minutes. The launch engines cut off. Suddenly the force is gone, and we lurch forward in our seats. During the next few minutes the empty fuel tank drops away and falls to Earth, and we are very busy getting the shuttle ready to enter orbit. But we're not too busy to notice that our books and pencils are floating in midair. We're in space! ✳

Elegy for Challenger

1991

Diane Ackerman

WIND-WALKERS,
how we envied you

riding a golden plume
on a glitter-mad trajectory

to watch Earth roll
her blooming hips below

and scout the shores
of still unnamed seas.

You were the Balboas
we longed to be,

all star-spangled grin,
upbeat and eager,

a nation's cameo.
When the sun went out

and you blew into your shadow,
horrors clanged

like falling bells.

You orbit our thoughts now
as last we saw you:

boarding a shuttle bound
out of this world,

quivering with thrill,
deadset, but tingling.

Challenger in White,
Greg Mort, 1986

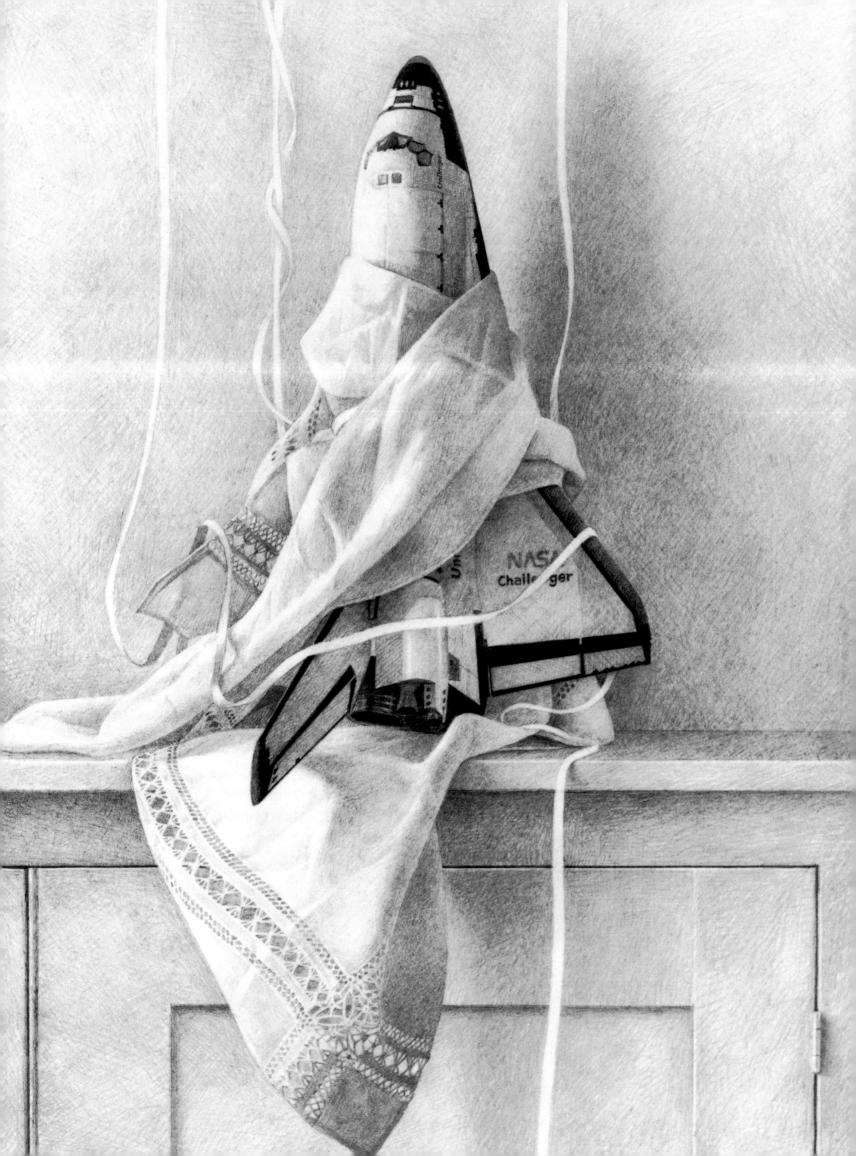

STS-71 (Mission to Mir), Edgar H. Sorrells-Adewale, 1997

Six Months on Mir

1998

Shannon W. Lucid

FOR SIX MONTHS, at least once a day, and many times more often, I floated above the large observation window in the Kvant-2 module of Mir and gazed at the earth below or into the depths of the universe. Invariably, I was struck by the majesty of the unfolding scene. But to be honest, the most amazing thing of all was that here I was, a child of the pre-Sputnik, cold war 1950s, living on a Russian space station. During my early childhood in the Texas Panhandle, I had spent a significant amount of time chasing windblown tumbleweeds across the prairie. Now I was in a vehicle that resembled a cosmic tumbleweed, working and socializing with a Russian air force officer and a Russian engineer. Just 10 years ago such a plot line would have been deemed too implausible for anything but a science-fiction novel.

In the early 1970s both the American and Russian space agencies began exploring the possibility of long-term habitation in space. After the end of the third Skylab mission in 1974, the American program focused on short-duration space shuttle flights. But the Russians continued to expand the time their cosmonauts spent in orbit, first on the Salyut space stations and later on Mir, which means "peace" in Russian. By the early 1990s, with the end of the cold war, it seemed only natural that the U.S. and Russia should cooperate in the next major step of space exploration, the construction of the International Space Station. The Russians formally joined the partnership—which also includes the European, Japanese, Canadian and Brazilian space agencies—in 1993.

The first phase of this partnership was the Shuttle-Mir program....

My involvement with the program began in 1994. At that point, I had been a NASA astronaut for 15 years and had flown on four shuttle missions. Late one Friday afternoon I received a phone call from my boss, Robert "Hoot" Gibson, then the head of NASA's astronaut office. He asked if I was interested in starting full-time Russian-language instruction with the possibility of going to Russia to train for a Mir mission. My immediate answer was yes. Hoot tempered my enthusiasm by saying I was only being assigned to study Russian. This did not necessarily mean I would be going to Russia, much less flying on Mir. But because there was a possibility that I might fly on Mir and because learning Russian requires some lead time—a major understatement if ever there was one—Hoot thought it would be prudent for me to get started.

I hung up the phone and for a few brief moments stared reality in the face. The mission on which I might fly was less than a year and a half away. In that time I would have to learn a new language, not only to communicate with my crewmates in orbit but to train in Russia for the mission. I would have to learn the systems and operations for Mir and Soyuz, the spacecraft that transports Russian crews to and from the space station. Because I would be traveling to and from Mir on the space shuttle, I needed to maintain my familiarity with the American space-craft. As if that were not enough, I would also have to master the series of experiments I would be conducting while in orbit.

It is fair at this point to ask, "Why?" Why would I wish to live and work on Mir? And from a broader perspective, why are so many countries joining together to build a new space station? Certainly one reason is scientific research. Gravity influences all experiments done on the earth except for investigations conducted in drop towers or on airplanes in parabolic flight. But on a space station, scientists can conduct long-term investigations in an environment where gravity is almost nonexistent—the microgravity environment. And the experience gained by main-taining a continuous human presence in space may help determine what is needed to support manned flights to other planets.

From a personal standpoint, I viewed the Mir mission as a perfect opportunity to combine two of my passions: flying airplanes and working in labora-tories. I received my private pilot's license when I was 20 years old and have been flying ever since. And before I became an astronaut, I was a bio-chemist, earning my Ph.D. from the University of Oklahoma in 1973. For a scientist who loves flying,

what could be more exciting than working in a labo-ratory that hurtles around the earth at 17,000 miles (27,000 kilometers) per hour?

Living in Microgravity
MY FIRST DAYS ON MIR were spent getting to know Onufriyenko and Usachev—we spoke exclusively in Russian—and the layout of the space station. Mir has a modular design and was built in stages. The first part, the Base Block, was launched in February 1986. Attached to one end of the Base Block is Kvant-1, launched in 1987, and at the other end is Mir's transfer node, which serves the same function as a hallway in a house. Instead of being a long corridor with doors, though, the transfer node is a ball with six hatches. Kvant-2 (1989), Kristall (1990) and Spektr (1995) are each docked to a hatch. During my stay on Mir, the Russians launched Priroda, the final module of the space station, and attached it to the transfer node. Priroda contained the laboratory where I conducted most of my experi-ments. I stored my personal belongings in Spektr and slept there every night. My commute to work was very short—in a matter of seconds I could float from one module to the other.

The two cosmonauts slept in cubicles in the Base Block. Most mornings the wake-up alarm went off at eight o'clock (Mir runs on Moscow time, as does the Russian mission control in Korolev). In about 20 minutes we were dressed and ready to start the day. The first thing we usually did was put on our head-sets to talk to mission control. Unlike the space shuttle, which transmits messages via a pair of com-munications satellites, Mir is not in constant contact with the ground. The cosmonauts can talk to mission control only when the space station passes over one of the communications ground sites in Russia. These "comm passes" occurred once an orbit—about every 90 minutes—and generally lasted about 10 minutes. Commander Onufriyenko wanted each of us to be "on comm" every time it was available, in case the ground needed to talk to us. This routine worked out well because it gave us short breaks throughout the day. We gathered in the Base Block and socialized a bit before and after talking with mission control.

After the first comm pass of the day, we ate breakfast. One of the most pleasant aspects of being part of the Mir crew was that we ate all our meals together, floating around a table in the Base Block. Preflight, I had assumed that the repetitive nature of the menu would dampen my appetite, but to my surprise I was hungry for every meal. We ate both Russian and American dehydrated food that we reconstituted with hot water. We experimented with mixing the various packages to create new tastes, and we each had favorite mixtures that we recommended to the others. For breakfast I liked to have a bag of Russian soup—usually borscht or vegetable—and a bag of fruit juice. For lunch or supper I liked the Russian meat-and-potato casseroles. The Russians loved the packets of American mayonnaise, which they added to nearly everything they ate.

Our work schedule was detailed in a daily time-line that the Russians called the Form 24. The cosmonauts typically spent most of their day main-taining Mir's systems, while I conducted experiments for NASA. We had to exercise every day to prevent our muscles from atrophying in the weightless environment. Usually, we all exercised just before lunch. There are two treadmills on Mir—one in the Base Block and the other in the Kristall module—and a bicycle ergometer is stored under a floor panel in the Base Block. We followed three exercise proto-cols developed by Russian physiologists; we did a different one each day, then repeated the cycle. Each protocol took about 45 minutes and alternated periods of treadmill running with exercises that involved pulling against bungee cords to simulate the gravita-tional forces we were no longer feeling. Toward the end of my stay on Mir I felt that I needed to be working harder, so after I finished my exercises I ran additional kilometers on the treadmill.

I'll be honest: the daily exercise was what I dis-liked most about living on Mir. First, it was just downright hard. I had to put on a harness and then connect it with bungee cords to the treadmill. Working against the bungees allowed me to stand flat on the device. With a little practice, I learned to

run. Second, it was boring. The treadmill was so noisy you could not carry on a conversation. To keep my mind occupied, I listened to my Walkman while running, but soon I realized I'd made a huge preflight mistake. I had packed very few tapes with a fast beat. Luckily, there was a large collection of music tapes on Mir. During my six-month stay, I worked through most of them.

When we had finished exercising, we usually enjoyed a long lunch, then returned to our work. Many times in the late afternoon we had a short tea break, and in the late evening we shared supper. By this point we had usually finished all the assignments on the Form 24, but there were still many house-keeping chores that needed to be done: collecting the trash, organizing the food supply, sponging up the water that had condensed on cool surfaces. Clutter was a problem on Mir. After we had unloaded new supplies from the unmanned Progress spacecraft that docked with the space station once every few months, we could put human wastes and trash into the empty vehicles, which would burn up on reentry into the atmosphere. But there was usually no room left on Progress for the many pieces of scientific equipment that were no longer in use.

After supper, mission control would send us the Form 24 for the next day on the teleprinter. If there was time, we had tea and a small treat—cookies or candy—before the last comm pass of the day, which usually occurred between 10 and 11 at night. Then we said good night to one another and went to our separate sleeping areas. I floated into Spektr, unrolled my sleeping bag and tethered it to a handrail. I usually spent some time reading and typing letters to home on my computer (we used a ham radio packet system to send the messages to the ground controllers, who sent them to my family by email). At midnight I turned out the light and floated into my sleeping bag. I always slept soundly until the alarm went off the next morning....

Safety in Space

THROUGHOUT MY MISSION I also performed a series of earth observations. Many scientists had asked NASA to photograph parts of the planet under varying seasonal and lighting conditions. Oceanographers, geologists and climatologists would incorporate the photographs into their research. I usually took the pictures from the Kvant-2 observation window with a handheld Hasselblad camera. I discovered that during a long spaceflight, as opposed to a quick space shuttle jaunt, I could see the flow of seasons across the face of the globe. When I arrived on Mir at the end of March, the higher latitudes of the Northern Hemisphere were covered with ice and snow. Within a few weeks, though, I could see huge cracks in the lakes as the ice started to break up. Seemingly overnight, the Northern Hemisphere glowed green with spring.

We also documented some unusual events on the earth's surface. One day as we passed over Mongolia we saw giant plumes of smoke, as though the entire country were on fire. The amount of smoke so amazed us that we told the ground controllers about it. Days later they informed us that news of huge forest fires was just starting to filter out of Mongolia.

For long-duration manned spaceflight, the most important consideration is not the technology of the spacecraft but the composition of the crew. The main reason for the success of our Mir mission was the fact that Commander Onufriyenko, flight engineer Usachev and I were so compatible. It would have been very easy for language, gender or culture to divide us, but this did not happen. My Russian crewmates always made sure that I was included in their conversations. Whenever practical, we worked on projects together. We did not spend time criticizing one another—if a mistake was made, it was understood, corrected and then forgotten. Most important, we laughed together a lot.

The competence of my crewmates was one of the reasons I always felt safe on Mir. When I began my mission, the space station had been in orbit for 10 years, twice as long as it had been designed to operate. Onufriyenko and Usachev had to spend most of their time maintaining the station, replacing parts as they failed and monitoring the systems critical

to life support. I soon discovered that my crewmates could fix just about anything. Many spare parts are stored on Mir, and more are brought up as needed on the Progress spacecraft. Unlike the space shuttle, Mir cannot return to the earth for repairs, so the rotating crews of cosmonauts are trained to keep the station functioning.

Furthermore, the crews on Mir have ample time to respond to most malfunctions. A hardware failure on the space shuttle demands immediate attention because the shuttle is the crew's only way to return to the earth. If a piece of vital equipment breaks down, the astronauts have to repair the damage quickly or end the mission early, which has happened on a few occasions. But Mir has a lifeboat: at least one Soyuz spacecraft is always attached to the space station. If a hardware failure occurs on Mir, it does not threaten the crew's safe return home. As long as the space station remains habitable, the crew members can analyze what happened, talk to mission control and then correct the malfunction or work around the problem.

Only two situations would force the Mir crew to take immediate action: a fire inside the space station or a rapid depressurization. Both events occurred on Mir in 1997, after I left the station. In each case, the crew members were able to contain the damage quickly.

My mission on the space station was supposed to end in August 1996, but my ride home—shuttle mission STS-79—was delayed for six weeks while NASA engineers studied abnormal burn patterns on the solid-fuel boosters from a previous shuttle flight. When I heard about the delay, my first thought was, "Oh, no, not another month and a half of treadmill running!" Because of the delay, I was still on Mir when a new Russian crew arrived on the Soyuz spacecraft to relieve Onufriyenko and Usachev. By the time I finally came back on the shuttle Atlantis on September 26, 1996, I had logged 188 days in space—an American record that still stands.... ✳

Satellite in Space, Lonny Schiff, 1989

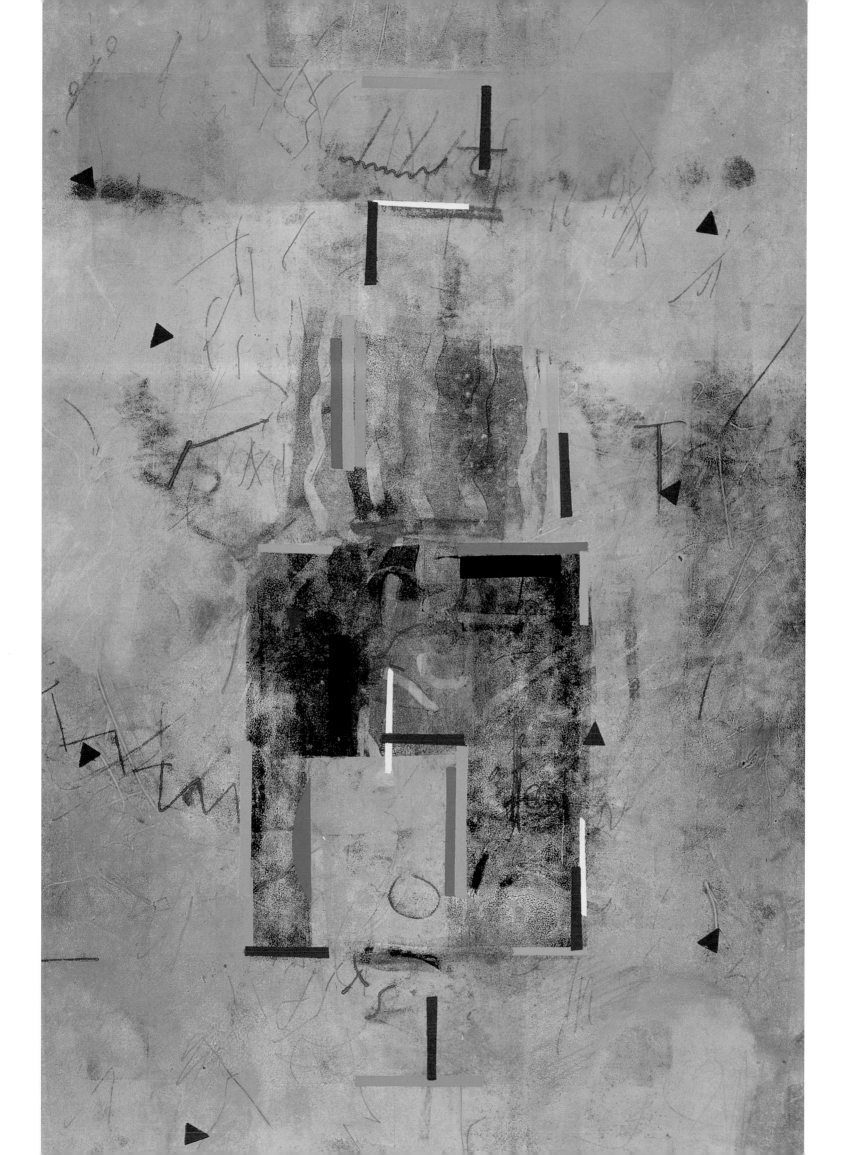

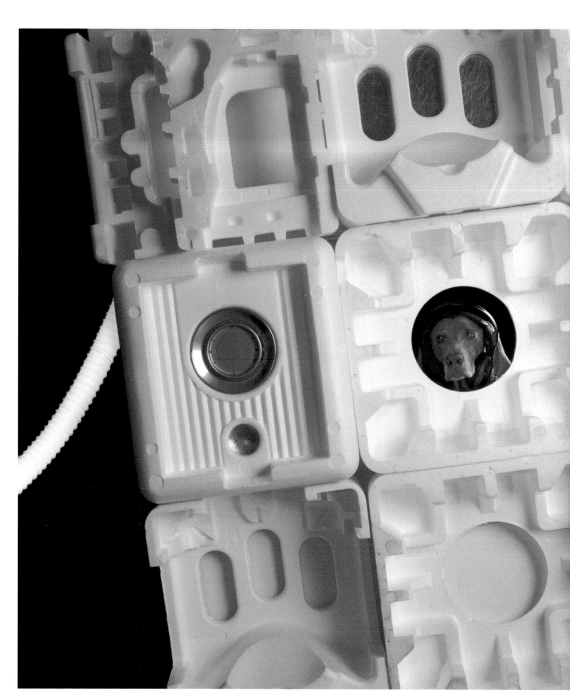

Chip and Batty Explore Space, William Wegman, 2001

Tourists on the Moon #2, Yoshio Itagaki, 1998

The Green Hills of Earth

1967

Robert A. Heinlein

Let the sweet fresh breezes heal me
As they rove around the girth
Of our lovely mother planet
Of the cool, green hills of Earth.

We rot in the moulds of Venus,
We retch at her tainted breath.
Foul are her flooded jungles,
Crawling with unclean death.

We've tried each spinning space mote
And reckoned its true worth:
Take us back again to the homes of men
On the cool, green hills of Earth.

The arching sky is calling
Spacemen back to their trade.
ALL HANDS! STAND BY! FREE FALLING!
And the lights below us fade.

Out ride the sons of Terra,
Far drives the thundering jet,
Up leaps a race of Earthmen,
Out, far, and onward yet —

We pray for one last landing
On the globe that gave us birth;
Let us rest our eyes on the friendly skies
And the cool, green hills of Earth.

Beyond the Sky

1999

Judy Collins

*Lyrics in honor of First Female Space Shuttle
Commander Eileen Collins*

Once there was a girl with a dream in her heart
Wild as the wind was her hope
In those far off days she could dream all she would
No one but her heart believed her hope
All she could do was to hold to her dream
Catching every rainbow's light
Praying for the miracle to come to pass
Even on the darkest night

And she would fly
Beyond the sky
Beyond the Stars beyond the heavens
Beyond the dawn she'd carry on
Until her dreams had all come true

Once there was a woman with stars in her eyes
Flying on the wings of her dreams
She had come so far it was hard to believe
Changed the world from what it seemed
Equal to the ones who had claimed the sky
Now she flew with them beneath the sun
But she dared a dream beyond all dreams
She would take the helm and be the one

And she would fly
Beyond the sky
Beyond the Stars beyond the heavens
Beyond the dawn she'd carry on
Until her dreams had all come true

She had led the way beyond darkness
For other dreamers who would dare the sky
She had led us to believe in dreaming
Given us the hope that we can try

Now in her grace of her dance of delight
Shining in her destiny
Here is the promise for all our hopes
Telling us we can be free

And we will fly
Beyond the sky
Beyond the Stars beyond the heavens
Beyond the dawn she'd carry on
Until her dreams had all come true

To those who fly—we sing to you

Into the sky

Beyond the stars

We'll reach our dreams

Eileen Collins, Annie Leibovitz, 1999

The Boy's First Flight

1999

Gary Soto

One side of our house was desert
And the other, the one facing east,
Was Eden itself.
I didn't know this until I bounced on a trampoline
And landed on the garage roof, me the unpaid astronaut,
Age nine, knees scuffed from a rough landing.
I looked about, stunned. A breeze lived
In the sycamore and a single-engine airplane
Hung by a thread of exhaust in the darkening sky.
This was 1961. I asked, "Is this for us?" meaning the bushel of stars,
Pitched and pulsating their icy thorns. The moon was a tiger's tooth,
Hooked in a frightening way. I walked back
And forth on the roof, arms out for balance.
I saw my cat and dog, and they saw me, perhaps in awe,
Because they did lift their eyes to me.

And now it's 1999, the end of the millennium,
And it's certainly the end of my knees,
Those springs long gone. A latch of rust groans in each knee—
How they would love that payload of a taut trampoline.
I see these children, how they jump, fall back, and jump again.
If only I could sit on a roof, in summer,
If only I could watch a Shuttle—what lever does the commander push
To make a smile on his face, her face? I'm in the dark, literally,
Ice cubes rattling in my tea. The crickets sing in the weeds,
And soon the Shuttle, dime-bright, will lift off
And pull away. My friends, my suited up pilgrims,
What news will you bring?

Blastoff, Alma Thomas, 1970

9/11

A VIEW OF THE SEPTEMBER 11TH TERRORIST ATTACKS FROM THE INTERNATIONAL SPACE STATION, 2001

Frank L. Culbertson

I HAVEN'T WRITTEN VERY MUCH about specifics of this mission during the month I've been here, mainly for two reasons: the first being that there has been very little time to do that kind of writing, and secondly because I'm not sure how comfortable I am sharing thoughts I share with family and friends with the rest of the world.

Well, obviously the world changed today. What I say or do is very minor compared to the significance of what happened to our country today when it was attacked by .... by whom? Terrorists is all we know, I guess. Hard to know at whom to direct our anger and fear....

I had just finished a number of tasks this morning, the most time-consuming being the physical exams of all crew members. In a private conversation following that, the flight surgeon told me they were having a very bad day on the ground. I had no idea...

He described the situation to me as best he knew it at ~0900 CDT. I was flabbergasted, then horrified. My first thought was that this wasn't a real conversation, that I was still listening to one of my Tom Clancy tapes. It just didn't seem possible on this scale in our country. I couldn't even imagine the particulars, even before the news of further destruction began coming in.

Vladimir [Dezhurov] came over pretty quickly, sensing that something very serious was being discussed. I waved Michael [Tyurin] into the module as well. They were also amazed and stunned. After we signed off, I tried to explain to Vladimir and Michael as best I could the potential magnitude of this act of terror in downtown Manhattan and at the Pentagon. They clearly understood and were very sympathetic.

I glanced at the World Map on the computer to see where over the world we were and noticed that we were coming southeast out of Canada and would be passing over New England in a few minutes. I zipped around the station until I found a window that would give me a view of NYC and grabbed the nearest camera. It happened to be a video camera, and I was looking south from the window of Michael's cabin.

The smoke seemed to have an odd bloom to it at the base of the column that was streaming south of the city. After reading one of the news articles we just received, I believe we were looking at NY around the time of, or shortly after, the collapse of the second tower. How horrible....

I panned the camera all along the East Coast to the south to see if I could see any other smoke around Washington, or anywhere else, but nothing was visible.

It was pretty difficult to think about work after that, though we had some to do, but on the next orbit we crossed the U.S. further south. All three of us were working one or two cameras to try to get views of New York or Washington. There was haze

Space Station, Nicky Enright, 2000

over Washington, but no specific source could be seen. It all looked incredible from two to three hundred miles away. I can't imagine the tragic scenes on the ground.

Other than the emotional impact of our country being attacked and thousands of our citizens and maybe some friends being killed, the most overwhelming feeling being where I am is one of isolation.

Next day....

I GUESS THE FATIGUE AND EMOTIONAL STRAIN got the best of me. I couldn't stay awake and continue to write. Today was still difficult, but we started getting more information, plus we had the honor of talking directly with the [Johnson Space] Center Director, Roy Estess, who assured us that the ground teams would continue to work and ensure our safety, as well as the safe operation of the Station. We also heard from our Administrator, Mr. [Daniel S.] Goldin, who added that the partners in the program are all totally committed to continuing safe operations and support. These were never questions for me. I know all these people! The ground teams have been incredibly supportive, very understanding of the impact of the news, and have tried to be as helpful as possible. They have all been very professional and focused though I can't imagine the distraction of this type of news coming in and the thought that government buildings might be at risk. They never skipped a beat, even when relocating control centers. And a group of senior personnel and friends gave us a pretty thorough briefing on what was known and what was being done in the government and at NASA on Tuesday afternoon, which was very helpful and kind of them to do in the midst of all the turmoil. The Russian TsUP has also been supportive and helpful, trying to uplink news articles when our own assets were inoperable, and saying kind words....

My crewmates have been great, too. They know it's been a tough day for me and the folks on the ground, and they've tried to be as even keeled and helpful as possible. Michael even fixed me my favorite Borscht soup for dinner. And they give me plenty of room to think when I needed it. They are

very sympathetic and of course outraged at whoever would do this.

I know so many people in Washington, so many people who travel to DC and NYC, so many who are pilots, that I felt sure I would receive at least a few pieces of bad news over the next few days. I got the first one today when I learned that the Captain of the American Airlines jet that hit the Pentagon was Chic Burlingame, a classmate of mine. I met Chic during plebe summer when we were in the D&B together, and we had lots of classes together. I can't imagine what he must of gone through, and now I hear that he may have risen further than we can even think of by possibly preventing his plane from being the one to attack the White House. What a terrible loss, but I'm sure Chic was fighting bravely to the end. And tears don't flow the same in space....

It's difficult to describe how it feels to be the only American completely off the planet at a time such as this. The feeling that I should be there with all of you, dealing with this, helping in some way, is overwhelming. I know that we are on the threshold (or beyond) of a terrible shift in the history of the world. Many things will never be the same again after September 11, 2001. Not just for the thousands and thousands of people directly affected by these horrendous acts of terrorism, but probably for all of us. We will find ourselves feeling differently about dozens of things, including probably space exploration, unfortunately.

It's horrible to see smoke pouring from wounds in your own country from such a fantastic vantage point. The dichotomy of being on a spacecraft dedicated to improving life on the earth and watching life being destroyed by such willful, terrible acts is jolting to the psyche, no matter who you are. And the knowledge that everything will be different than when we launched by the time we land is a little disconcerting. I have confidence in our country and in our leadership that we will do everything possible to better defend her and our families, and to bring justice for what has been done. I have confidence that the good people at NASA will do everything necessary to continue our mission safely and return us safely at the right time. And I miss all of you very much. I can't be there with you in person, and we have a long way to go to complete our mission, but be certain that my heart is with you, and know you are in my prayers.

Humbly,
Frank

September 14, 2001; 22:49
*An update to the last letter....*Fortunately, it's been a busy week up here. And to prove that, like our country, we are continuing on our intended path with business as usual (as much as possible). Tonight the latest addition to the station, the Russian Docking Compartment, will be launched from Baikonur, Kazakhstan. On Saturday night (U.S. time), it will dock with us, at a port never used before on the nadir side of the Service Module. This new module will give us another place to dock a Progress or Soyuz and will provide a large airlock with two useable hatches for conducting EVA's in Russian Orlan suits, which we will do a few of before we come home.

The problem before in dealing with this week was too little news. The problem now is too much. It came all at once when email was restored, and there's not enough time to read it all! Plus it's too hard to deal with all of it at once. But I appreciate getting it, and I really appreciate the great letters of support and friendship I am receiving.

We are doing well on board, getting our work done, and talking about things. Last night we had a long discussion over dinner about the significance of these events, the possible actions to follow, and what should be done. After dinner, Michael made a point of telling me that every email he received from friends in Russia said specifically to tell me how sorry they were that this happened, extending their condolences, and asking how I was doing. Vladimir taught me the Russian word for "condolences" after talking to the previous CDR, Yuri Usachev, on the phone in Star City. (Both the Russian and the English words are much too long to pronounce easily.) Very kind people.

For the last two days, the Russian MCC has been good enough to transmit live broadcasts of radio news about the event and associated stories, to make sure I was well informed. Every specialist who has come on the line to discuss a procedure or a problem has at some point extended greetings to me with kind words. Tonight the Russian capcom told us that because of the special day of remembrance in the U.S., all day people had been bringing flowers and lining all the walls of the U.S. embassy in Moscow, and this evening they were lighting candles in the street outside the embassy. How the world has changed.

People everywhere seem to recognize the sense-lessness and horror in this attack. And the tremendous loss. Moscow has dealt with these kind of problems in the last few years with apartment and subway bombings, so they are as anxious to get rid of this threat as we are. But the bottom line is that there are good people everywhere who want to live in peace. I read that a child asked, "America is so good to other countries, we always help everyone, how can they hate us so much?"

I hope the example of cooperation and trust that this spacecraft and all the people in the program demonstrate daily will someday inspire the rest of the world to work the same way. They must!

Unfortunately, we won't be flying over the U.S. during the time people are lighting candles. Don't know if we could see that anyway. We did, how-ever, see a very unusual and beautiful sight a few minutes ago: the launch of our Docking Compartment on a Soyuz booster. We were overtak-ing it and it came into view about three minutes after its launch from Baikonur as the sun hit our sta-tion, so it was still in the dark. It looked like a large comet with a straight, wide tail silhouetted against the dark planet beneath. Despite some bad lighting for a while as the sun hit our window at a low angle, I managed some video of it as first we passed the rocket, and then watched it begin to catch up as it gained altitude and speed. I filmed until main engine cutoff and booster separation occurred—just as we approached sunrise on the Himalayas. An unforgettable sight in an unforgettable week...

Life goes on, even in space. We're here to stay...

Frank ✳

Go for the Stars, P. A. Nisbet, 1990
PRECEDING PAGES: *A New Frontier*, Keith Duncan, 2001

Our Infinite Journey

2000

Walter Cronkite

WE ARE EXTRAORDINARILY LUCKY, we of the generation that participated in and witnessed the birth of the space age. We were there at the concept as the military tested the first American rockets in the New Mexico desert. We were there as President Kennedy put a new focus on the space program. He inspired a nation and spoke the American dream—within the decade we would land men on the Moon and bring them safely home.

And we were there on the beaches of Florida and, the lucky few, at Cape Canaveral as we watched our rockets and spacecraft grow and eventually soar toward the Moon. And the world, through television, shared the American adventure, and the American success.

The Moon landing was dramatic and important but it was, after all, only a step along the way. The shuttle was to follow—our first reusable spacecraft, one that soon would be on the frequent schedule of a commuter as it orbited Earth, photographing Earth as it never had been shown before, revealing the stars as we had never seen them, enabling unprecedented predictions of our weather below, providing the satellite communication links that forever changed the world, aiding the nations in assuring peace by keeping a friendly eye on each other's neighbors, and proving humans' capabilities to work in the rare environment of space.

With the closing of the remarkable century that saw space opening up to the conquering miracles of human flight, sixteen nations were participating in building the first space station that would be continually occupied by humans—a station that would open new possibilities for further exploration and uses of the near gravity-free environment for medical treatment and manufacturing techniques that still are only dreams.

And parallel to the accomplishments of human flight, we have lived with the exciting development of robotic exploration of deep space. Those amazing craft conceived by the best brains of humans and directed by them are today circling the distant planets at the edge of our universe and telling us what they see and feel and sense.

Our successes in space were, for Americans, a powerful antidote at a time when we needed it badly. The 1960s, when we first launched humans into space and went on to the Moon, were in other ways a terrible drain on our spirit. The civil rights battles, the frightening divisiveness of the Vietnam War, the horrible assassinations—they drained the American spirit. It is no exaggeration to say the space program saved us.

Yes, indeed, we are the lucky generation. Not only were our achievements in space important in restoring our self-respect; they enabled us as well to enter the history books. Thanks to our hero scientists, technicians, and astronauts, we will be remembered hundreds of years from now as those who first broke our earthly bonds and ventured into space. From our descendants' perches on other planets or distant space cities, they will look back at our achievement with wonder at our courage and audacity and with appreciation of our accomplishments, which assured the future in which they live. *

Courage

1937

Amelia Earhart

COURAGE IS THE PRICE THAT LIFE
    exacts for granting peace.
The soul that knows it not,
    knows no release
From little things:

knows not the livid loneliness of fear,
Nor mountain heights where bitter joy
    can hear
The sound of wings.

How can Life grant us boon of living,
    compensate
For dull gray ugliness and pregnant hate
Unless we dare

The soul's dominion? Each time we
    make a choice, we pay
With courage to behold resistless day,
And count it fair.

Early Biplane in Flight

About the Authors

Diane Ackerman was born in Waukegan, Illinois in 1948. During the late 1970s and 1980s, she published three volumes of poetry and a verse drama. Ackerman gained recognition for her for creative non-fiction with the publication of *A Natural History of the Senses* in 1990. In *A Natural History of Love* (1994), and, most recently, *A Slender Thread* (1997), Ackerman continued her meditative exploration of the interconnection between the natural and human worlds. Her poetry has appeared in numerous anthologies.

Ernest Archdeacon was a rich French lawyer and sportsman. He founded the Aero-Club de France after hearing Octave Chanute speak in March 1903. The goal of the club was to promote heavier-than-air flying, but if, along the way, it could beat the Wrights in the race to achieve the powered airplane, so much the better. Archdeacon built a copy of the Wright No. 3 glider of 1902—which was completed in March 1904—but had only limited success flying it.

Richard Bach is the author of twelve books, including the best-selling *Jonathan Livingston Seagull*, *Illusions*, and *Rescue Ferrets at Sea*. A former USAF fighter pilot, gypsy barnstormer, and airplane mechanic, he flies a seaplane today.

Paul Bewsher was a Sub-Lieutenant in the Royal Naval Air Service. During the war, the first operational unit to receive the big Handley Page was the R.N.A.S-5th Wing at Dunkerque, which received its first O/100 in November 1916. This was flown to France by Squadron Commander John Babington, with Lieutenant Jones and Sub-Lieutenant Paul Bewsher as crew. During the war he began writing poetry and published "The Dawn Patrol" in 1917.

Louis Blériot was born in Cambrai, France in 1872. He was an inventor, aircraft designer, and pilot. Although interested in aviation since 1900, he is best known for his flight over the English Channel on July 25, 1909—the world's first over a large body of water in a heavier-than-air craft. Blériot then became president of the floundering aircraft company Société pour les Appareils Deperdussin, renamed it Société Pour Aviation et ses Derives (SPAD), and turned it into one of France's leading manufacturers of combat aircraft. After World War I, Blériot formed a commercial aircraft company, Blériot-Aéronautique. He died in 1936.

Ray Bradbury is a prolific science fiction writer and futurist who is well known for his more than five hundred published works—short stories, novels, plays, screenplays, television scripts, and verse—each exemplifying a uniquely American imagination. He is best known for his novel, *The Martian Chronicles* (1950), but he has also been at the forefront of space exploration advocacy throughout the second half of the twentieth century.

Joe Brainard was born in Arkansas in 1942, and grew up in Tulsa, Oklahoma. He moved to New York City after graduating from high school, and found early success in his debut solo exhibition in 1965 with assemblages made of logos and sequins, and garish altarpieces made of dolls, boxes, and price tags. Brainard stopped exhibiting his art in 1979 and turned his attention to writing poetry and prose. His memoir, *I Remember*, is a book-length poem about pop culture and universal moments of feeling odd. Brainard died of AIDS in 1994.

Wernher von Braun, born in 1912, was the leader of the "rocket team," which developed the V-2 ballistic missile for the Nazis during World War II. The V-2s were manufactured at the forced labor factory, Mittelwerk. Scholars are still assessing von Braun's role in these activities. After the war, von Braun came to Fort Bliss in El Paso, Texas, to work on rocket development and use the V-2 for high altitude research. In 1950, his team built the Army's Jupiter ballistic missile, and before that the Redstone, used by NASA to launch the first Mercury capsules. He also oversaw development of the Saturn V Moon rocket. He died in 1977.

Eugene Cernan is an astronaut who served as commander of Apollo 17, the last mission to land on the Moon. His career is relayed in his autobiography, written with Don Davis, *The Last Man on the Moon: Astronaut Eugene Cernan and America's Race in Space* (1999).

Octave Chanute was born in Paris and came to the United States as a child. He spent most of his life as an engineer in the railroad industry, but later gained international fame in the study of aeronautics. He published *Progress in Flying Machines* in New York in 1894, which summarized and thoroughly analyzed the technical accomplishments of the world's aviation pioneers up to that time. The book became a classic and a guidebook for the efforts of many would-be aviators around the world, including the Wright brothers. They acknowledged Chanute's key role as a mentor, saying his research paved the way for their success. Chanute corresponded with them for many years and even visited their camp at Kitty Hawk.

Tena R. Clarke is a songwriter/singer who has composed music for many well-known performers, including Patti LaBelle and Gladys Knight. She is also chief executive officer of Disc Marketing, a music production and packaging firm in Pasadena, California.

Arthur C. Clarke, born in England in 1913, is one of the most well known science fiction authors. He has also been an eloquent writer on behalf of space exploration. In 1945, before the invention of the transistor, Clarke wrote an article in *Extraterrestrial Relays* describing the possibility of geosynchronous orbit and the development of communication relays by satellite. He also wrote several novels, the most famous being *2001: A Space Odyssey*, based on a screenplay he prepared for director Stanley Kubrick. The movie is still one of the most realistic depictions of space flight ever filmed.

Judy Collins is a singer/songwriter whose music has been popular for more than thirty years.

Michael Collins was command module pilot during the Apollo 11 mission to the Moon. He later served as the first director of the Smithsonian Institution's National Air and Space Museum from 1976-1979, and wrote several important books on space flight. These include *Carrying the Fire* (1974), *Liftoff: The Story of America's Adventure in Space* (1987), and *Mission to Mars* (1990).

Robert L. Crippen was the pilot for STS-1, the maiden flight of the Space Shuttle *Columbia* on April 12-14, 1981.

Walter Cronkite is a veteran journalist whose career spanned six decades. He covered the space program from its formative years to the first flights of the space shuttle. He became a special correspondent for CBS in 1981, when, after 19 years, he stepped down as anchorman and managing editor of the CBS Evening News. He continues to serve as a Special Correspondent for CBS and hosts many public affairs and cultural programs. In 1993 he co-founded The Cronkite Ward Company, a documentary production company which has produced more than 25 award-winning documentary hours.

Frank L. Culbertson, a NASA astronaut who is a veteran of three space flights, has logging over 142 days in space. Most recently, he was commander of the Expedition-3 crew to the International Space Station (ISS) between August and December 2001. Culbertson lived and worked aboard the station for a total of 125 days.

Elizabeth Daryush was born in England in 1887, the daughter of Robert Bridges. She published three books of verse, numerous critical essays, and an anthology. She died in 1977.

Benjamin O. Davis, Jr. graduated from West Point in 1936, and got his pilot's wings in March 1942, after becoming the first black officer to solo an Army Air Corps aircraft. He led the famous Tuskegee airmen of the 99th Pursuit Squadron, later taking command of the 332d Fighter Group. The distinctive 332d "Red Tail" P-51 Mustangs under Davis flew more than 15,000 sorties against the Luftwaffe, shot down 111 enemy aircraft, and destroyed another 150 on the ground, losing only 66 of their own aircraft. Davis later achieved the rank of Brigadier General, becoming the first African American to earn a star. He retired in 1970, gained a fourth star in 1998, and died in 2002.

Don Davis is an author and co-author of numerous publications including "The Last Man on the Moon" and "Dark Waters: An Insider's Account of the Nr-1, the Cold War's Undercover, Nuclear Sub."

General James H. "Jimmy" Doolittle was born at Alameda, California, in 1896. He enlisted as an Army flying cadet during World War I. He earned a B.A. degree in 1922 and then studied aeronautical engineering at M.I.T., where he received both a Masters and Doctors degree in science. During World War II, he was awarded the Medal of Honor and was promoted from Colonel to Brigadier General for leading the first carrier-based bomber attack on mainland Japan in 1942. Doolittle died in California in 1993.

Amelia Earhart was born in 1897 in Atchison, Kansas. Her flying career began in Los Angeles in 1921 when, at 24, she took flying lessons from Neta Snook and bought her first airplane, a Kinner Airstar. She sold her plane in 1924 and moved east, where she worked as a social worker. Four years later, she bought an Avro Avian airplane and became the first woman to make a solo-return transcontinental flight. She continued to set and break her own speed and distance records in competitive events as well as personal stunts promoted by her husband George Palmer Putnam. Earhart's name became a household word in 1932 when she became the first woman—and only the second person—to fly solo across the Atlantic in a Lockheed Vega. She died during an attempted around-the-world flight in 1937.

Antoine de Saint-Exupéry was born in Lyon, France in 1900. At the age of 26 he became pilot of mail service from Toulouse to Dakar, and was named a chef of the Port Juby office. In 1938, after German troops occupied France, he moved to United States. His experiences are described in *Night Flight* (Vol de Nuit, 1931), *Southern Mail* (Courrier Sud, 1929), *Flight to Arras* (Pilote de Guerre, 1942) *Airman's Odyssey, Wisdoms of the Sands, Letter to a Hostage (Lettre à un Otage, 1943)* and *Wind, Sand and Stars* (Terre des Hommes, 1939). In America he wrote several novels, among them *The Little Prince* (Le Petit Prince), published in 1940. At the beginning of World War II, Exupery moved back to France and joined the army. On July 31, 1944, he was shot down over the Mediterranean.

Robert Frost was born in San Francisco in 1874, but moved to Lawrence, Massachusetts at the age of eleven, and by the 1920s had become one of America's most celebrated poets. By his death in 1963, Frost had received four Pulitzer Prizes and a host of other awards.

Lord Gorell was born in 1884 in England. The author of numerous works of poetry and prose, he became a barrister and journalist who served as an almost professional chair of numerous official committees from the 1920s until his death in 1963.

Charles J. Gross is the historian of the Air National Guard in Washington, D.C. He has recently published *American Military Aviation in the 20th Century: The Indispensable Arm* (2002).

E. Vine Hall was a British poet, musician, and cleric. The Vicar of St. John's Church in Bromsgrove, England, he published "The Airman" in *Icarus: An Anthology of the Poetry of Flight* (1938).

Marie-Lynn Hammond founded in 1971 the Canadian folk group, Stringband. In 1978, she embarked on a parallel solo career. In the early 1980s, her songs about her family grew into a play, "Beautiful beaux gestes," that received much critical acclaim. She has written or co-written four more plays and a screenplay, and has hosted two national radio shows for the Canadian Broadcasting Corporation. Half English, three-eighths French, and one-eighth Aboriginal (Abenaki), she embodies the amalgam that is Canada. These days, Hammond earns her living primarily as a writer and editor in Toronto.

John Norman Harris was a Canadian author born in 1915. He is the author of *Knights of the Air: Canadian aces of World War I* (1958). Harris died in 1964.

Robert A. Heinlein was a well-known science fiction author who began publishing stories before World War II and continued a celebrated career until his death in 1988. He published more than sixty books, among the best known were *Starship Troopers* (1952), *Stranger in a Strange Land* (1961), and *Time Enough for Love* (1974).

John F. Kennedy was President of the United States from 1961-1963. In his 1960 presidential campaign, Kennedy used the slogan, "Let's get this country moving again," to criticize the Eisenhower Administration for doing nothing about the myriad social, economic, and international problems in the 1950s. On May 25, 1961, President Kennedy announced the goal of sending an American to the Moon before the end of the decade. The human space flight imperative was a direct outgrowth of it; Projects Mercury (in its latter stages), Gemini, and Apollo were each designed to execute it.

Rudyard Kipling was born in Bombay, India, in 1865. After completing his education, Kipling began to write, and his short stories and verses gained success in the late 1890s when he was hailed as a literary heir to Charles Dickens. His work expressed in the best possible terms the glory of the British Empire. His novels, *The Jungle Book* (1894) and *Kim* (1901)—as well as the *Just So Stories* (1902)—have now become widely translated classics. He received the Nobel Prize for literature in 1907. Kipling died in London in 1936.

Samuel Pierpont Langley was born in Roxbury, Massachusetts, in 1834, and became one of America's most accomplished scientists. His work in astronomy, physics, and aeronautics was highly regarded. In 1887, after a career at several educational institutions, Langley became Secretary of the Smithsonian Institution in Washington D.C. There he undertook research on flying machines, attempting a flight on December 8, 1903, just a few days before the Wright brothers, which crashed into the Potomac River.

Anne Morrow Lindbergh was born in 1906 in Englewood, New Jersey. The daughter of diplomat and U.S. Senator Dwight Morrow, she married Charles A. Lindbergh in 1929. Anne served as her husband's co-pilot, navigator, and radio operator on history-making explorations, charting potential air routes for commercial airlines across the continent and the Caribbean. In 1931, they journeyed in a single-engine plane over uncharted routes from Canada and Alaska to Japan and China, which she chronicled in her first book, *North to the Orient*. They then completed a five-and-a-half-month, 30,000-

mile survey of North and South Atlantic air routes in 1933 (the subject of her next book, *Listen! the Wind*). Lindbergh published eleven other books including *Earth Shine, The Steep Ascent*, and *Gift from the Sea*, and five volumes of diaries and letters from the years 1922-1944. She died in Vermont in 2001.

Charles A. Lindbergh was born in Detroit, Michigan, in 1902. He entered a Lincoln, Nebraska, flying school in 1922. After purchasing a war surplus Jenny trainer in 1923, he made his first solo flight and barnstormed for a year. On May 20-21, 1927, Lindbergh made history by piloting his Ryan monoplane, "The Spirit of St. Louis," solo across the Atlantic from New York to Paris. Overnight, he became an international hero, receiving the Congressional Medal of Honor and the first-ever Distinguished Flying Cross by the U.S. government, and high honors from many other countries. He married Anne Morrow in 1929. After the kidnapping and death of their son in 1932, the Lindberghs moved to England, but in 1939 Lindbergh returned to the United States to make antiwar speeches. Upon U.S. entry into the war, he volunteered and subsequently flew combat missions for the Air Force in the Pacific. He died in 1974.

Vachel Lindsay was born in central Illinois in 1879 and first received recognition in 1913, when *Poetry* magazine published his poem "General William Booth Enters into Heaven," about the founder of The Salvation Army. Lindsay's verse is characterized by its lyric quality and its simple, forceful rhythms. Among his volumes of poetry are *The Congo and Other Poems* (1914) and *Every Soul Is a Circus* (1929). He committed suicide in 1931.

Shannon W. Lucid was born in 1943, and after completing advanced science degrees entered the NASA astronaut corps in 1978. A veteran of five space flights, she has logged 5,354 hours (223 days) in space. She set the initial United States single mission space flight endurance record while on the Russian Space Station Mir, where she has spent more than a 100 consecutive days.

Archibald MacLeish was born in 1892 in Glencoe, Illinois. A Yale gradute and Wolrd War I veteran, he became a lawyer but then moved to Paris with his family to be a poet. There he wrote *The Happy Marriage* (1924), *The Pot of Earth* (1925), *Streets on the Moon* (1926), and *The Hamlet of A. MacLeish* (1928). MacLeish returned to the United States to research the Spanish conquest of Mexico, and the result, *Conquistador* (1932), won him a Pulitzer Prize. From 1920-1939, he was a member of the editorial board of *Fortune* magazine; from 1929-1944, he served as Librarian of Congress. MacLeish's *Collected Poems* (1952) won him a second Pulitzer and his poetic drama, *J.B.*, was a Broadway success. He died in 1982.

John Gillespie Magee Jr. was born in Shanghai, China in 1922, the son of missionary parents; his father was an American and his mother was originally British. He came to the U.S. in 1939 and earned a scholarship to Yale, but in September 1940, enlisted in the Royal Canadian Air Force and was graduated as a pilot. He was sent to England for combat duty in July 1941. In August or September 1941, Pilot Officer Magee composed *High Flight* and sent a copy to his parents. Several months later, on December 11, 1941, his Spitfire collided with another plane over England and Magee, only 19 years old, crashed to his death.

Norman Mailer is one of America's best-known writers. In 1948, he published his first novel at age 25, *The Naked and the Dead*. He won a Pulitzer Prize (1969) for *The Armies of the Night*—a journalistic novel in which he was the main character in the march on the Pentagon to stop the war. *Of a Fire on the Moon* (1970) is an interesting work by Mailer that captures some insights into rocket technology and the people who produced it in Project Apollo.

F. T. Marinetti and Fillia published their *Manifesto of Futurist Sacred Art* in Italy in 1931. They were representative of a group of futurists who sought to use modern themes, including aviation, in their work.

James Michener was born in 1907 and became one of the best-selling American novelists of the twentieth century. His regionally- oriented, multi-generational stories such as *Hawaii* (1959) and *Centennial* (1974) earned him world-wide acclaim. His novel, *Space* (1982) emphasizes how the lives of politicians and astronauts were intertwined in the story of the development of the American space program.

Joni Mitchell is a songwriter, singer, musician, poet and painter. Her output of 21 albums over 30 years is widely regarded as one of the most significant and consistent collections of work by any artist of her generation. Her unique interpretation of divergent styles creates an intriguing, often unclassifiable musical landscape, captivating music lovers and keeping pundits guessing.

David Moolten won the 1994 Morse Poetry Prize for his first collection *Plums & Ashes*. He has received numerous grants and fellowships including a Pennsylvania Council of the Arts fellowship for literature.

Frank O'Hara was born in Baltimore, Maryland, in 1926 and served in the U.S. Navy during World War II. Afterward, O'Hara received a graduate fellowship in comparative literature at the University of Michigan, where he earned an M.A. in 1951. His collection of poems, "A Byzantine Place" and *Try! Try!*, a verse play, won O'Hara the Avery Hopwood Major Award in poetry. In 1952 he published *A City Winter and Other Poems*, a collection of thirteen poems with two drawings by Larry Rivers. Several collections of poetry followed, some published after his death in 1966.

Susan Okie is a medical journalist for the Washington Post who received her MD from Harvard Medical School. She has known Sally Ride since they were students at the Westlake School in Los Angeles.

Dominick Pisano is chair of the Aeronautics Department at the National Air and Space Museum, Smithsonian Institution, Washington, D.C. He is the author of several books including, *Charles Lindbergh and the Spirit of St. Louis* (2002), *To Fill the Skies With Pilots: The Civilian Pilot Training Program, 1939-46* (1993), and *Legend, Memory, and the Great War in the Air* (1992).

Harriet Quimby was born in Michigan in 1875, and became the first woman in the United States—and the second in the world—to obtain a pilot's license. She received Federation Aeronautique Internationale license No. 37 from the Aero Club of America on August 1, 1911. On April 16, 1912, Quimby became the first woman to cross the English Channel, flying from the Cliffs of Dover to Hardelot, France. On July 1, while flying the manager of the Harvard-Boston Aviation Meet, William A.P. Willard, around the Boston Light, her Blériot plane was caught in turbulent air and nose-dived, plummeting both Willard and Quimby to their deaths.

Captain Edward V. Rickenbacker was born in Columbus, Ohio, in 1890. Prior to World War I, he gained fame as a race car driver. During the war he served with the 94th Aero Squadron, becoming the United States' leading ace with 26 confirmed victories. He received the Medal of Honor for attacking seven enemy airplanes on September 25, 1918, and shooting down two. After the war, Rickenbacker became chief executive officer of Eastern Airlines. He died in 1973.

Sally K. Ride was the first American woman to fly in space, and in veteran of two shuttle flights (STS-7 and STS-41G). She served as a member of the Presidential Commission on the Space Shuttle Challenger Accident.

Cornelius Ryan was an influential journalist who worked with *Collier's* magazine in the 1950s and was in large measure responsible for the issues of the magazine devoted to space that appeared between 1952 and 1955. He became best known for his World War II trilogy: *The Longest Day: June 6, 1944* (1959); *A Bridge Too Far* (1974); and *The Last Battle* (1966).

Carl Sagan was the David Duncan Professor of Astronomy and Space Sciences and Director of the Laboratory for Planetary Studies at Cornell. He has played a leading role in the Mariner, Viking, and Voyager spacecraft expeditions, for which he received the NASA Medals for Exceptional Scientific Achievement and (twice) for Distinguished Public Service. He was best known for his many books and articles—especially *Broca's Brain: Reflections on the Romance of Science* (1979), *Cosmos* (1980), *Contact: A Novel* (1985), and *Pale Blue Dot: A Vision of the Human Future in Space* (1994). *Cosmos*—was accompanied by an award-winning TV series—became the best-selling science book ever published in the English language.

Russell Schweickart was an astronaut who served as lunar module pilot for Apollo 9. He later served as backup commander for the first Skylab mission and as Director of User Affairs in the Office of Applications at NASA Headquarters.

Louis Simpson was born in Jamaica, West Indies, in 1923. During World War II, he served in the 101st Airborne Division in France, Holland, Belgium, and Germany. After the war he published his first book of poems, *The Arrivistes* (1949). He worked first as a editor in New York, and then earned a Ph.D. at Columbia and went on to teach at Columbia, UC Berkeley, and the State University of New York at Stony Brook. He has published seventeen books of original poetry, recently including *Nombres et poussière* (1996); *There You Are* (1995); *In the Room We Share* (1990); *Collected Poems* (1988); and *People Live Here: Selected Poems 1949-83* (1983). He received the Pulitzer Prize for *At the End of the Open Road: Poems* (1963).

Richard Snyder, born in 1916, was a pilot in World War II. As the title suggests, "The Aging Poet, on a Reading Trip to Dayton, Visits the Air Force Museum and Discovers There a Plane He Once Flew," describes his own experience. He died in 1997.

Gary Soto is the author of ten poetry collections, most notably *New and Selected Poems*, a 1995 finalist for both the *Los Angeles Times* Book Award and the National Book Award. His recollections *Living Up the Street* received a Before Columbus Foundation 1985 American Book Award. His poems have appeared in many literary magazines, including *The Nation*, *Ploughshares*, *The Iowa Review*, *Ontario Review*, and most frequently *Poetry*, which has honored him with the Bess Hokin Prize and the Levinson Award.

Louise Stewart was a British poet of the interwar period.

Charles E. Taylor was a close associate of the Wright brothers during the time that they were working on their flying machines. Taylor was their only employee and built the engines for the Wright's first planes according to their designs.

John Travolta was born in 1954, and became an actor in the 1970s in the sitcom "Welcome Back, Kotter." He went on to star in several films, including *Saturday Night Fever* (1977), *Grease* (1978), and *Pulp Fiction* (1994). An avid aviator, Travolta owns his own aircraft

and has completed 747-400 First Officer simulator training. He also serves the airline Qantas as its "Ambassador-at-Large."

Neil de Grasse Tyson was born and raised in New York City. He earned his B.A. in physics from Harvard and his Ph.D. in astrophysics from Columbia. His professional research interests are varied, but they primarily address problems related to star formation models for dwarf galaxies, exploding stars, and the chemical evolution history of the Milky Way's galactic bulge. He is the author of several works, including *The Sky Is Not The Limit: Adventures of an Urban Astrophysicist* (2000) and *One Universe: At Home in the Cosmos* (2000).

David K. Vaughan lives in Dayton, Ohio. He is the author of *Runway Visions: An American C-130 Pilot's Memoir of Combat Airlift Operations in Southeast Asia, 1967–1968* (1998), and co-author of *MiG Alley to Mu Ghia Pass* (2001).

Jules Verne was born in 1828 and became one of the leading writers of his time, and one of the founders of the literary genre of science fiction. He described in his novels the possibility of space flight, the use of submarines for travel beneath the ocean, and a variety of other visionary technologies that were realized in the twentieth century. He died in 1905.

Trevor Winkfield was born in 1944 in Leeds, England, but moved in 1969 to New York City to pursue a career in the arts. He has created several important artistic works, held several exhibitions, and published *In the Scissors' Courtyard: Selected Writings 1967-75* (1994) and *Analytical Dottiness* (1978).

Orville Wright, along with his brother **Wilbur**, first demonstrated the capability of controlled, heavier-than-air powered flight on December 17, 1903, on the dunes of Kitty Hawk, North Carolina, in the process beginning a century of flight.

Chuck Yeager enlisted in the U.S. Air Force in 1941 at age 18. He worked as an aircraft mechanic and pilot before fighting in World War II. After the war he entered test pilot school and was selected over 125 senior pilots to fly the X-1. On October 14, 1947, Yeager broke the sound barrier over the town of Victorville, California. Six years later, on another test flight, Yeager pushed his X-1A to new heights, but almost lost his life as the plane came within feet of crashing. During the fifties, he flew experimental aircraft for the Air Force and investigated various accidents. In 1960, he was appointed director of the Space School at Edwards Air Force Base, went to Vietnam as a wing commander in 1966, and flew over 120 combat missions. In 1986, Yeager was appointed to the Presidential Commission investigating the Challenger accident.

William Butler Yeats was born in Dublin, Ireland, in 1865. Born into the Anglo-Irish landowning class, Yeats became involved with the Celtic Revival, a movement against the cultural influences of English rule in Ireland, which sought to promote the spirit of Ireland's native heritage. He was deeply involved in Irish politics and his verse reflected pessimism about the political situation in his country and the rest of Europe. Yeats was awarded the Nobel Prize in 1923 for his large body of influential work. He died in 1939 at the age of 73.

B.P. Young was an Air Vice Marshal with the Royal Air Force. He is the author of several works of poetry relating to aviation.

John W. Young is a career astronaut who has flown in the Gemini, Apollo, and Space Shuttle programs. He was the commander of STS-1, the maiden flight of the Space Shuttle *Columbia* on April 12-14, 1981.

CREDITS

Literary

Page 28: "Kitty Hawk" from *The Poetry of Robert Frost* edited by Edward Connery Lathem. © 1957 by The Estate of Robert Frost, © 1962 by Robert Frost. Reprinted by permission of Henry Holt and Company, LLC.

Page 40: "Ode tor Orville and Wilbur Wright" by David Moolten, appeared in *The Southern Review*, reprinted by permission of the Poet.

Page 59: "Amelia" Copyright 1977 Crazy Crow Music. All rights administered by Sony/ATV Music Publishing, 8 Music Square West, Nashville, TN 37203. All rights reserved. Used by permission.

Page 60: From *I Could Never Be So Lucky Again* by General James H. Doolittle with Carroll V. Glines, copyright © 1991 by The John P. Doolittle Family Trust. Used by permission of Bantam Books, a division of Random House, Inc.

Page 66: Excerpt from "New York to Paris" reprinted with the permission of Scribner, an imprint of Simon & Schuster Adult Publishing Group, from *The Spirit of St. Louis* by Charles A. Lindbergh. Copyright © 1953 by Charles Scribner's Sons; copyright renewed © 1981 by Anne Morrow Lindbergh.

Page 86: "Poem XXVII" by Elizabeth Daryush. Reprinted with the permission of Carcanet Press Limited.

Page 91: Excerpt from *Benjamin O. Davis, Jr., American: an autobiography*. © 1991 by Benjamin O. Davis, Jr. Permission to reprint granted by L. Scott Melville, Executor.

Page 94: © 1975 Marie-Lynn Hammond. www.marielynnhammond.com

Page 96: PP. 347–54 from *Across The High Frontier* by William B. Lundgren. Copyright © 1955, renewed 1983 by William B. Lundgren. Reprinted by permission of HarperCollins Publishers Inc. William Morrow.

Page 101: *Practicing Our Sighs, The Collected Poetry of Richard Laurence Snyder 1925–1986* Edited by Mary Snyder and Robert McGovern/The Ashland Poetry Press 1989 First appeared in *Commonweal*, Vol. CIV, No. 8 April 15, 1977. Permission to reprint granted by Mary Snyder.

Page 103: "'A Lonely Impulse of Delight'—W. B. Yeats" by David K. Vaughan. Reprinted by permission of the Poet.

Page 106: Excerpts from *Wind, Sand and Stars*, copyright 1939 by Antoine de Saint-Exupéry and renewed 1967 by Lewis Galantiere, reprinted by permission of Harcourt, Inc.

Page 109: Excerpt from *North To The Orient*, copyright 1935 and renewed 1963 by Anne Morrow Lindbergh, reprinted by permission of Harcourt, Inc.

Page 114: "Air Crash" by Elizabeth Daryush. Reprinted with the permission of Carcanet Press Limited.

Page 117: "Aeropictorial Dinner in a Cockpit" by Marinetti and Fillia from *Stung By Salt and War: Creative Texts of the Italian Avant-Gardist* by F.T. Marinetti. Copyright 1987 Peter Lang Publishing, Inc. Reprinted with permission of the publisher.

Page 118: "Aerial Palette" © 1975 Trevor Winkfield. Permission granted by the Poet.

Page 127: "Tuesday, December 8, 1970" by Joe Brainard. Permission granted by John D. Brainard, Executor, The Estate of Joe Brainard.

Page 128: Excerpt from *Propeller One-Way Night Coach* by John Travolta. Copyright © 1992, 1997 by John Travolta. By permission of Warner Books, Inc.

Page 131: "Sleeping on the Wing" from *Collected Poems* by Frank O'Hara, copyright © 1971 by Maureen Granville-Smith, Administratrix of the Estate of Frank O'Hara. Used by permission of Alfred A. Knopf, a division of Random House, Inc.

Page 145: © Estate of Archibald MacLeish and reprinted by permission of the Estate.

Page 153: "The Shores of Infinity" by Arthur C. Clarke from *First On The Moon: A Voyage with Neil Armstrong, Michael Collins and Edwin E. Aldrin, Jr.* Reprinted by permission of the author and the author's agent, Scovil Chichak Galen Literary Agency, Inc.

Page 162: Copyright © 1994 by Carl Sagan. Reprinted with permission from the Estate of Carl Sagan.

Page 178: Excerpt from "Chapter 13" from *Carrying The Fire: An Astronaut's Journey* by Michael Collins. Copyright © 1974 by Michael Collins. Reprinted by permission of Farrar, Straus & Giroux, LLC.

Page 185: "Voyage to the Moon", from *Collected Poems, 1917–1982* by Archibald MacLeish. Copyright © 1985 by the Estate of Archibald MacLeish. Reprinted by permission of Houghton Mifflin Company. All rights reserved.

Page 186: Excerpt from "Whose Earth?" by Russell Schweikart from *The Next Whole Earth Catalog* edited by Stewart Brand. Reprinted with the permission of Mr. Schweikart, Mr. Brand, and Brockman, Inc.

Page 188: "Why Do They Become Astronauts?" from *Of A Fire On The Moon*. Copyright © 1969, 1970 by Norman Mailer, reprinted with the permission of The Wylie Agency, Inc.

Page 194: "The Heron and the Astronaut" *LIFE* 2/28/69 © 1969 TIME Inc. reprinted by permission.

Page 199: Copyright © 1999 by Eugene Cernan and Don Davis, from: *The Last Man on the Moon* by Eugene Cernan and Don Davis, Reprinted by permission of St. Martin's Press, LLC.

Page 206: Excerpt from *To Space & Back*. Copyright © 1986 by Sally Ride and Susan Oakie. Reprinted by permission of HarperCollins Publishers.

Page 208: From *Jaguar of Sweet Laughter* by Diane Ackerman, copyright © 1991 by Diane Ackerman. Used by permission of Random House, Inc.

Page 211: Text only of article "Six Months on Mir," by Shannon W. Lucid, May 1998. Reprinted with permission. Copyright © 1998 by *Scientific American*, Inc. All rights reserved.

Page 231: "Foreword" by Walter Cronkite from *The Infinite Journey: Eyewitness Accounts of NASA and the Age of Space* by William E. Burrows. Permission to reprint granted by Walter Cronkite.

Art

Page 2: Yvonne Jacquette, *Boston III*, 1995, oil on linen, 66 x 54 ^{1}/$_2$ inches, Courtesy DC Moore Gallery, NYC.

Page 6: Gerhard Richter, *Phantom Interceptors*, 1964, oil on canvas,140 x 190 cm / 55 ^{1}/$_8$ x 74 ^{3}/$_4$", Courtesy of the Artist and Marian Goodman Gallery, New York.

Pages 10–11: Pablo Picasso, *Nature morte: "Notre Avenir est dans l'Air"*, 1912 (Still Life: Our Future is in the Air). Oil on oval canvas. 38 x 55.2 cm, Private Collection. © 2003 Estate of Pablo Picasso/Artist Rights Society (ARS), New York.

Page 13: *Spectre of Kitty Hawk* by Theodore Roszak, 1946, pen & ink, brush & ink, and ink on wash paper, 29 ^{3}/$_8$ x 33 ^{1}/$_{16}$ inches irregular, Hirshhorn Museum and Sculpture Garden, Smithsonian Institution, gift of Joseph H. Hirshhorn, 1966, photographer, Lee Stalsworth, © Estate of Theodore Roszak/Licensed by VAGA, New York, NY.

Page 15: Richard Serra, *Kitty Hawk*, 1983, cor-ten steel, unframed: 48 x 72 x 4" (121.92 x 182.88 x 10.16 cm.). 2 pieces, Albright-Knox Art Gallery, Buffalo, New York, Mildred Bork Connors, Edmund Hayes, George B. and Jenny R. Matthews, and General Purchase Funds, 1991.

Page 16: Robert Rauschenberg, *Stoned Moon Poster, 1969*, offset Litho, 39 ^{1}/$_4$ x 32 ^{1}/$_4$ inches, © Robert Rauschenberg/Licensed by VAGA, New York, NY.

Pages 18–19: AC1992.154.1, *Picasso and Braque*, 1992, Mark Tansey, 80" x 108" inches, Los Angeles County Museum of Art, Modern and Contemporary Art Council Fund, Photograph © 2003 Museum Associates/LACMA.

Page 20: *Figurine Honoring Gordon-Bennett* © National Aviation Museum/CORBIS.

Pages 22–23: *Lieutenant Frank Lahm-1st Serviceman to Fly*, Richard M. Green, COURTESY, UNITED STATES AIR FORCE ART COLLECTION.

Page 27: *Photo of the first Wright brother's flight, December 17, 1903*. Digital file from The Library of Congress.

Page 28: Roszak, Theodore (1907–1981). *Airport Structure*, 1932. Copper, aluminum, steel and brass, 19 ^{1}/$_8$" h. Collection of the Newark Museum, 77.23. © Copyright must be cleared. Copyright The Newark Museum/Art Resource, NY, The Newark Museum, Newark, New Jersey, U.S.A., © Estate of Theodore Roszak/Licensed by VAGA, New York, NY.

Page 33: Wright brother's telegram to their father, December 17, 1903. Reproduction from The Library of Congress.

Pages 34–35: *Orville Wrights First Powered Flight-Kitty Hawk, North*, Harvey K. Kidder. COURTESY, UNITED STATES AIR FORCE ART COLLECTION.

Page 37: Bolle, Leon (1870–1913). *Wilbur Wright with plane*. Gelatin silver print, 11.9 x 16.3 cm. (pre-conservation). Copyright National Portrait Gallery, Smithsonian Institution/Art Resource, NY, National Portrait Gallery, Smithsonian Institution,Washington, D.C. U.S.A.

Page 40: Photograph of Robert Rauschenberg's *Pelican (Dedicated to the Wright Brothers)*, Photograph by Peter Moore, 1963, © Estate of Peter Moore/Licensed by VAGA, NYC.

Page 44: *Charles Augustus Lindbergh*, 1927. Poster, 48.6 x 37 cm. Copyright National Portrait Gallery, Smithsonian Institution/Art Resource, NY.

Pages 46–47: © L&M SERVICES B.V. Amsterdam 20030204 "Hommage à Blériot".

Page 49: Leger, Fernand (1881–1955) © ARS, NY. *Propellers*. 1918. Oil on canvas, 31 ^{7}/$_8$ x 25 ^{3}/$_4$". Katherine S. Dreier Bequest. (171.1953) Digital Image © The Museum of Modern Art/Licensed by SCALA/Art Resource, NY, The Museum of Modern Art, New York, NY, U.S.A.

Page 53: DH.60T *Trainer Biplane in Flight* © Museum of Flight/CORBIS.

Page 54: Gellert, Hugo. *Portrait of Amelia Earhart (1897–1937)*, c. 1932. Litho crayon on paper, 21 x 19 cm. Copyright National Portrait Gallery, Smithsonian Institution/Art Resource, NY, National Portrait Gallery, Smithsonian Institution, Washington DC, U.S.A.

Page 58: *Aviator Amelia Earhart in Fl* © CORBIS.

Page 60: Buehler (b. Unknown, active c. 1932). *Smash All Records Flying for Shell*, with portraits of Gen. James Harold Doolittle (1896–1993) and James G. Haizlip (c.1900–?), 1932. Color lithograph poster, 77.4 x 140.5 cm. Copyright National Portrait Gallery, Smithsonian Institution/Art Resource, NY, National Portrait Gallery, Smithsonian Institution, Washington DC, U.S.A.

Page 62: Malevich, Kazimir (1878–1935). *Suprematist Composition: Airplane Flying*, 1915 (dated 1914). Oil on canvas, 22 ^{7}/$_8$ x 19". Purchase. Acquisition confirmed in 1999 by agreement with the Estate of Kazimir Malevich and made possible with funds from the Mrs. John Hay Whitney Bequest (by exchange). (248.1935) Digital Image © The Museum of Modern Art/Licensed by SCALA/Art Resource, NY, The Museum of Modern Art, New York, NY, U.S.A.

Page 65: *Seaplane* by Charles Bell, Gift from the Stuart M. Speiser Photorealist Collection, National Air and Space Museum, Smithsonian Institution. 1973. Oil on canvas.

Page 66: Alexander Calder, *Spirit of St. Louis, 1929*/wire sculpture, 17 x 24 x 4", courtesy of Vance Jordan Fine Art, New York.© 2003 Estate of Alexander Calder / Artist Rights Society (ARS), New York.

Pages 70–71: Rousseau, Henri (1844–1910). *The Line-fishers* or *"Les Pêcheurs à la ligne,"* c. 1908. Oil on canvas, 55 x 46 cm. Photo: C. Jean. Copyright Réunion des Musées Nationaux/Art Resource, NY, Musee de l'Orangerie, Paris, France.

Page 75: Lichtenstein, Roy (1923–1997) © Estate of Roy Lichtenstein. *Whaam!*, 1963. Magna acrylic and oil on canvas. 2 canvases, each 68 x 80" (172.7 x 203.2 cm.). 1963. © COPYRIGHT CONTEMPORARY ARTS SERVICES, NY. Copyright Tate Gallery, London/Art Resource, NY, Tate Gallery, London, Great Britain.

Pages 76–77: *Aeroplane Fight over the Verdun Front*, Henri Farre, COURTESY, UNITED STATES AIR FORCE ART COLLECTION.

Page 80: F.T. Marinetti, "The bombardment of Adrianople," from: *Zang tumb tuuum*, 1912. Research Library, Getty Research Institute, Los Angeles.

Page 81: Malcolm Morley, *Flight of Icarus*, 1995, oil and wax on canvas; oil and wax on paper with wood and steel structure, 45 x 113 x 91 inches (114.3 x 287 x 231.1 cm.) overall, Timothy Eggert Collection, Washington, D.C., Courtesy Sperone Westwater, New York.

Page 82: PEANUTS © United Feature Syndicate, Inc.

Pages 84–85: Nash, Paul (1889-1946). *Totes Meer* (Dead Sea), 1940–41. Oil on canvas, 101.6 x 152.4 cm. © The Estate of Paul Nash c/o Tate, London 2003/ Art Resource, NY, Tate Gallery, London, Great Britain.

Page 87: 1970.31.1. (2534)/PA: Hartley, Marsden, *The Aero*, Andrew W. Mellon Fund, Photograph © 2002 Board of Trustees, National Gallery of Art, Washington, 1914, oil on canvas, without frame: 1.003 x .812 (39 $^1/_2$ x 32); framed: 1.067 x .877 (42 x 34 $^1/_2$).

Pages 88–89: Gerhard Richter, *Mustang Staffel*, 1964, 34 $^3/_4$ x 59 inches, oil on canvas, courtesy of the artist and Marian Goodman Gallery, New York.

Page 90: *Woody Driver...Black Birdman* by Roy LaGrone, 1988, acrylic, 36" x 30", (NASA Art Program).

Page 94: Vija Celmins, *Burning Plane*, 1965, oil on canvas, 14 $^1/_2$ x 24 inches, courtesy McKee Gallery, New York.

Pages 96–97: *Compression and Penetration* by Nixon Galloway, 1985, oil painting, (NASA Art Program).

Page 100: *Bombing of The Haruna*, Peter Hurd, COURTESY, UNITED STATES AIR FORCE ART COLLECTION.

Pages 102–03: Kiefer, Anselm, *Angel of History* , Eugene L. and Marie-Louise Garbéty Fund, Photograph © 2002 Board of Trustees, National Gallery of Art, Washington, 1989.

Pages 106–07: Georgia O'Keeffe, American, 1887–1986, *Sky Above Clouds IV*, 1965, oil on canvas, 243.8 x 731.5 cm, Restricted gift of the Paul and Gabriella Rosenbaum Foundation; gift of Georgia O'Keeffe, 1983.821, reproduction The Art Institute of Chicago. © 2003 The Georgia O'Keeffe Foundation/Artist Rights Society (ARS), New York.

Pages 108–09: Sheeler, Charles, American, 1883–1965, *Yankee Clipper*, 1939, oil on canvas, 24" x 28", Museum of Art, Rhode Island School of Design, B. Jackson Funds.

Page 112: *Fluid Dynamics* by Tina York, mixed media, 1995, 44" x 35 $^1/_2$", (NASA Art Program).

Page 115: Vija Celmins, *T.V.*, 1964, oil on canvas, 26 x 36 inches, courtesy McKee Gallery, New York.

Page 116: Carlo Carra, *Manifestazione Interventista*, 1914, tempera and collage on cardboard, (15 $^3/_8$ x 12 in.) 38.5 x 30 cm. Gianni Mattioli Collection (on long-term loan to the Peggy Guggenheim Collection, Venice), " photograph © 2002 The Gianni Mattioli Collection" © 2003 Artists Rights Society (ARS), New York/SIAE, Rome.

Page 119: Yvonne Jacquette, *Oregon Valley, Overcast Day II*, 1995, oil on linen, 60 $^1/_2$ x 50 $^1/_4$ inches, courtesy DC Moore Gallery, NYC.

Page 120: Stanton Macdonald-Wright (American, 1890–1973), *Aeroplane Synchromy in Yellow-Orange*, 1920, oil on canvas, 24 $^1/_4$ x 24 in "The Metropolitan Museum of Art, Alfred Stieglitz Collection, 1949. (49.70.52), photograph © 1995 The Metropolitan Museum of Art."

Page 123: *Propeller Reflections* by John Rummelhoff, Gift from the Stuart M. Speiser Photorealist Collection, National Air and Space Museum, Smithsonian Institution. Oil on canvas and measures 7.62 x180.34 x 119.38 cm. 1973.

Pages 126–27: *Host* by John Salt, Gift from the Stuart M. Speiser Photorealist Collection, National Air and Space Museum, Smithsonian Institution. Watercolor on paper and measures 2.54 x 76.56 x 58.42 cm. 1973.

Page 129: *707* by Ben Schonzeit, Gift from the Stuart M. Speiser Photorealist Collection, National Air and Space Museum, Smithsonian Institution. Oil on canvas and measures 3.81 x184.15 x 184.15 cm. 1973.

Page 130: John Schabel, *Untitled (Passenger #3 - 463)*, 1994–1995. Toned gelatin silver print, 23 $^1/_8$ x 19 $^1/_6$ in. Whitney Museum of American Art, New York; gift of the Artist and Morris-Healy Gallery 97.82 © 1995 John Schabel.

Pages 132–33: *X-15* by Stan Stokes, Acrylic, 1986, 45" x 60", (NASA Art Program).

Pages 134–35: *The Spirit of Flight Research* by Robert T. McCall, © 1977 by McCall Studios, Inc., Mural on display at the Dryden Flight Research Center, Lancaster, CA.

Page 140: *Illustration of Rocket Approaching* © Bettmann/CORBIS.

Page 143: *View of Earth* by Dennis Davidson, oil, 1992, 72" x 20" panels, Total: 72" x100", (NASA Art Program).

Page 144: *Lunar Confrontation (with Jules Verne)* by Robert Shore, 1970, (NASA Art Program).

Page 147: *Mars Part 1* by Russell Crotty, 2000, ink on paper, 59" x 47", (NASA Art Program).

Page 148: *Mars Part 2* by Russell Crotty, 2000, ink on paper, 18" x 17 $^1/_2$", (NASA Art Program).

Pages 150–51: *View from Mimas* by Ron Miller, 1981, (NASA Art Program).

Page 152: *2001: A Space Odyssey* by Robert McCall, Gift from Metro-Goldwyn-Mayer, Inc., National Air and Space Museum, Smithsonian Institution. Oil on masonite and measures 110.5 x 141 cm. "2001: A SPACE ODYSSEY © 1968 Turner Entertainment Co. An AOL Time Warner Company. All Rights Reserved."

Pages 156–57: © Bonestell Space Art

Page 160: *Lift Off From The Moon. Look* April 1965, printed by permission of the Norman Rockwell Family Agency, copyright © 1965 the Norman Rockwell Family Entities.

Page 162: *Burned Retina* by Doug and Mike Starn, 2000, mixed media, 28 $^1/_2$" x 28 $^1/_4$", (NASA Art Program).

Page 164: Panamarenko (°1940), *Bing of the Ferro Lusto X*, 1997, Glass, quartz, pop mixture, pompon, epoxy resin, engine, aramide, magnetic ball bearings, engine for compressed air, 300 x 700 cm, photo credit: Panamarenko, courtesy: Gallery Ronny Van de Velde, Antwerp.

Pages 166–67: Alexis Rockman, *Biosphere (Primates)*,1993 © Alexis Rockman, 1993. Courtesy Gorney Bravin + Lee, New York.

Pages 170–71: *Strange Encounter for the First Time* by Clayton Pond, 1981, silkscreen, (NASA Art Program).

Page 172: *Dragonfly Above Io* by Yvonne Jacquette, 2000, (NASA Art Program).

Page 176: Robert Rauschenberg, *Retroactive I*, 1963, oil on silkscreen ink on canvas, 84 x 60 inches, © Robert Rauschenberg/Licensed by VAGA, New York, NY.

Page 179: Andy Warhol, *Moonwalk 1*, silkscreen, 1987, (NASA Art Program), © 2003 Andy Warhol Foundation for the Visual Arts/ARS, New York.

Pages 184–85: Nancy Graves, *Part of Sabine D Region of The Moon, Southwest Mare Tranquilitatis*, 1972, acrylic on canvas, 72 x 85 in. (182.9 x 215.9 cm), collection Museum of Contemporary Art San Diego, museum purchase with matching funds from the National Endowment for the Arts, Art © Nancy Graves Foundation/Licensed by VAGA, New York, NY.

Page 188: *Astronauts on the Moon*, 1972, Red Grooms, Mimi Gross, with the Ruckus Contruction Company, 13 x 30 x 15, © 2003 Red Grooms/Artist Rights Society (ARS), New York.

Pages 190–91: *Grissom and Young Suiting Up. Look* April 1965, printed by permission of the Norman Rockwell Family Agency, copyright © 1965 the Norman Rockwell Family Entities.

Page 192: *First Steps* by Mitchell Jamieson, 1963, acrylic on canvas, 79" x 61", originally commissioned by NASA, National Air and Space Museum, Smithsonian Institution.

Pages 194–95: Robert Rauschenberg, *Local Means (Stoned Moon Series)*, 1970, color lithograph, 32 $^3/_8$ x 43 $^5/_{16}$ inches, © Robert Rauschenberg/Licensed by VAGA, New York, NY.

Page 198: *Astronauts Explore the Moon* by Pierre Mion, 1979, 10" x 40", (NASA Art Program).

Page 201: *Columbia Launch Fantasy* by Andreas Nottebohm, 1982, mixed media painting, (NASA Art Program).

Page 203: *Challenger, Edwards Air Force Base, July 4 1982* acrylic painting by Ron Cobb. 45 x 32, 1982, (NASA Art Program).

Pages 204–05: *From the Seeds of Change...a Discovery* by Robert A.M. Stephens, 1984, oil, 30" x 48", (NASA Art Program).

Page 206: *Flight out of Time* by Susan Kaprov, 1980, color xerox prints mounted on museum ragboard, (NASA Art Program).

Page 209: *Challenger in White* by Greg Mort, 1986, pencil drawing, 21" x 18", (NASA Art Program).

Page 210: *STS-71 (Mission to Mir)* by Edgar H. Sorrells-Adewale, 1997, mixed media, 81 $^1/_2$" x 31", (NASA Art Program).

Page 215: *Satellite in Space* by Lonny Schiff, 1989, monoprint chine colle with silk screen on Arches paper, 27" x 20 $^1/_2$", (NASA Art Program).

Pages 216–17: *Chip and Batty Explore Space*, Iris print, photograph by William Wegman, 2001, reprinted by permission of the Artist.

Pages 218–19: Yoshio Itagaki, *Tourists on the Moon #2 (Triptych)*, 1998, 40 x 90 inches, Fuji-Flex Crystal Archival print, courtesy of the Artist and Cristinerose Gallery, NYC.

Page 221: *Eileen Collins* by Annie Leibovitz, 1999, C Print, Johnson Space Center, Houston, Texas, reprinted by permission of the Artist.

Page 222: *Blast Off* by Alma Thomas, Gift of Vincent Melzac, National Air and Space Museum, Smithsonian Institution. Acrylic on canvas and measures 137.2 x 188 cm. 1970.

Page 225: *Space Station* by Nicky Enright, 2000, (NASA Art Program).

Pages 228–29: *A New Frontier* by Keith Duncan, 2001, (NASA Art Program).

Page 230: *Go for the Stars (Study)* by P.A. Nisbet, 1990, field study in oil, 5 $^7/_8$" x 8 $^1/_2$", (NASA Art Program).

Pages 232–33: *Early Biplane in Flight* © Corbis.

The editors and publisher gratefully acknowledge the assistance of the various institutions and individuals who supplied text and art for this book.

Every attempt has been made to obtain permission to reproduce materials protected by copyright. Where omissions may have occurred, the publisher will be happy to acknowledge this in future printings.

Acknowledgements — The editors would like to thank the following for making this book possible:

First and foremost is Lena Tabori who first had a vision for this book years ago. Everyone else at Welcome Books has been extremely helpful and diligent in making this book possible including Natasha Fried, Gregory Wakabayashi, Larry Chesler, Jon Glick, and Alice Wong.

At NASA, we would like to thank Sherry Foster, Glenn Mahone, Evelyn Thames, and Beverly Falmarco for their management support. Particular thanks goes to Arocena Kennedy at NASA who spent many hours preparing texts for publication. For their many contributions in completing this project, we wish especially to thank Jane Odom, Colin Fries, and John Hargenrader, who helped track down information and correct inconsistencies; Stephen J. Garber offered valuable advice; Nadine Andreassen and Louise Alstork, who helped with proofreading and compilation; the staffs of the NASA Headquarters Library and the Scientific and Technical Information Program who provided assistance in locating materials.

We also thank the archivists at various presidential libraries, and the National Archives and Records Administration in helping with research. In addition to these individuals, we wish to acknowledge the following scholars or experts who aided in a variety of ways: George W. Bradley, Lynn Cline, Tom D. Crouch, James Dean, Tom Dixon, Frank Goodyear, Dwayne A. Day, Fred Durant, Charles Gross, John F. Guilmartin, Jr., Barton C. Hacker, R. Cargill Hall, Richard P. Hallion, Roger Handberg, T.A. Heppenheimer, Francis T. Hoban, David A. Hounshell, Perry D. Jamieson, Stephen B. Johnson, W.D. Kay, Richard H. Kohn, Sylvia K. Kraemer, John Krige, Alan M. Ladwig, W. Henry Lambright, John M. Logsdon, John Lonnquest, John L. Loos, Howard E. McCurdy, Jonathan C. McDowell, Renee McKee, George E. Mueller, Valerie Neal, Allan A. Needell, Michael J. Neufeld, Karen Olsen, Frederick I. Ordway III, Dominic Pisano, Robert Schulman, Mary Beth Smalley, and Stephen P. Waring.

We also thank the aviators, astronauts, artists, writers, academics, and historians who have been the inspiration behind this book. Last but not at all least, we would like to thank our families and friends for their support in this endeavor.

TITLE PAGE: *Boston III*, Yvonne Jacquette, 1995

Published in 2003 by Welcome Books®
An imprint of Welcome Enterprises, Inc.
6 West 18th Street
New York, NY 10011
(212) 989-3200; Fax (212) 989-3205
e-mail: info@welcomebooks.biz
www.welcomebooks.biz

Publisher: LENA TABORI
Project Director: NATASHA TABORI FRIED
Designer: GREGORY WAKABAYASHI
Picture Researcher: LAWRENCE CHESLER

Distributed to the trade in the U.S. and Canada by
Andrews McMeel Distribution Services
Order Department and Customer Service (800) 943-9839
Orders Only Fax: (800) 943-9831

Design & Compilation Copyright © 2003 Welcome Enterprises, Inc.
Book Introduction and Part 4 Introduction © 2003 by Anne Collins Goodyear; Part 1 Introduction © 2003 by Anthony Springer; Part 2 Introduction © 2003 by Dominick Pisano; Part 3 Introduction © 2003 by Charles Gross; Part 5 Introduction © 2003 by Michael H. Gorn; Part 6 Introduction © 2003 by Roger D. Launius

Additional copyright information and credits available on page 238

All rights reserved. No part of this book may be reproduced or utilized in any form or by any means, electronic or mechanical, including photocopying, recording, or by any information storage or retrieval system, without permission in writing from the publisher.

Library of Congress Cataloging-in-Publication Data

Flight: a celebration of 100 years in art and literature / edited by Anne Collins Goodyear.
     p. cm.
     ISBN 0-941807-83-5
     1. Flight in art. 2. Arts, Modern—20th century. I. Goodyear, Anne Collins.

NX650.F55 F55 2003
700'.456—dc21

                   2002193350

Printed in Singapore

FIRST EDITION

10 9 8 7 6 5 4 3 2 1